Crime
International Agenda

This volume was written
in commemoration of the 100th
anniversary of the First
International Prison Congress
London 1872

Crime:
International Agenda

Concern and Action in the Prevention of Crime and
Treatment of Offenders, 1846-1972

Benedict S. Alper
Jerry F. Boren

Department of Sociology
Boston College

With a Foreword by
William Clifford
United Nations

Lexington Books
D.C. Heath and Company
Lexington, Massachusetts
Toronto   London

To our wives
Ethel and Linda,
respectively—
and affectionately.

Table of Contents

List of Exhibits

Foreword,*
William Clifford

Avant-Propos

There is an international dimension to crime which modern travel and communications, transnational business networks, and a common urban culture are making a new reality. There is a new generation of international offenders—mobile, daring, better educated and certainly not deterred by national boundaries. There are organized rings which direct this illegality with branch offices in different capitals: and inevitably in a situation like this, politics gets mixed with conventional crime as the respect for national controls declines and the real advantages of a politico-criminal make themselves apparent. Skyjacking, currency dealing, counterfeiting, the kidnapping or killing of diplomats, drug trafficking, and more recently the stealing and foreign disposal of national art treasures, have all combined to internationalize crime and expose the limitations of countermeasures which are nationally restricted or politically hesitant.

The problem has mushroomed as the world has shrunk: but the international character of crime and the elements obviously common to our legal regulation of behavior and the treatment of offenders in any country have been appreciated and internationally studied as this book shows, for a hundred and fifty years. Long before the accelerated transformation of contemporary society heightened the dangers and intensified the need for international cooperation there were people looking for ways of coordi-

---

*This is a personal statement which in no way conveys the official position of the United Nations or indicates a United Nations endorsement of this work.

nating penal action on a world scale. It seems that the nineteenth century in particular created a world consciousness of the need for cooperation.

The story of world concern with crime could be carried even further back. From the Hammurabi Code and the Mosaic Law through Roman Law and the Napoleonic Code there has been a continuing preoccupation with law-making which like the *jus gentium* or the Canon Law has been international in character. Countries have borrowed and adapted liberally in the attempt to achieve a higher level of efficiency and civilized order in their distribution and protection of rights and obligations. The numerous legal systems of the world are reducible to common and civil law simply because in the efforts to deal with this complex problem there has been a regular export and borrowing of codes, precedents and statutes. Of course, the Shariah—Moslem family—courts, rabbinical or various customary legal systems, exist to provide exceptions to any general rule but these have also been widely adopted or imposed by conquest, and their complication hardly detracts from the vast correspondence of legislative substance and practice which obtains across the continents of the world. There may not have been quite the same thought given to the treatment of offenders, but if legislation and procedure be included, then international cooperation to deal with crime, like world efforts to ensure peace, can be said to have a venerable tradition. Court procedures and even styles of prison architecture are recognizable between nations and have been for hundreds of years. Crimes of an international character have not been numerous, but treaties on piracy or the recognized procedures for the ransoming of prisoners and the protection of trade caravans show that national boundaries have never limited the scope of criminal activity.

There is of course a universality of human nature which makes internationalism inevitable—given the appropriate communications: crime flows naturally from those qualities and perversities of human conduct and from the defects of social organization which are well known in all parts of the world.

Not surprisingly then, in our own times penal reformers, lawyers, judges and correctional personnel have found an affinity despite national boundaries and the differences of political systems. They have not hesitated to borrow from each other so that Walnut Street-type penitentiaries, reformatories, Borstals, juvenile courts, *sursis* and probation systems, child welfare boards and scientific methods in police and prison services have emerged in countries widely dispersed. They have not always operated in the same way, of course, and the adaptation to the local cultures has been free and often imaginative. Nevertheless the international cooperation for crime prevention and control has been based on a wide ranging similarity not only of crime problems but of the laws, their enforcement, and the methods for dealing with offenders.

What is surprising is that this range of international interest in a common problem and its national as well as extra-national ramifications has received so little attention in the vast literature on crime and criminality. The authors of this volume are therefore to be congratulated on the production of a very useful handbook for those who seek to enter a field frequently crossed but so rarely cultivated. The variety of international, regional, official and nongovernmental organizations concerned with crime are described, and their preoccupations at their numerous congresses explained. While this work makes no pretence of being exhaustive, it is clearly innovative in that a collection of this kind has not been offered before.

At first sight the picture is rather depressing. It seems that for the 150 years or so spanned by this volume the giants have labored largely in vain. When one looks at the subjects discussed in 1872 and 1970 it might appear that there has been little headway made, and these people might be described as plodding the kind of futile endless treadmill that had been abolished in the prisons even before their organizations were founded. In some respect this is true. Impressive conferences are no substitute for the allocation of adequate resources for action. It cannot be claimed that nations have yet taken crime prevention seriously. Indeed the Declaration adopted by the United Nations Kyoto Congress in 1970 made this charge internationally explicit. It affirmed that

> inadequacies in the attention paid to all aspects of life in the process of development are manifest in the increasing seriousness and proportions of the problem of crime in many countries [and it felt] an inescapable obligation to alert the world to the serious consequences for society of the insufficient attention which is now being given to measures of crime prevention which by definition include the treatment of offenders. . . .

As a result of Kyoto, the United Nations Economic and Social Council has established a new Committee on Crime Prevention and Control with greater status and position than the Advisory Committee which existed before. It has also improved the level of the Social Defence Section which has now become part of a wider Social Defence Programme designed to serve the new Committee and develop action across the world. But this has coincided with a financial crisis in the United Nations Organization which has restricted the practical action available to the Secretariat. Any real developments in the United Nations leadership therefore await the decision of the different countries to make greater and more effective use of the United Nations to mobilize international action for the prevention of crime.

More serious perhaps is the evidence which this brief survey of international cooperation provides of the dearth of ideas and the slowness of their implementation. Attica and the study of prison problems in France has drawn attention to the fact that the treatment of offenders still languishes in nineteenth century structures and concepts even older; and as crime rises with the growth of towns, the criminal justice systems of most countries are beginning to burst at the seams. Police rates of efficiency decline, courts are so overcrowded that justice is intolerably slow, and the overburdened correction systems are becoming increasingly incapable of producing the individual and social reforms for which they were designed. Yet many of the reforms now demanded were being discussed fifty or more years ago. The evidence has been available for years—though it attracted little public attention—that the enlightened ideas of these international meetings were ideas only and far from being translated into practical effect in so many of the countries represented.

There is now a demand for improved legislation, for a reorganization of the police and more community-based solutions to the treatment of offenders. But to those with any inkling of the international work in this field there is nothing particularly novel about these demands. They have all been worked over before and many of them were supposed to have been carried into effect. It is doubtful whether the present ferment will achieve much if it is not backed by solid administrative knowledge and the will to give practical effect to principles which have been enunciated before. The fact that these have more public support now does not remove the difficulties of applying them in societies where aims, conflict and methods are disputed.

Another consequence of this review of international events in crime prevention and treatment is the circularity of concepts. For instance, it is sometimes thought that the confusion about aims and objects is a consequence of the new age of situational ethics and permissiveness. But as this account shows, the conflict of principles goes back for a century or more: the fact that penitentiaries and societies to mitigate their effects were set up at about the same time is striking evidence of this confusion of aims. Hillaire Belloc once said that the "sentimental man" would equally abhor crime and its necessary punishment, disorder and an organized police. Humanitarianism and the realities of crime prevention have been intermingled for centuries. In modern times this has sharpened into a confrontation between the protection of human rights and the minimal requirements of effective rehabilitation. It is significant that, at the 8th Congress of the Society for Social Defence, held in Paris in November 1971 (on the theme of "The Individuation of Treatment"), the whole concept of the individuation of treatment was challenged on the grounds that authorities have no moral right to do more than administer a punishment according to the offense—thus reintroducing—on the basis of human rights and after more than 200 years—Beccaria's calculus of punishments according to the gravity of the crime.

It could be that the debates renew themselves over the years simply because the options for dealing with crime and criminals are more limited than might have been supposed. The understandable tendency to look for new perspectives and more scientific methods for dealing with crime problems may reflect the expectations of a technological age without doing sufficient justice to the prevalence of human nature. The issues probably do not change very much over the years. Human rights were as important two hundred years ago as they are today, and what to do with people in prison is a problem which may differ in content but not in nature from the seventeenth to the twenty-first centuries. The real differences lie in the communications media and the higher expectations of a more involved and better-educated population. Similarly, the basic principles seem to apply across national boundaries and though there are obvious differences of culture, the humanity and fairness of treatment binds men closely in every part of the world.

This was recently demonstrated when, at the regional meetings to prepare for the United Nations Congress in Kyoto in 1970, the Standard Minimum Rules for the Treatment of Prisoners (originally formulated for European conditions) were held by experts from many cultures to be of universal relevance. If this be true, then it is natural that the discussions over the years have had a kind of circularity. Both national and international conferences will tend to talk about the same things simply because man is struggling to find solutions to problems which persist everywhere and over the years—and which have not yet been adequately dealt with. Crime prevention like peace is a long familiar road, but man is always losing his way. If he keeps coming back to the basic issue he may yet find a way of keeping to the road.

Allowing for all this, the achievements of international exchanges and discussions have been remarkable, given the lack of official attention and, often, of public support for effective international action to prevent crime. Undoubtedly the Standard Minimum Rules for the Treatment of Prisoners represent a landmark: and it is significant that copies of these Minimum Rules are in great demand at this time of prison unrest. Similarly, the gradual improvement of conditions in prisons all over the world and the spread of new ideas and innovative measures owe much to the climate of opinion created by international debate.

As already indicated, the development of international work for crime prevention may be expected to increase with the growing internationalism of crime itself and the world-wide appreciation of the common nature of the fundamental issues in crime prevention and control. Kyoto provided, under the aegis of the United Nations, an important example of the unification of policy as between countries East and West—developed and developing—and it is difficult to propose machinery more effective than the United Nations for drawing together these diverse systems and interests in the world. Considerable progress has already been made in a very complicated situation in obtaining general agreement to devote resources to the application of the decisions made by the community of eighty-five nations at Kyoto in 1970.

Whatever the future, the information offered by this book should be of value to all those interested in the international scene.

William Clifford, Chief of Crime Prevention Programs at the United Nations, was Executive Secretary of the Fourth UN Crime Congress in Kyoto in 1970. Trained in law, sociology, and economics at the University of London, he has been both administrator and consultant in problems of social development in Cyprus, the Congo, Togo, Laos, Jordan, The United Arab Republic, Kenya, Trinidad and Tobago, Iran, and Dahomey. He founded, and was the first principal of the Oppenheimer College of Social Service in Zambia—the first multiracial college in central Africa. He is currently engaged in planning and preparation for the next UN Crime Congress in Toronto in 1975.

Preface

The convening of the Fourth United Nations Congress on Prevention of Crime and Treatment of Offenders in Japan in August of 1970 marked almost a century and a half of international effort in this field. It may indeed be said that no other social problem has a longer continuous record of world-wide concern and action than the phenomenon of crime in its manifold ramifications.

This book has been in preparation since the United Nations Consultative Group on Prevention of Crime and Treatment of Offenders met in Geneva in 1968. It examines and reviews the major contributions made by regional and international congresses, conventions and agencies that have one interest in common—the solution of the myriad problems surrounding the commission of crime and the treatment of offenders.

It was hoped that this book would be ready for distribution at the Fourth United Nations Crime Congress held in Kyoto in 1970. The plan originally encompassed only the work of the International Penal and Penitentiary Commission (IPPC) up to 1950, and the contributions of the United Nations thereafter.

But once embarked on an historical journey, a strict itinerary is not easily maintained. Behind the first International Congress on the Prevention and Repression of Crime, held in London in 1872, lay almost fifty years of preliminary groundwork. The selection of 1872 as a point of departure could hardly be justified simply on the grounds that it was the arbitrary base year for a centenary which would end in the decade of the 70s. Furthermore, the IPPC and the United Nations were not the only organizations at work in this field. The League of Nations had made major contributions, as had many inter- and non-governmental agencies, especially after World

War II. A proliferation of regional groups working in this field had also taken place. All these extended the inquiry, as the date for its starting point was pushed back in time. When it appeared that the broadened scope of this inquiry would make it impossible for this book to appear in time for the 1970 Congress, completion was postponed until after that meeting had been held.

In exploring the path of development of international concern and action in this field, no direct or single course has become manifest. While the amount of international interchange, debate and even advocacy has been tremendous, these are not the only influences which have been brought to bear in this area. To whatever has been the effect of international activity in the field of crime prevention and treatment must be added the impress of academic studies, inquiries by national governments, and the vagaries and pressures exerted by public opinion. The resulting totality may appear to some to be a clear, well-paced and orderly development—to others, rather as a maze or zig-zag, compounded of all the elements which are, or have been, brought to bear over these years on the development of criminological and penological thought and practice. To not a few, the most apt summation may be expressed in the adage *plus ça change, plus c'est la même chose*.

While no claim is made that what follows includes all that has transpired during the past 150 years, no major contribution has been knowingly omitted. To the writers' knowledge this is the most comprehensive work of its kind, up to 1972. Its chief merit may well lie in that fact.

If, after reviewing what follows, it is seen that some progress has been made, a spur to further effort may result. If the record is interpreted rather to show that the same problems, largely unresolved, still persist, and that few definite solutions have been forthcoming, perhaps this may serve as a goad to the innovative. The already discouraged need no record of history to support their discouragement, in any area. As Erik H. Erikson once said, "Hope is the basic attribute of being alive."

Benedict S. Alper
Jerry F. Boren

Acknowledgments

Any study of this kind must derive from the work and the ideas of many others. The main printed sources consulted will be found listed in the bibliography at the end of this book. We did not want similarly to relegate to the back of the book the names of those persons whose help has made this publication possible. Their contributions we here acknowledge with appreciation: G. Richard Bacon, Executive Director of the Pennsylvania Prison Society, Philadelphia; Dr. Carlos G. Basalo, Inspector, Federal Prison Service, Buenos Aires; Norman Bishop, Chief, Planning and Development Unit, National Correctional Administration, Stockholm; Dr. P. Ramón E. Coo Baeza, Secretary-General of the Movimiento Penitenciario Latino-Americano, Santiago de Chile; Professor Paul Cornil of the University of Brussels; Dr. Adolfo Beria di Argentina, Secretary-General of the Centro Nazionale di Prevenzione e Difesa Sociale, Milan; Jean Dupréel, Secretary-General of the Ministry of Justice, Brussels; Hon. Duncan Fairn, Lord Chancellor's Office, London; Professor Albert G. Hess, Brockport State University, New York; Professor Hermann Mannheim, Emeritus from the University of London; Ynonne-Renée Marx, Institute of Comparative Law, Paris; Dr. Sean McBride, Secretary-General of the International Commission of Jurists, Geneva; Professor Norval Morris, Director of the Center for Studies in Criminal Justice, University of Chicago Law School; Professor Gerhard O.W. Mueller, Director, Criminal Law Education and Research Center, New York University Law School; Patterson Smith, publisher, Montclair, New Jersey; Sir Leon Radzinowicz, Director, Institute of Criminology, Cambridge University; Professor Thorsten Sellin, Emeritus from the University of Pennsylvania, Gilmanton, New Hampshire; Dr. Jan Stepan, Librarian of the International Law Library, Harvard Law School,

Cambridge; Professor Negley K. Teeters, Hartwick College, Oneonta, New York; Jan van Nuland, Executive Secretary, International Programme for Prisoner's Children, Louvain; Professor Severin-Carlos Versele, Director of Research, Institute of Sociology, Brussels.

Our thanks go also to the following friends at the United Nations who, in both personal and professional capacity, rendered signal assistance and invaluable advice: William Clifford, Executive Secretary of the Fourth U.N. Crime Congress and Chief of United Nations Social Defence Programmes; Torsten Eriksson and Edward Galway, U.N. interregional advisors in social defence; Irene Melup, V.N. Pillai and Minoru Shikita of the U.N. Section of Social Defence; as well as Atsushi Nagashima, Director of the United Nations Asia and Far East Institute for Prevention of Crime and Treatment of Offenders, Fuchu (Tokyo).

We gratefully acknowledge the faculty research grant generously extended by Boston College, which facilitated our study, as well as the help of those nimble-fingered and dedicated colleagues at Boston College who patiently ground out the various drafts through which it went: Rose Bayes, Lorraine Bone, Martha Caraker, Alice Close, and Elfriede Malloy. To Elizabeth Grudin and Sandra Reitman go our thanks for deciphering the first draft.

For his interest in the message of this book and for his expert counsel, we acknowledge with gratitude the editorial assistance of Sidney Seamans.

Prelude

1 Overview

Between 1846 and 1970 more than eighty major international conferences on the subject of crime, its prevention, and the treatment of offenders are recorded as having taken place. The number of their participants, even if duplications were to be excluded, must surely run into the tens of thousands.

What has it all added up to and how should one approach an appraisal of their accomplishments during all these years?

A beginning will be made by proceeding from the general to the specific. It is interesting to realize at the outset that the subject of crime has been the object of international concern and action longer than any other major social problem. It is certain that this problem has been higher on the international agenda than it has been, historically, on the list of national priorities of most countries, even those which consider themselves advanced.

A further observation may bear directly on any attempt to evaluate the results of these many years of international effort: the penitentiary (a term coined by John Howard) was matched not long after its establishment by the organization of national societies to cope with the recognized evils which flowed from it. As a dramatic example may be cited the fact that the good Quakers of Philadelphia, who were responsible for the erection of the first prison on Walnut Street, were also responsible—almost at the same time—for the founding of a society of citizens concerned with improving it. Seldom has a social innovation been accompanied, *pari passu*, by the organization of measures of critique.

It is clear that the birth of international organizations to deal with penitentiary matters came about as an amalgam of the sentiments and ef-

3

forts on the national level in several places in the world at almost the same point in time. A contemporary parallel, the concern—until recently—with questions of mental health, may throw some light on the way in which citizens of the early 19th century banded together to improve the lot of the convict consigned to their most recent, yet hardly humane, penitentiary. There is the added fact that men of good will and of high standing in their communities lent their names and their energies to the movement to improve the conditions under which prisoners were being confined. It may be of more than passing interest to note, briefly, that the two individuals most responsible for catalyzing the movement that led to the convening of the 1872 London Congress were a spokesman from Russia and one from the United States, both leading contenders in other arenas of international life today.

But to go back two centuries, the writings of the philosopher-leaders of the Enlightenment had ushered in a new humanism and an increased respect for the rights of man, leading to the diminution of corporal punishment and limitations on the application of the death penalty. This led to a search for alternative forms of sanctions, which was quickened when transportation by Great Britain of its convicts to colonies overseas was abruptly brought to almost a complete halt by the outbreak of the American Revolution. Compassionate men in the late 18th century now began to lend their efforts to the amelioration of the conditions suffered in the new penal stations by persons confined in them. It was small consolation that in a still earlier day such prisoners might have been maimed, tortured or hung.

Beginning with an initial concern for penitentiaries and convicts, the ambit of international interest and action has widened enormously until in the end it has encompassed the full range of the criminal court-correctional process: from prevention of crime through apprehension, trial, sentence, institutional confinement, alternatives to imprisonment, and finally, aftercare.

Questions Discussed at International Congresses

While it is difficult to categorize all of the issues which have arisen at the various international congresses because of the degree to which many of them overlap, a middle level of generality may nevertheless be perceived among them. Proceeding from this realization, the issues discussed over the years at international congresses of the International Penal and Penitentiary Commission (IPPC) and the United Nations may be ranked as follows:

1. Juvenile delinquency;
2. Rules for treatment of prisoners;
3. Parole and indeterminate sentence;
4. Probation and alternatives to imprisonment;
5. After-care agencies and programs;
6. Individualization of sentence and treatment;
7. Prison labor (also wages and savings);
8. Recidivists and recidivism.

Turning now from rank order at this general level to frequency of appearance, the following questions, first raised at London in 1872, seem to have been those most frequently discussed thereafter:

Number
10 — Alternatives to imprisonment;
12 — Remission of sentences and conditional discharges;
13 — Supervision of discharged prisoners;
14 — Treatment of recidivists;
15 — Prison labor;
18 — Reformation of juvenile offenders;
20 — Aid to discharged prisoners;
21 — Rehabilitation of discharged prisoners;
25 — Treatment of prisoners before conviction;
26 — Cooperation between states and extradition.

The following questions, also initially posed at the London Congress, seem not to have recurred:

Number
1 — Maximum prison population;
11 — Privation of liberty for natural life;
16 — Administrative control of prisons by visiting justices and boards;
17 — Central authority for prisons;
22 — Repressing criminal capitalists;
24 — Maximum imprisonment for less than life.

Finally, to complete the tally, are listed the important issues discussed at subsequent congresses which were not on the agenda of London in 1872:

Individualization of punishment and treatment;
Alcoholics and alcoholism;

Concern for non-delinquent minors;
Children's courts;
Open institutions;
Social change and crime;
Research and evaluation of existing programs and policies;
Prevention of crime.

For the picture to be completed, several other trends should be noted. The first and most obvious is a change in international emphasis from a concern with the nature of punishment to consideration of the best methods for bringing about correction and rehabilitation. The early wrangles over the reformatory idea and the indeterminate sentence were at first more concerned with the latter than with the former. Out of it all came the swing toward reformation as the goal of imprisonment. In the process the shift in concern is from systems for dealing with prisoners to programs for prevention of crime.

Similarly, as the records of the past century's history unfold, increasing attention is seen to have been paid to the other two ends of the court-correctional process of which prison is only the center: the plight of the detainee before trial, and the need to prepare the prisoner for discharge and for programs of after-care. Overwhelming evidence is also adduced that preoccupation with the special needs of young people runs from the first international crime congress in London to the most recent in Kyoto, not always in the same groove, not always at the same pace, but never totally ignored. A parallel course is discernible when viewing the total concept of crime prevention, while questions relating to research and evaluation, except for the matter of crime statistics, are the most recent arrivals of all.

If in the earlier meetings there appears to have been a preponderance of scholars, lawyers and professors, with lesser representation from the ranks of actual administrators, as the years passed persons interested in alternatives to imprisonment seem to have been represented in larger numbers. This may be partially responsible for the apparent shift in emphasis, during the course of the past century, from prisons and punishment to reformatories and classification. This last preoccupied late-19th century penologists in their attempts to understand the causation of crime by devising typologies of criminals, leading ultimately to the movement for greater variety and opportunity for the incarcerated offender. Involvement in improving the educational and vocational aspects of prison life in turn ushered in the rehabilitative school of penology. Ultimately there emerged the search for a theory and a methlodogy which could predict the onset of delinquent behavior among children, as well as the probability of recidivism with regard to the released offender.

Any appraisal of past efforts should also include the citation of at least a sampling of specific examples of the results of international interchange of ideas and their sponsors.[1] The idea of training schools for juveniles, apart from adult offenders, may be traced to Pope Clement XI and the institution he established, the Hospice of San Michele, in 1703. While the idea of the reformatory is usually associated with Elmira, its establishment derived from work done in Spain, Ireland, Germany and Australia. Today's system of fingerprinting as a means of human identification was the joint product of ideas from an even larger number of countries: China, France, England, Japan, India and Argentina.

Sir Evelyn Ruggles-Brise has acknowledged the debt owed by the original idea of Borstal—the provision of a variety of institutions offering a wide range of custodial, treatment, and completely open facilities for young and young-adult offenders—to the example of the Elmira Reformatory.[2] The Borstal experiment, in turn, spread from England to India, Canada and New Zealand. The idea of the open Borstals in the country at Hollesley Bay, at the ocean at North Sea Camp and in the woods of Usk, was further extended as the result of a visit to the forestry camps in the United States by Sir Alexander Paterson in 1932.[3]

The honor system at Sing Sing, originated by Thomas Mott Osborne, was replicated for a time in Belgium. The ideas of Lombroso, and later of Garofalo and Ferri, of the Italian Positivist School (the doctrine, oversimplified and exaggerated, that a criminal represents a distinct anthropological type with definite physical and mental stigmata, a product of heredity, atavism and even degeneracy) like those of the Vienna psychoanalysts, have been universal in their ultimate effect and their direct application to an understanding of criminal behavior. Probation and the juvenile court, originating in Boston and Chicago, respectively, have made their way around the world. The non-court dealing with delinquent children embodied in the Scandinavian child welfare boards is only just now, after 200 years, having an impact on new attitudes toward child offenders. The program for coping with the mentally retarded and disturbed, initiated by the helping villagers of Gheel in Belgium, has proliferated into the halfway house, the hostel and other forms of residential and nonresidential community dealing with offenders, young and old, at all stages of the court-correctional process.

Work release, conjugal visits, furloughs, after-care, the role of the child guidance clinic, victimology, the contributions of endocrinology and pharmacotherapy, and research methods for evaluating the results of correctional treatment, have been put forward from a large number of national sources, and seen themselves adopted in many other countries. Numerous further examples of the contagious stimulation of new ideas and experi-

Exhibit 1
Main International Congresses Relating to Crime —
1846-1970

1846 — First Penal and Penitentiary Congress — Frankfort
1847 — Second International Penitentiary Congress — Brussels
1856 — International Congress of Philanthropy — Brussels
1857 — Congress of Charities, Correction and Philanthropy — Frankfort-am-Main
       — First International Statistical Conference — Vienna
1860 — Second International Statistical Conference — London
1870 — Third International Statistical Conference — The Hague
       — The National Congress of Penitentiary and Reformatory Discipline —
       Cincinnati
1872 — First International Congress on the Prevention and Repression of Crime
       — London
1878 — Second International Penal and Penitentiary Congress — Stockholm
1885 — Third International Penal and Penitentiary Congress — Rome
       — First International Congress of Criminal Anthropology — Rome
1889 — Second International Congress of Criminal Anthropology — Paris
1890 — Fourth International Penal and Penitentiary Congress — St. Petersburg
1892 — Third International Congress of Criminal Anthropology — Brussels
1895 — Fifth International Penal and Penitentiary Congress — Paris
1896 — Fourth International Congress of Criminal Anthropology — Geneva
1900 — Sixth International Penal and Penitentiary Congress — Brussels
       — Congress of Comparative Law — Paris
1901 — Fifth International Congress of Criminal Anthropology — Amsterdam
1905 — Seventh International Penal and Penitentiary Congress — Budapest
1906 — Sixth International Congress of Criminal Anthropology — Turin
1910 — Eighth International Penal and Penitentiary Congress — Washington
1911 — Seventh International Congress of Criminal Anthropology — Cologne
       — International Congress of Children's Courts — Paris
1925 — Ninth International Penal and Penitentiary Congress — London
1926 — First International Congress of Penal Law — Brussels
1927 — First International Conference for the Unification of Penal Law —
       Warsaw
1928 — Second International Conference for the Unification of Penal Law —
       Rome
1929 — Second International Congress of Penal Law — Brussels
1930 — Tenth International Penal and Penitentiary Congress — Prague
       — Third International Conference for the Unification of Penal Law —
       Brussels
       — First International Congress of Children's Court Judges — Brussels
1931 — Fourth International Conference for the Unification of Penal Law — Paris

1933 — Fifth International Conference for the Unification of Penal Law — Madrid
    — Third International Congress of Penal Law — Palermo
1935 — Eleventh International Penal and Penitentiary Congress — Berlin
    — Second International Congress of Children's Court Judges — Brussels
    — Sixth International Conference for the Unification of Penal Law — Copenhagen
1937 — Fourth International Congress of Penal Law — Paris
1938 — Seventh International Conference for the Unification of Penal Law — Cairo
    — First International Congress of Criminology — Rome
1947 — First International Congress of Social Defence — San Remo
    — Fifth International Congress of Penal Law — Geneva
    — Eighth International Conference for the Unification of Penal Law — Brussels
    — Pan American Congress of Criminology — Rio de Janeiro
1949 — Second International Congress of Social Defence — Liége
1950 — Twelfth International Penal and Penitentiary Congress — The Hague
    — Third International Congress of Children's Court Judges — Liége
    — Second International Congress of Criminology — Paris
1951 — International Congress of High Police Officers — The Hague
1952 — First Congress of International Association of Workers with Maladjusted Children — Amersfoort
1953 — Sixth International Congress of Penal Law — Rome
1954 — Third International Congress of Social Defence — Antwerp
    — Second Congress of International Association of Workers with Maladjusted Children — Brussels
    — Fourth International Congress of Children's Court Judges — Brussels
1955 — First United Nations Congress on the Prevention of Crime and the Treatment of Offenders — Geneva
    — Third International Congress of Criminology — London
1956 — Fourth International Congress of Social Defence — Milan
    — Third Congress of International Association of Workers with Maladjusted Children — Fontainebleau
1957 — Seventh International Congress of Penal Law — Athens
    — Congress of the International Federation of Senior Police Officers — Antwerp
1958 — Fifth International Congress of Social Defence — Stockholm
    — Fifth International Congress of Youth Magistrates — Brussels
    — World Child Welfare Congress — Brussels
    — Fourth Congress of International Association of Workers with Maladjusted Children — Lausanne

1960 — Second United Nations Congress on the Prevention of Crime and the
       Treatment of Offenders — London
     — Fourth International Congress of Criminology — The Hague
     — Fifth Congress of International Association of Workers with Maladjusted
       Children — Rome
1961 — Sixth International Congress of Social Defence — Belgrade
1962 — Sixth International Congress of Youth Magistrates — Naples
1963 — Sixth Congress of International Association of Workers with Maladjusted
       Children — Breisgau
1964 — Ninth International Congress of Penal Law — The Hague
1965 — Third United Nations Congress on the Prevention of Crime and the
       Treatment of Offenders — Stockholm
     — Fifth International Congress of Criminology — Montreal
1966 — Seventh International Congress of Social Defence — Lecca
     — Seventh International Congress of Youth Magistrates — Paris
1970 — Fourth United Nations Congress on the Prevention of Crime and the
       Treatment of Offenders — Kyoto
     — Sixth International Congress of Criminology — Madrid
     — Seventh Congress of International Association of Workers with
       Maladjusted Children — Versailles
     — Eighth International Congress of Youth Magistrates — Geneva

mental approaches toward the treatment of the offender could be cited without adding to the value or the validity of international exchange.

All of these issues have been raised at one time or another at the many international congresses held since 1872 (see Exhibit 1). What follows will detail their development.

Notes

1. Such specific examples in the case of the London Congress of 1872 can be found in Enoch C. Wines, "International Prison Congresses," pp. 31-52.

2. See his *English Prison System* (London: Macmillan & Co., 1921), p. 91.

3. "The Prison Problem of America (with admiration for those who face it)," printed at Maidstone Prison for private circulation, 1932.

2   Early Origins

From today's point in time it is not easy to ascertain with any degree of precision the impelling factors behind the first efforts, in the mid-19th century, to place the problems of penology and criminology on the international agenda. As good a reason as any is, perhaps, that it had not been too many decades previous that the death penalty had begun to be greatly curtailed—and even abolished for many crimes—and that the frequency of corporal punishment for lesser offenses was also being somewhat reduced. The need to substitute some alternative form of sanction (such as incarceration) had led quite directly to the growth of the penitentiary movement.

It is equally difficult to recapture today the intense degree of interest and involvement of a very large number of citizens of many countries in a movement to bring a greater measure of humaneness to bear on the plight of the incarcerated offender. To cite but three examples, in inverse historical order, the writings of Charles Dickens in England; the reports of investigations by those advanced observers and social thinkers, de Toqueville and de Beaumont of France; and the pioneering efforts of the Quakers in Pennsylvania and its neighboring states in the United States, stemming from the revelations by that indefatigable prison visitor and observer, John Howard, in his "State of Prisons."

The Enlightenment had borne fruit partly in the revolutions in the North American British Colonies and in France. It is as much a matter of philosophical and political, as of penological interest, that the Bastille had been the symbol of the *ancien régime*, and that its destruction (although at the time it confined only seven prisoners) on July 14, 1789 by a "mob" of 1,000 persons, including 49 Italians, Germans, Belgians, Dutch and Swiss,

11

helped to usher in—as it bespoke—a new international humanism.[1] The turn
into the 19th century had been marked by a new concern for human rights,
and, in the process, both the "lunatic" and the condemned convict of that
day benefitted, to some degree, from the new attitudes that were being advanced in behalf of the rights of all men.

Dr. Benjamin Rush of Philadelphia, who pioneered efforts for more
humane treatment for the mentally deranged as well as for the convicted
prisoner, was also a signer of the Declaration of Independence. From these
diverse and varied origins, from a wide range of legal, philosophical, scientific and moral approaches, from Voltaire and Rousseau, Montesquieu,
Diderot and Victor Hugo; no less than from Beccaria, Bentham and Locke,
Lessing and Herder, Franklin and Paine, may be said to have arisen the
applied concern for the condemned man in confinement which ushered in
the 19th century.

Seemingly caught up in a common solicitude for the plight of the
prisoner confined in the new experimental penal stations, concerned citizens organized under a variety of titles and auspices. The first association
recorded was the Philadelphia Society for Alleviating the Miseries of Public
Prisons, established in May 1787, only three years after the construction of
the Walnut Street Jail, the first penitentiary in the world. Dr. Rush had
been one of its incorporators. There followed, in London, the Society for
the Improvement of Prison Discipline and for the Reformation of Juvenile
Offenders, in 1815; the Royal Prison Society of France, in 1819; and in
1824 the Prison Discipline Society in Boston. Four other states on the eastern seaboard of the United States were soon to follow suit.

One of the first recorded efforts between widely separated nations to
exchange information about prison matters took place in 1825 when the
London Society for the Improvement of Prison Discipline sent a tract published in Spanish to the Argentine, entitled "Ideas for the Governing of
Prisons."[2] This contained detailed suggestions for the construction and
management of prisons and for the discipline of prisoners. A reference
under the heading of "General Considerations" casts light on the standards
prevailing at the time: "As regards punishment, the imposition of chains or
fetters is definitely forbidden, except in cases of absolute necessity, and
even then, for a period not to exceed two days. Underground cells are also
proscribed."[3]

Given the abundance and diversity of national sources from which
sprang the ideology of the new humanism of the early years of the 19th
century, and the concomitant reaction to the increasing tempo of industrialization which found expression in the Utopian cooperative movement
of its early decades, it is perhaps no wonder that newer and less repressive
ways were now being sought for dealing with the problems of offenders,

both young and old. The stem of this concern can be traced from three specific, yet related, 18th century roots—impatience with the conditions of penal institutions as they had been earlier revealed by such reformers as John Howard; insistence on separation of young offenders from adults, as exemplified in the Hospice of San Michele under Pope Clement XI; and the growth of workhouses and houses of correction.

It is of interest, then, that concern for the general condition of the vagrant, the poor, and what we would term today "the unemployed," found expression at a meeting in 1835 of the Swiss Society of Public Utility where the suggestion was offered that consideration of the problems of pauperism should be combined with the problems of crime, which "occasioned a very important and lively debate." The years immediately after—1842 and 1843—saw two consecutive conferences held in Italy, at Florence and thereafter at Lucca, in which the related problems of sanitation and penitentiary reforms were discussed. These presaged the 1846 conference held in Frankfort, Germany.

Frankfort — 1846

After 1843 the first recorded International Penitentiary Conference was convened in Frankfort am Main in September of 1846.[4] The initiators of this conference appear to have been Ducpetiaux of Belgium and Russell of Great Britain. The invitation was signed by representatives of Switzerland, Denmark, Germany, France and the Netherlands. Delegates from these countries—as well as from Russia, Sweden, Norway, the United States, Poland, Austria and Italy—totalling over eighty in all, met for three days; passed eight resolutions and published their proceedings in both German and French during the following year.[5]

In addition to reports from delegates describing the status of the penal system and its reform in their home countries, the delegates had before them an agenda of twenty-two questions. These concerned chiefly the relative merits of various penal systems: notably those of Geneva, Auburn and Philadelphia. The rule of silence, the role of religion, the value of isolation and its effect on health and morale, were among the subjects discussed. An early hint as to the value of followup studies and the first mention of "recidivism" appears here in the form of the question: "What are the results of the various systems in regard to the betterment of the prisoners, the decrease of recidivism and convictions in general?" The first question posed, "What is the purpose of imprisonment," has been, of course, whether formally recognized as an agenda item or not, a topic for concern and argument at every international crime congress ever since, and still awaits a consistent and definitive answer.

The eight resolutions adopted by the Congress approved the policy of separate confinement "in such a way that there can be no kind of communication between themselves or with other prisoners. . . ." Useful labor, education and religious instruction, daily exercise, and open air were urged as adjuncts to this solitary and silent regimen. A vague and early indication of later community concern and participation in programs for prisoners is found in the references to visits to the solitary convict by warden, physician and clergyman, as well as by members of outside committees of inspection and of "patronage." The implication of this for released convicts may be viewed as an example of early thinking in the area of after-care, as well as the present emphasis on community dealing with offenders.

The only association permitted to prisoners under the system endorsed at Frankfort was during the time of religious worship. Contemporary pictures of such services—with each prisoner separated from his fellow by a three-sided box, open in front so as to permit him to see or hear no one but the clergyman straight ahead on the pulpit—are illustrative of the ingenuity employed by prison administrators to enforce the rule of complete isolation and absolute silence.

Despite the overwhelming support which the penitentiary resolution won, the proceedings do reflect an absence of complete unanimity. The Auburn system also had its strong advocate, Rev. Dwight of Boston, who urged upon his unsympathetic audience a regimen of solitary confinement only at night—the days to be spent in congregate labor under conditions of silence.

Brussels — 1847

The Frankfort delegates must have returned home with a feeling that there still remained a sizeable number of questions to be resolved, for the record shows a second Congress convening the following year at Brussels, with more than 200 delegates in attendance.[6] The list includes several countries not previously represented: Luxembourg, Spain and Portugal. Noteworthy was the presence of one woman delegate—from France—and the round of dinners, concerts and soirees arranged for the delegates. Special programs for the wives of delegates—premonitory of today's usual conference arrangements—included attendance at these functions, as well as at the expositions.

The gist of the resolutions adopted at this Brussels Conference was summarized by one of the delegates as follows:

It is worth noting that while much detailed consideration was given to problems connected with the imposition of the rigors of the isolated penitentiary regime, the delegates also had before them—for consideration at a conference to be convened the following year—such matters as the establishment and publication of uniform statistics on prisons, manner of appointing prison personnel, comparative criminal law, classification of offenses, and the limitations to be placed on pardon.

But the political upheavals of 1848 took precedence over the proposed conference, to have been held in Switzerland. E.C. Wines makes a brief reference to an 1856 conference convened in Brussels on the twin problems of philanthropy and crime, but it seems to have adjourned without leaving any record of its proceedings.[7]

Frankfort — 1857

Interest in the proposed subject matter of the abortive 1848 gathering carried over into the next decade. It is not surprising, therefore, to learn that when the third international meeting convened, again at Frankfort, in September of 1857, it was titled "Congress of Charities, Correction and Philanthropy."[8] Three separate sections of the conference reflected the triple concern—one was devoted to "benevolence," a second to "educational instruction" and the last to "penal reform."

The president and the chief officers came from the German States, as did three-fifths of all the delegates, who represented, in all, some twenty countries. Interestingly enough, all of the resolutions were adopted unanimously or by a vote of at least three-quarters of the delegates. These referred to such matters as had previously won approval at earlier congresses, and related to separate confinement in silence; provision of work, exercise, religious services and instructions; and visits by authorized persons from the outside.

One is struck, on reviewing the two-volume report of the transactions of this Congress, as with those of earlier and later years, by the continued reappearance of what might be called the lowest common denominator of penal standards and practices prevailing in any of the lands represented by the delegates. In order for any gathering of penologists, lawyers or jurists, scholars and administrators, to conclude any international assembly with even a measure of assent, they are seemingly inclined (with what degree of reluctance, we are not privileged to know) to vote for a series of minimal propositions which tend to be unrepresentative of the thinking and the programs which might be emerging in some of the more innovative jurisdictions from which some of the delegates come.

As in every conference on crime since these early years, many a delegate finds it difficult to resist the urge to place before his colleagues the best possible picture of penal conditions in his home country. When the time comes to vote on resolutions, however, these same delegates are sometimes found to be lacking in official instructions or power—or are otherwise loath—to support propositions which embody the claims which they may have vaunted in their public addresses.

So it is that today's chroniclers of these gatherings are struck with the high degree of daring which is represented by questions raised, but which never find embodiment in resolutions, nor, thereafter, in implementation. This is to say nothing of the matters exchanged in private discussions which, while unrecorded, are likely to be—as every conference-goer knows— the most fruitful results of any gathering of persons with a common professional interest.

Thus one finds that at the second Frankfort conference of 1857 suggestions such as the following were made at the sessions—though no hint of them finds its way into the official resolutions which fix the proceedings in their historic setting. These included the idea of commutation of sentence by one-third when it is served in separate confinement; the establishment of agricultural colonies for aged and invalid convicts; abolition of corporal punishment and public labor; "the establishment of intermediate institutions between strict imprisonment and full liberty both for habitual criminals and for those who after discharge have no employment and, consequently, no means of honest support."[9] From today's vantage point one may care to read into this partial list of unofficial suggestions some pioneering notions which are only now winning recognition in the field of penology: prerelease centers and halfway houses and hostels; together with some which have found their way into more general acceptance—commutation of sentence for good behavior, the reformatory, forestry camps, and so on.

The president of the Penal Reform Section of the 1857 Conference, Dr. Karl Joseph Mittermaier of Heidelberg, struck at the end a note which, while somewhat pessimistic, nevertheless serves as a portent of the slow progress which has marked this field since his day. He pointed out that "while he would like to see universal understanding of penal matters, he had little hope that such would be attained for a long period of time, due to the wide differences of opinion expressed and cherished."[10] It is the word, cherished, it is suggested, which holds the key.

An historian of preceding international conferences on penology was later to report to the 1870 congress in Cincinnati that despite this less-than-optimistic note struck by the president of the 1857 congress, its participants nevertheless recommended the adoption of a charter

> ... for an international philanthropic association, whose object would be to bring together men from all countries, devoted to the

work of relieving and improving the poorest classes of the people; and who would also communicate their views to each other on subjects of this kind in order to arrive, in a more easy way, to the solution of certain problems more intimately connected with crime and misery.[11]

Cincinnati — 1870

Passage of the years between 1857 and 1872 marks what appear, in retrospect, to be the longest stretch without some record of international action in the field, unless one includes the formation, in 1866 in London, of the Howard Association, which was to collaborate with other international organizations for the advancement of improved penal standards and practices.

Further evidence that these years were not entirely barren may be drawn from the fact that when the first National Conference on Penitentiary and Reformatory Discipline in the United States opened on 12 October 1870, under the presidency of Governor Rutherford B. Hayes of Ohio, it was at least partly as a result of the earlier international congresses which had been attended by some American delegates.[12] One representative each is recorded for Canada and from Colombia, but there were no representatives from any of the European countries in attendance at Cincinnati, although papers were read by others at the conference, written by eleven leading penologists from Great Britain, France, Denmark and India.

The immediate precipitating factor in the convening of this congress can be ascribed to an essay on the prison question in Russia written by Count Wladimir Alexandrowitsch Sollohub, who was at the time president of the Commission for Penal Reform in Russia, and director of the House of Correction and Industry in Moscow. His essay appeared in the 1869 annual report of the Prison Association of New York, and closed with

> ... the proposition, submitted to all who are interested in the future of prisons, to convoke an international reunion of specialists and jurisconsults, who, under the patronage of their respective governments, should be charged with the duty of giving to penitentiary science its definitive principles.[13]

Rev. Enoch Cobb Wines, secretary of the Prison Association of New York at the time, was evidently moved by the Count's "auspicious initiative," and with assistance from some prison reform colleagues, notably Rev. Theodore Dwight of New York, Franklin Benjamin Sanborn of Boston, and Zebulon R. Brockway of Detroit, began to organize support for it both in the United States and abroad. Because the established state prison associations appeared hesitant to give such a national conference the necessary sponsorship in preparation for an eventual international meeting, Wines and his associates thereupon issued a call for "a national congress or conference on criminal punishment and reformatory treatment. . . ."[14]

The response was encouraging, and since both the preparations and the congress itself were carefully planned and controlled by its initiators, the outcome was predictable. For a full week Wines and his supporters—in 40 papers—informed and exhorted the gathering of 236 persons from 23 states with the message of reformation, moral treatment and individualization of punishment. The advocates of the idea of the reformatory drew their inspiration from the so-called Irish-progressive system, which combined the principle of the indeterminate sentence with the provision that the release of prisoners should be directly related to improvement in their conduct within the institution. The delegates must at times have thought they were participating in a tent revival meeting, for the religious language as reported in the *Transactions* seems to have flowed in such abundance that one participant later described the experience as similar to that undergone by the Disciples on the Mount of Transfiguration.[15]

A paper contributed by Edwin Hill, an Englishman who had been an early though unheeded advocate of probation in his country, was read to the congress on the electrifying topic of "Criminal Capitalists."[16] Today we refer politely to this as white-collar crime, under Edwin Sutherland's influence.[17] But Hill was more blunt when he warned against the increasing seriousness of crime as an organized business, requiring the cooperation of real estate owners, investors, manufacturers and other "honest" people.

A pioneering declaration of thirty-seven principles adopted by the conference was the most important single result constituting a landmark in penological thought (see Exhibit 6, p. 169). In addition, the delegates voted to establish a national organization, elected Dr. Wines as its secretary, and charged him to organize an international congress.

While the Cincinnati Conference was organized and held in the United States, its convening can be clearly linked to the previous international gatherings and the communication which had been established earlier between the American prison reformers and their colleagues in Great Britain and on the Continent. The special pleaders for some counterpart to the solitary regimen of the penitentiary had been deeply influenced by the work of Colonel Manuel Montesinos in Spain, von Obermaier in Bavaria, and Sir Walter Crofton, founder of the Irish system of "Intermediate Stages" and director of the famous Montjoy system, and Alexander Maconochie in Australia. It was in great part the ideas and the work of such men as these which motivated the desire to bring the representatives of as many countries as possible together in an international gathering. From a distance of 100 years it is difficult to see accurately all the forces that were at work, but it seems fair to note that Wines was committed to the reformatory idea, as embodied in the new institution erected at Elmira in 1869, and that he made no secret of his admiration for the innovators whose ideas helped to form the basis for the Elmira program. After all, Maconochie, Obermaier, Crofton and Montesinos[18] had laid the groundwork for the reformatory, but the idea caught on best in the United States under Brockway, along the lines that Enoch Wines had been preaching—to any one who would listen. The three principles—indeterminate sentence, limitation to persons between the ages of 18 and 30, and reformative treatment programs—were inseparable from one another.

Wines and Crofton had been in correspondence in 1870 regarding the possibility of an international conference on prison problems, the latter offering some practical advice which may have validity today: "Philanthropists are so small a body that it will not do to depend on them. Sooner or later we must go to the government, if reforms are to be carried out. . . ."[19] The proposition was thereupon submitted to the conference at Cincinnati, and overwhelmingly approved. The early efforts were further rewarded when Wines called the attention of the United States government to the project, and worked to secure the passage by both Houses of Congress of a resolution to the effect that it would be useful to hold an international conference on prison questions and that London would be a suitable place for such an assembly. The resolution further authorized the President of the United States to appoint a special committee which named Dr. Wines to head the mission. In the summer of 1871 Wines sailed for Europe to reap the harvest of the unflagging efforts which had been expended by him and his colleagues. He travelled to every European nation, and through his activity national committees were formed in each.[20]

Notes

1. See Jacques Godechot, *The Taking of the Bastille*, p. 225.
2. Originally published in London in 1825 by R. Taylor. Reprinted as part of a special issue, "John Howard—A Century and a Half After His Death," *Revista Penal y Penitenciaria* 5 (Jan. 1940): 7-18.
3. Ibid., p. 17.
4. We are aware of only three brief discussions of these early conferences. The first is by Martino Beltrani-Scalia, Inspector-General of Prisons in Italy, "Historical Sketch of National and International Penitentiary Congresses in Europe and America," pp. 267-77. The second is Enoch C. Wines, *State of Prisons and of Child-Saving Institutions in the Civilized World*, pp.

42-45. The third is the account by Negley K. Teeters, "The First International Penitentiary Congresses: 1846-47-57," pp. 190-211.

5. Beltrani-Scalia, "Historical Sketch," p. 170; Wines, *State of Prisons*, p. 44; Teeters, "First International Congresses," pp. 191, 197-200.

6. See Beltrani-Scalia, "Historical Sketch," p. 270; Wines, *State of Prisons*, p. 44; and Teeters,"First International Congresses," pp. 193-4; 200-206.

7. Wines, *State of Prisons*, p. 44.

8. For discussions of this congress, see Beltrani-Scalia, "Historical Sketch," p. 270; Wines, ibid., pp. 44-45; and Teeters, "First International Congresses," 195-6, 207-11.

9. Teeters, "First International Congresses," p. 196, quoting Enoch C. Wines.

10. Ibid.

11. Beltrani-Scalia, "Historical Sketch," p. 271.

12. The basic document to consult here is *Transactions of the National Congress on Penitentiary and Reformatory Discipline, Cincinnati, Ohio, October 12-18, 1870,* ed. Enoch C. Wines. Hereafter referred to as *Cincinnati Transactions.*

13. Quoted in E.C. Wines, "International Prison Congresses," in *Transactions of the Fourth National Prison Congress Held in New York, June 6-9, 1876,* ed. Enoch C. Wines, p. 34. Hereafter cited as *New York Transactions.*

14. Ibid., p. 35.

15. Blake McKelvey, *American Prisons: A Study in American Social History Prior to 1915* (Montclair, N.J.: Patterson-Smith, 1968), p. 71.

16. For an excellent discussion of this subject, see Gilbert Geis, *White Collar Crime* (New York: Addison Press, 1968).

17. Edwin H. Sutherland, *White Collar Crime.*

18. For an example of the work done by this great pioneer, see "Homenaje al Coronel Montesinos," *Revista de Estudios Penitenciaros* [Madrid] 18 (Oct.-Dec. 1962): 43-67.

19. Wines, ed., *Cincinnati Transactions*, p. 638.

20. For his own discussion and evaluation of this trip, see Wines, ed., *New York Transactions*, pp. 36-37.

The First Half Century

3 The 1872 London Congress and the Early Work of the IPC

The main stem of what is recorded in this chapter derives from the minutes, proceedings and transactions of regular quinquennial congresses called by the International Prison Commission in the years after 1872. Those years represent the longest uninterrupted period of international action in the field of crime under the aegis of a single body. But for a broader view, our research revealed that other forces and other ideas had been at work and that other groups were struggling for recognition. The attempt has been made to weave these, in later chapters, into the main web of historical development, represented by the work of the International Prison Commission.

London — 1872

The result of Wines' efforts in Europe was the participation of more than a score of governments in the calling of what has since been hailed as the first International Congress on the Prevention and Repression of Crime, held in London from 3-13, June 1872.[1] It represents, in retrospect, a point linked by a line to the decades of international concern which preceded it, and reaches into the future, specifically to the call for the Fifth United Nations Congress on Crime, to take place in Toronto in 1975. The link had been forged through the ceaseless efforts of a handful of dedicated men on both sides of the Atlantic; the resulting chain has endured for a full century.

Wines had been commissioned by the United States Government to organize an international congress on penal reform and related matters. With the aid of diplomatic and consular representatives, as well as numerous private advocates of international action throughout Europe, cooperation was received from every government in Europe—except Portugal—in a period of but half a year.

This formal diplomatic approval, together with the genuine enthusiasm evidenced by penal authorities, signalled that the time was indeed ripe for a congress which might well inaugurate a new era in prison reform. Encouraging indications of support were forthcoming even before the congress began, from almost a score of governments which ". . . appointed special commissions to examine into and report upon their respective prison systems, and personally to lay before the Congress . . . the information thus obtained."[2]

The London Congress thus proved to be a milestone in international gatherings: not only were the meetings being thoroughly prepared in advance by the leading thinkers and workers in the field from more than a score of sovereign states; it was also to be the first international conference aimed to bring together the representatives of governments as well as scholars and practitioners.

The congress opened on July 3, presided over by the Earl of Carnarvon, with the purpose "to collect reliable prison statistics, to gather information, and to compare experiences as to the working of different prison systems, and the effect of various systems of penal legislation; to compare the deterrent effects of various forms of punishment and treatment, and the methods adopted both for the repression and prevention of crime."[3]

An English committee with the Right Hon. Sir Walter Crofton as chairman was responsible for local preparations. A second committee consisting of one representative from each participating nation arranged the program with the commendable resolve "not to occupy the time of the Congress by the reading of papers, but to leave such accounts as each country had prepared, together with the papers which had been contributed, and a full report of the discussions, for publication in the volume of the *Transactions*."[4] Thus the bulk of the delegates' concern was devoted to discussion of the twenty-six questions placed before it in three major categories relating to the prisoner: 1) before conviction; 2) during the time of punishment; and 3) his treatment when discharged. Two "minor" sections were concerned with the role of women in the management of prisons, and the wages of prisoners. Dividing into English- and French-speaking sections, the participants spent the greater part of two days vigorously debating the relative merits of the variety of congregate and separate prison systems which had been presented to them.

The groundwork had been laid for the discussion of measures to gather and compile international criminal statistics in several international congresses of statisticians which convened prior to 1872: at Brussels in 1853, Paris in 1855, Vienna in 1857, London in 1860, Florence in 1866, and the Hague in 1870. "Unity in official [crime] statistics, so that the results may be compared" was the consensus of Brussels.[5] Paris unanimously voted in favor of "A uniform compilation of penitentiary statistics" as well as accurate information from each country as to its penal system, the various degrees of punishment, and pardons.[6] Florence went further than any of its predecessor congresses in debating the causes of delinquency and the best ways of classifying such data. At London in 1860 an internationally representative committee was named, charged with the responsibility of recommending measures for the permanent gathering of international penal statistics, a goal which still beckons a century later.

The provisional committee which had set up the London Congress had been headed by Beltrani-Scalia of Italy. His successor in that post, later confirmed as its permanent chief executive, was Dr. Louis Guillaume of France, under whose leadership this pioneer conference reflected a true microcosm of world opinion and practice in the field of penology. The delegates and other participants from twenty-two countries might well have been expected to differ widely in their opinion with regard to the fundamental questions before them. Nevertheless, the draft of the final report prepared by the International Committee was unanimously adopted at the concluding meeting. This report favored reformation rather than deterrence, and leniency of punishment rather than severity. For this unanimity to be rightly viewed in the context of 1872, we cite a behind-the-scenes report by an English delegate, speaking to an American audience less than two years later:

> Whilst there are abundant signs that the Congress of London has given a world-wide impulse to public sentiment and official action, there are not wanting other evidences that its influence on several very important points was far less than some persons looked for. This was particularly the case with reference to the long-standing controversy on the respective merits of congregate and separate imprisonment. . . . This was owing mainly to some local influences temporarily prominent on the occasion; as, for instance, the circumstance that the arrangements of the Congress were somewhat specially in the hands of certain strongly pronounced friends of one particular system . . . and in this, and various other ways, it is incontestable that one side of the question was placed before the Congress under favorable auspices, which were largely lacking to independent critics, and to the advocates of the separate system.[7]

While admitting that "as it appeared through the majority of American and Continental voices, the congress enunciated the principle that 'the moral regeneration of the prisoner should be a primary aim of prison discipline','" one commentator added that "this conclusion has met with many dissentients, especially in England, both at the Congress and at various discussions since."[8] Thus it would appear that a spirit of diversity characterized the conference, and was voiced in open and healthy expression of basic differences, which were resolved—or perhaps only submerged—by the time the final report was acted upon.

As one leafs through the written transactions of this and subsequent crime congresses, he derives a sense that the influence of any such international gatherings is inevitably, and closely, related to the stage of development of the penal code and system at which a specific country finds itself. For example, a representative from a Latin American or African nation would probably find it easier to be objective in his evaluation of the congregate versus cellular issue, or to accept the controversial notion of the reformatory, than it would be for a delegate from a country with a longer-established legal and penal tradition, and a more rigid point of view.

Judging from the reporters' summaries, an unusual amount of time was spent considering "what is the treatment likely to be most effective for the reformation of juvenile offenders?" The answer to this question, item 18 on the agenda, was fairly conclusive: "All [the discussants] were in agreement that large congregate schools were to be deplored and that schools on the cottage or family plan were highly desirable."

A parallel objection to the confinement of large numbers of adult prisoners in any one institution was also voiced: while some spoke in favor of prisons with a capacity up to 1,000, the majority expressed a preference for a maximum of 500, holding that larger prisons were unwieldy. Discussions of the problems of juveniles and of penitentiary systems appear to have occasioned the liveliest meetings of the congress. Strong disagreement centered around the question of flogging, which was advocated by the British delegates, while American and Continental delegates were as firmly opposed.

The impact of this conference may be thought of more as a step in a process than as an independent event with only isolated results. The London Congress represented a vast reservoir of concern, ideals, and desire for change in some of the major countries around the world, providing a source for international discussions which continue to this day.

At this first conference a precedent was set for future meetings: participants were extended the privilege of visiting prisons and jails of the host country. If it may be thought that only the best penal stations were thus thrown open for inspection, it may be countered that delegates needed no exposure to the worst; there was hardly a country that did not contain places of incarceration which failed to come up to the standards advocated in the conference sessions. Participants were more likely to benefit—and hopefully so would the prisons of their countries as well—by being shown those places of which the host country was most proud.

Several women were in attendance at this first congress—another precedent which was followed in all subsequent international gatherings. They were superintendents of institutions, as well as representatives of agencies involved in dealing with discharged prisoners.

While the final report of the executive committee of the congress was endorsed unanimously, "it did not mean that everyone voting in the affirmative gave his assent to every proposition contained in the report; still less that the official delegates thereby intended their Governments to any opinions or any action whatsoever. It was intended simply to convey the idea that the voters believed that the report of the committee embodied the *general sentiment* [italics in original] of the congress, as gathered from the delegates."[9]

The principles of reform adopted at London, patterned after the 37 Cincinnati principles, were broad enough to include a wide variety of legal, institutional, and programmatic forms (see Exhibit 2). In these principles may be found the beginning of what were later to be known as the Standard Minimum Rules for Prisoners which, 100 years later, were still high on the agenda of the centennial Crime Congress of the United Nations in 1970. If some delegates saw the road to penal progress as requiring severe discipline and the progressive system, others, equally opinionated, preferred to emphasize leniency and the progressive system. One government advocated the strictest separation plan as the superior method of prison discipline; its next-door neighbor was equally eloquent in urging a modified "corporate" method as the alternative.

Concern for arresting the development of lives of crime was also expressed by the executive committee's report when it states "that it is in the field of preventive agencies—such as general education, the establishment of industrial and ragged schools,[10] and of other institutions designed to save children not yet criminal but in danger of becoming so—that the battle against crime is in a great degree to be won."

In an age when trans-Atlantic travel was slow and tedious, many delegates had in London experienced their first opportunity to meet their professional counterparts and to visit unfamiliar facilities and programs, with a resultant stimulating interchange of ideas and information. More tangible currents flowed, too, out of the congress: books, articles and pamphlets in addition to the voluminous *Transactions* which were to receive wide distribution. Reform in national penal codes, the easing of prison discipline, and increased attention to discharged prisoners were results later reported in almost every country which had participated.[11]

Exhibit 2
Questions Considered at the First International Congress on the Prevention and Repression of Crime — London, 1872

1. What ought to be the maximum number of prisoners or convicts detained in any prison?
2. Ought classification of prisoners according to character to be considered as the principal basis of any penitentiary system, whether associated or separate?
3. Should the prison system be regulated by legislative act?
4. Ought corporal punishment to be admitted in the disciplinary code of a penitentiary system?
5. What should be the kind and limit of instruction for reformatory treatment applied to convicts?
6. Ought training schools for prison officers to be formed, and for what class of officers?
7. Ought transportation to be admitted as a punishment? If so, what ought to be its nature?
8. Ought the punishment of privation of liberty to be uniform in nature, and differing only in length; or ought several kinds, different in denomination and discipline, to be admitted? In the latter case, what kinds are to be admitted?
9. Ought a kind of imprisonment consisting only in a mere privation of liberty, without obligation to work, and without contact with other kinds of prisoners, to be admitted for special crimes not implying any great perversity?
10. Is it possible to replace short imprisonments and the nonpayment of fines by forced labour without privation of liberty?
11. Ought any kind of privation of liberty to be imposed for the term of natural life?
12. What is the best mode of giving remission of sentences, and regulating conditional discharges?
13. Is the supervision of discharged prisoners desirable? If so, what are the most efficient means of accomplishing it?
14. Ought prisoners, on reconviction, to be subjected to more severe disciplinary treatment than on their first entrance?
15. Should prison labor be merely penal, or should it be industrial?
16. How far should the visiting justices, or boards of prison managers, control the administration of prisoners?
17. Ought the government of prisons to be placed wholly in the hands of one central authority?
18. What is the treatment likely to be most effective for the reformation of juvenile offenders?
19. Is it desirable to establish international prison statistics? And if so, how may this be accomplished?

20. What is the best mode of giving aid to discharged prisoners?
21. What are the best means of securing the rehabilitation of discharged prisoners?
22. What are the best means of repressing criminal capitalists?
23. Ought all penitentiary systems to exclude all kinds of corporal punishment?
24. What ought to be the maximum of imprisonment, cellular or otherwise, for terms less than life?
25. What should be the treatment of prisoners before conviction?
26. Is it in the interest of the prevention and repression of crime that treaties of extradition should be concluded between civilized nations?

Of equal importance was the permanent mark made by the London Congress on the subsequent history of international action in the field of criminology and penology. The principle of combining official members, designated by governments, and nonofficial members, invited by the National Committee of each particular country "on account of their special knowledge of or interest in the subjects to be considered," has been maintained to this day. This congress also affirmed the desirability of holding regular meetings—usually quinquennially—coordinated by a permanent committee or organization. Thus it was that London in 1872 ushered in a new era of cooperative international action in the field of crime and delinquency.

The experience of this first major international gathering taught its advocates other important lessons. It demonstrated that genuine cooperation across national boundaries was not always a matter of ready agreement, for example, in behalf of a universal penal code, a model prison system or even a philosophy of punishment. Cooperation on an international scale, it became clear, was inevitably to entail a long process of conflict and compromise and the realization that different—"cherished"—national cultures both necessitated and evoked different penal practices.

Progress along international lines would not come by way of one nation leading the rest toward a "true and final faith." It would come, rather, by bits and pieces, through an idea borrowed from here, a practice emulated there, and occasionally a principle newly advocated, which might suddenly—or eventually—win an unexpected degree of adherence.

At the close of the London Congress the permanent International Prison Commission (IPC) was formed, composed of one member from each participating country, in an evident effort to create a strong organizational framework for this international movement. Its purpose, as stated at the time, was threefold: to devise a comprehensive scheme of international penitentiary statistics on a uniform basis; to be responsible for general over-seeing of penitentiary reform in its international aspects; and to prepare for, and call, the next congress. Dr. Enoch Wines was named its first president.

Accordingly in 1874, an interim meeting of the original promoters of the London Congress met in Brussels and unanimously voted to hold a second. A subcommittee was elected and charged with responsibility for its organization.

Stockholm — 1878

The international crime congress in London was widely acclaimed as a success. In the following six years, no less than eight participating countries reported such improvements as introduction of a new penal code, the establishment of a cellular system, the formation of prisoner aid societies, opening of a school for the training of prison officers, and the founding of agricultural colonies for prison inmates.[1,2]

But the "permanent organization" which the first congress had called for was not to be easily achieved. Its first and most immediate problem was to secure the financial backing of governments in order to underwrite the next meeting. The International Prison Commission had met at least five times after London to arrange for this second congress. In the process, the commission broadened its membership base and proposed regulations which defined its scope and purpose. These regulations, drawn up at a meeting held in Paris shortly before the opening of the Stockholm meetings (and to be revised in 1886), were an attempt to secure the official participation and financial support of governments, without impairing their autonomy by requiring them to become "adhering" members of the commission.

The first official draft of this document was thereafter submitted to the Stockholm Congress for consideration. Eight nations accepted it without qualification, and five conditionally. The financing of the commission was to be accomplished by dues based on 170 Swiss francs per 1 million of population. The major function of the commission between the quinquennial congresses was to conduct annual meetings of its members at headquarters, at which time the next congress was planned, statistics were amassed, and documentation was prepared.[13] During the next two years, the King of Sweden and Norway was to send these regulations to governments, recommending their adoption. By the time of the next congress in Rome in 1885, eleven States had adopted them.

The deliberations at Stockholm, read from this point in time, mark it as a hard-working and serious followup to the London meeting.[14] A genuine international penal movement was underway, it appeared. The three-part agenda considered sixteen questions under sections on penal legislation, penitentiary establishment, and preventive institutions. The conference was designed to emphasize practical results and to avoid "speculative and theoretical discussions."

Six days were spent in section and general assembly debate of the agenda questions; the remainder of the time was presumably spent in listening to official speeches, in attending social affairs and going on tours. More representative than London had been, some 300 delegates were in attendance from 30 different governments, states and colonies. More than three-fourths of all the prisons in Europe were represented, and numerous reports on the penitentiary question were prepared and distributed in advance. The congress again affirmed its intention to devise a system of international penitentiary statistics; expressed skepticism concerning the efficacy of transportation for convicts (finally abolished in Great Britain just a decade before); and reversed the position taken at London, with the advocacy of some formal training for prison officers and employees prior to their appointment. In this regard, Italy was commended for having established the first "normal school" for the training of prison officers and the professional education of other prison employees in 1873, five years before the congress was convened.

Rome — 1885

The Rome Congress was the first to meet without the leadership of Mr. Wines, of the United States[15] and Count Sollohub of Russia, both of whom had died since the previous meeting.[16] The highlight of this third congress was an elaborate exposition of types of prison construction and equipment from all over the world by means of small-scale models. The section on penitentiary establishments, as a result, devoted a great deal of time to discussion of prison construction.

Bertillon's system of registration and identification of offenders, introduced in 1881, was here discussed for the first time in an international congress. Several delegates seem to have been impressed with the system and expressed their intention to recommend its adoption to the appropriate authorities in their government. Some time between this congress and the Paris meeting in 1895, the states of Illinois, New York, and Massachusetts are reported to have put the system into operation.

Sessions were held in the Palace of Fine Arts; the twenty-two questions were considered under a three-part agenda of penal legislation, penitentiary establishments and prevention. The record reflects some concern on the part of delegates for the protection of children from immoral parents and other deleterious influences, but this topic would have to wait another ten years before receiving full consideration by the congress.

Early Activities of the IPC and the
Union/International de Droit Pénal

One year after the Rome Meeting of the International Prison Commission (IPC), the purpose of the Commission, first enunciated in 1880, was expanded and confirmed. It was now announced to be: "to collect documents and information relative to the prevention and repression of crime, and to prison management for the purpose of informing governments upon general methods for preventing the violation of penal laws, and to secure the repression of crime by the reformation of criminals."[17]

The publication of its *Bulletin* had begun in this same year, 1880. It was to continue to publish news of the activities of the IPC, reports on new legislation and administrative developments, bibliographies and statistics. While it appeared more or less irregularly (suspending publication entirely between 1910 and 1925), it tended in its later years to concentrate almost exclusively on materials relating to, or prepared for, the quinquennial congresses called by the IPC. It reappeared in 1931 under the title *Recueil de Documents en Matiére Pénal et Pénitentiare*. Interrupted by World War II, it again resumed publication, issuing its last—and fiftieth—volume in 1951.

International collaboration in the related area of criminal law had taken an important forward step in 1889 when the *Union International de Droit Pénal* was formed under the leadership of three outstanding penal law scholars, Professors F. Von Liszt of Germany, Adolph Prins of Belgium and G.A. van Hamel of the Netherlands. National groups affiliated with the *Union* were formed in nearly all of the countries of Europe as well as abroad. The work of Lombroso was having a profound effect on jurists and criminal law theorists, and the full import of the so-called "Italian School," which had resulted in the first gathering of the International Society of Criminal Anthropology,[18] was also being reflected in the realization that reforms within the penal systems of all countries could no longer be postponed.

The basic view of the *Union* is as pertinent today as it was when it was set out eighty years ago: "Crime is viewed more and more as a social phenomenon; its causes and the means to be employed in suppressing it, are then plainly as much the concern of sociological investigators as of judges and lawyers."[19] Inclusion in the first list of members of the *Union* of such outstanding names as Ferri and Garofalo of Italy, of Brockway and Wines from the United States, among the fifty-three representatives from fifteen other countries, gave evidence of the importance which was attached to the need for the creation of the *Union*, and the esteem in which it was held.

The basic purpose mirrored the growing revolt, in Europe mainly, against the rigidities of the criminal law as it represented a challenge to the classical notion of retribution. The coming together of judges, lawyers and penologists provided a forum for the interchange of ideas, while the *Bulletin* gave currency to their proposals for changes in penal legislation which would implement their legal and philosophical convictions (see Exhibit 3).

Congresses of the *Union* were held annually. Their deliberations, debates and resolutions are faithfully reported in the 20 volumes of the *Bulletin* issued between 1889 and 1913, and represent an avant-garde approach to penal and criminological questions not only for their own time, but, in many quarters of the globe, for today as well. It may suffice to cite but two areas of their concern relating to juvenile offenders and to habitual or mentally abnormal offenders.

The *Union* did not survive beyond World War I. Though subsequent attempts to reconstitute the organization were never fully successful, its example of bold leadership continues to provide a challenge to our times.[20]

But these diversionary accounts have overrun events. . . .

St. Petersburg — 1890

In view of the active part which the Russian delegate, Count Wladimir Sollohub, had played in the advocacy of international gatherings at Cincinnati, and his full participation in the first London Congress in 1872, it is not surprising to find that his country was now chosen to play host to 740 delegates, representing 28 countries, who held their sessions in the Hall of the Nobles.[21] The meeting coincided with the centenary of the death of John Howard:[22] the proceedings record that the contributions of his life and work were appropriately commemorated. Two prizes were offered in Howard's honor, one by the organizing committee and one by the Italian delegation. As in Rome, a prison exposition was again a featured attraction, together with displays of the products of prison labor in cellular institutions, models of correctional institutions for minors, as well as specimens of the work done by them. The exhibits came from all over Europe.

Among the recommendations which emerged was one urging that "a chair of penal science be established in the universities of the various countries, and that the penal administrations should offer the necessary facilities to support and encourage that study."

Exhibit 3

Propositions Adopted by the Union International de Droit Pénal " . . . as the fundamental basis of its labors," 1899

1. The purpose of criminal law is a struggle against crime viewed as a social phenomenon.
2. Penal science and penal legislation should take into consideration the results of anthropological and sociological studies.
3. Punishment is one of the most efficacious means at the disposal of the State in combatting crime. It is not the only means. It should not be separated from other social remedies, and especially from preventive measures.
4. The distinction between habitual and occasional delinquents is essential in practice as well as in theory, and should be at the base of provisions of the penal law.
5. As the administrations of criminal courts and of prisons pursue the same end, as the significance of the sentence depends upon the mode in which it is carried out, the distinction common in modern law between the repressive organs and the prison organs is irrational and hurtful.
6. Restraint of liberty occupying justly the first place in our system of punishments, the association devotes special attention to all that concerns the improvement of prisons and allied institutions.
7. With respect to punishments by imprisonments of short duration, the association considers that the substitution for imprisonment of measures of an equivalent efficacy, is possible and desirable.
8. With respect to punishment by imprisonments of long duration, the association holds that the length of the imprisonment should depend not only upon the material and moral gravity of the offense committed, but also upon the results obtained by the penitentiary system.
9. With respect to incorrigible, habitual delinquents, the association holds that the penal system should aim at placing such delinquents beyond the possibility of harm for as long a time as possible, and this independently of the gravity of the offense, even including the conviction of minor offenses.

Source: Roland P. Faulkner, "The International Criminal Law Association," reprinted from the *Annals of the American Academy of Political and Social Science* [Philadelphia] , July 1890, p. 2.

The plight of children was raised again, as it had been at Rome, and the decision taken that a special section on minors be prepared for the next congress. Nine years before the first juvenile court was to be established, the St. Petersburg Congress recommended that:

It would be necessary to eliminate questions of guilt and discernment, as relating to children, i.e., to individuals under sixteen years of age, and to replace them by the following questions: Does the child need the guardianship of public authority? Does it need mere education or a correctional regime?

The choice of a measure should be determined by the incentive which induced the child to commit the offense, and by the seriousness of the offense; by the degree of his intellectual development; by the surroundings in which he was brought up; by his antecedents and character. The age of the child is also of great importance as indicating his moral development.

The advantages of foster-home care and "the system of small groups" over institutional commitment were also commended to the interim committee charged with the preparation of the special report on children for the next congress to be held in Paris. A general increase in the emphasis placed on prevention seems to have marked this congress, related perhaps to the growing development and sophistication of the social and behavioral sciences which were beginning to emerge at this time.

As 1900 neared, there began to be evidenced the kind of forward-looking attitude with which mankind tends to mark the guideposts by which we measure time. The approach of the new century was like the advent of a new year in the private lives of persons who express their dissatisfaction with last year by resolving that in the next they will do decidedly better. It is during this decade that dissatisfaction with child labor conditions, the plight of women and the poor, and the evils of industrial exploitation generally was being openly voiced. The trade union movement was becoming stronger. There was a stirring of new hope as the old century approached its end. Edward Bellamy's best-seller, "Looking Backward" (1888), had been translated into many languages, and a feeling of the perfectability of men, of the infinity of progress (which was not to survive beyond the First World War) was still very much on the order of that day.

At St. Petersburg the state-use system of prison labor was favored over the contract system. In regard to an age-old controversy, the congress concluded that "the progressive system which begins with cellular confinement together with labor corresponds to the nature of penalties of medium length." The importance of prisoner's aid societies, some of whose antecedents went back for more than a century, was reaffirmed, and it was recommended that some kind of international cooperation among these societies, on a more organized basis, be initiated.

A significant instance of the effect of international concern in penal matters, however long the delay between initiation and later adoption, should be noted here: the system of probation had had its chief beginnings in the state of Massachusetts, where it was first practiced in 1841[2 3] and embodied into law as early as 1878. Its adoption in Belgium took place in 1890, and two years later in France. England had accepted the principle of probation by 1887, although not until 1907 did it pass the first probation law for offenders.

Paris — 1895

With this congress the regular five-year pattern which was to be the schedule for future meetings seems to have won acceptance.[2 4] The Sorbonne hosted over 500 participants from France itself. In his opening remarks, the President, M.F. Duflos, emphasized "the growing attention to the moral side of the work and to the necessity of the prevention of crime," and went on to describe international cooperation in the field as a fusion of the "charity" approach (presumably referring to the United States and perhaps England) with the "scientific" approach (evidently referring to the Continent). According to one of the American delegates, "one of the things which distinguished Paris from its predecessors was the great emphasis laid upon preventive work and the establishment of a special department for discussion of all questions relating to children and minors."[2 5] The new century was now only five years away.

The congress divided into four sections: three traditional—penal legislation, prison administration and preventive means—and, for the first time, a section on children and minors. In all, thirty questions were discussed.

The French anthropologist Bertillon personally demonstrated his system of individual measurement, and the congress resolved that "it would be of great advantage to reach some prompt international agreement as to the unification of anthropometric processes."

Cellular imprisonment for women was recommended. The question of prisoners' rights to wages for their work was recognized in a resolution which affirmed that "the prisoner has no right to wages, but it is for the interest of the State to give him some recompense. The remuneration assigned the prisoner should not be left to the decision of the administration, but fixed by general rule." This last question aroused "the most animated debate of the congress." "It was seen that the concession of the prisoners' rights to wages would carry with it a good many other rights which the

Congress was not prepared to concede and which it might be dangerous to affirm."[26] It was also noted that this practice was, in effect, not so radical as the debates regarding it would suggest, having been accepted in much of Europe, though not yet in the United States.

This was a period—as in the related field of psychiatry—when experts, whether criminologists or alienists, expended much of their time and effort in discussion of questions of "classification" of offenders—by offence, physical and moral characteristics, or suitability for various types of imprisonment. In this tradition, much congress attention seems to have been devoted to differentiating between "the competent" and "incompetent" criminal, and resolutions were passed urging separation of the two types, as well as special consideration for the "mentally alienated." As at previous congresses, much attention was given to problems of vagrancy and drunkenness as crimes, though here again the classifiers insisted on the distinction between indigent or infirm invalids; accidental mendicants or vagrants; as against persons who pursued this kind of life as professionals.

The section on children discussed eight questions with such unusual number and divergency of opinions that a special committee was formed to reconcile the different views. As one delegate reported: "This section proved to be one of the most popular. The largest hall in the College of France was assigned to it. While the first section was largely composed of lawyers and the second of prison officials, the fourth (children's) section was more general in its membership, having a representation of the bar, the clergy, and of prison experts, directors of educational and correctional institutions for the young, and a large delegation of women."[27]

The questions ranged over such topics as the legal age of minority, guardianship by the state, schools and houses of correction, physical education for minors, minimum or maximum penalties, the supervision of children placed in families, and the prevention of prostitution.

The resolutions which emerged were detailed, hesitant and frequently qualified. Two of them are worthy of quotation, for they marked the entrance of this congress into new areas of concern. Stated one: "It is desirable to fix the limit of penal minority at 18 years, on condition that children sent to houses of correction after the age of 16 shall not mingle with the others." Declared a second: "Children who are placed in families under administrative guardianship or who are wards of the Government can only be effectively supervised through societies of patronage." This increased interest shown by the Paris Congress in the problems of children may be seen either as a response to or as responsible for the noticeable increase in participation by women at this Paris Congress.

Success of the congress was also attributable to the large volume of documentation published and distributed by the International Prison Commission three months in advance of the gathering. These "represented opinions and experiences of 240 writers, and amounted to 2,500 pages in print." The financial condition of the IPC—due, at least in part, to large printing costs—continued precarious. A number of governments continued to balk at official representation on the IPC because of fears that they would somehow lose their autonomy in criminal and penal matters. Ironically, these included the United States (which named its first official commissioner in 1895) and Great Britain, among the prime movers of the first IPC. But funds were desperately needed in order to continue to finance the congresses, the publication of their *Proceedings*, and the *Bulletin*.

It was against this background that the Paris Congress decided to restate its "explanation" of 1886 and instructed the American delegation to invite and urge its government to become an adhering member. "It should be said that the rules of the Commission do not require that the delegate shall commit his Government to any action taken by the Commission: it simply secures the support and cooperation of the different nations represented in the study of the great problems relating to the suppression of crime, the protection of society, the proper treatment of the criminal, the moral rescue of children, the organization of every means for preventing the discharged prisoner from relapsing into the life of crime."[28] Fortunately, Rutherford B. Hayes, who was the new American President, had long been a friend of prison reform, and it was shortly after this congress adjourned that, with his support, the United States became an official member of the permanent IPC. It should be noted that the British government had recently given official sanction to the IPC and had appointed Sir Evelyn Ruggles-Brise as its first representative. Thus Paris represents an important point in the history of the IPC—marking its transition to financial stability.

While perhaps a bit over-long and by standards of today a bit flowery, two quotations from the opening records at Paris may here permit the reader to recapture some of the flavor of this *fin-de-siècle* criminological gathering. The first is from the welcoming address, the second from one of the responses to it:

> It seemed at first that your ideal was placed too high. You were reproached with attempting the impossible; your generous conceptions were greeted as chimeras; you were accused of sentimentalism and feebleness. Nothing could shake your faith. . . . You have affirmed that human nature is at bottom right, loyal and generous. . . . The questions is not of substituting for penal laws a sort of philosophical indifference which will compromise public security. It is the question of stimulating moral forces and developing generous instincts, which are able to prevent the offense or the crime, and, after the downfall,

of raising and rehabilitating the guilty. . . . It is true that physical constitution, education, heredity, and misery exercise a direct influence on criminality. Legislators have taken account of these inevitable reactions in the preparation of laws and the gradation of penalties . . . but you made an innovation when, breaking with ancient errors, you said that intimidation and fear are not the only means of assuring the amendment of the culpable, but that education and hope are also sure means of obtaining it.

That simple affirmation was a revolution.

* * *

We are, happily, very far from the time when it was thought that justice was honored in being represented as cold and impassible, the sword and the scales in her hand, but her eyes bandaged. That symbol of the partiality and integrity of ideal justice was often badly supported by the facts. The bandage symbolized better, perhaps, another quality of justice as formerly conceived, that of not seeing clearly in weighing the crime, but of striking blindly and without discernment the criminal; penitentiary science, whose triumphant advance marks the great progress of humanity, has dethroned cold, blind, and impassible justice. . . . Seeking to determine the causes and the movements of crime, it has been quick to see that the responsibility is not to be attributed alone to the material author of the crime. It has recognized the complicity of human nature and of society, the necessity of a complete revolution in the weapons of combat and in the means of attack and defense.

Our beginnings were very modest; but from London to Stockholm, Stockholm to Rome, and Rome to St. Petersburg the work of the Congress has not only gradually expanded, but has more and more conciliated the favor of the Governments and public opinion.

Brussels — 1900

The tone for this congress was set by the Belgian Minister of Justice who welcomed the 400-odd delegates with the note of caution that the twin perils most to be feared in penal discipline are "fixed indifference in routine and feverish restlessness in reform."[29] His warning was influenced, perhaps, by the inclusion on the agenda of two of the most controversial questions raised in the history of these international congresses: that of the indeterminate sentence and the cellular prison system.

While the American delegates arrived armed with a host of reports and an enthusiastic commitment to the indeterminate sentence, they left for home much sobered by an awareness that "the indefinite sentence will not find full scope and acceptance until every vestige of the idea of retaliation or social vengeance disappears from our criminal codes and judicial administration. This is far from realization at present, either in Europe or in the United States."[30]

The congress resolved after eight days of deliberation that:

A. As to penalties, the system of indeterminate sentences is inadmissible. It may be advantageously replaced by conditional liberation combined with a progressive lengthening of sentences for recidivists.

B. As to measures of education, protection or safety, the system of indeterminate sentences is only admissible under such restrictions as involve the abandonment of the principle itself. It will be more logical, more simple, and more practical to preserve the system of prolonged imprisonment with the corrective of conditional release.

C. In case of irresponsible delinquents affected with mental disease, the principle of the indeterminate duration of treatment must necessarily prevail; but measures taken in such cases have no penal character.

Belgium, the host country, was the leading proponent and practitioner of separation in cellular imprisonment. As twenty-eight years earlier, when the first London Congress had held the Irish-Crofton progressive system up as a model, so Brussels now endorsed the cellular system, with a degree of affirmation less enthusiastic, more restrained, and falling far short of outright endorsement of separation: "The Congress holds that the results of the cellular system as to criminality and recidivism, so far as they can be experimentally ascertained, respond to the expectations of the promoters of this form of imprisonment, to the extent allowed by the action of prison methods."

Experience in Belgium had shown "that cellular imprisonment even prolonged ten years or beyond, assuming the previous or subsequent elimination of certain elements, has no more unfavorable effect upon the physical or mental health of prisoners than any other mode of imprisonment."

In addition to the sections on penal legislation, prison administration and preventive measures, one section was again devoted to children and minors. The relationship between alcoholism and crime was discussed with less assurance than heretofore, while the medical approach to problems of crime received greater emphasis. Some heat appears to have been re-generated over the efficacy of the reformatory system in the United States and the possibility of its adoption by the European nations. The idea of the reformatory continued to win a larger measure of success in its country of adoption than it ever had in Europe where it had first been launched.

The congress resolution was polite on this subject but left little doubt as to its real sentiments: "The Congress, while taking into very serious consideration the organization of the reformatories of the United States of America, holds that the results known up to the present time cannot be regarded as sufficient to justify, without further study, the adoption of that organization in the countries of Europe." The resolution ended with an expression of hope that the IPC would continue to be kept informed on the subject in order to enable future congresses to come to a more conclusive opinion.

Budapest — 1905

By 1905, the International Prison Commission had established a schedule of meeting during alternate summers to plan the next congress: at Berne in 1902 and Budapest in 1904. Jules Rickl de Bellye presided over the deliberation of delegates from twenty-nine countries at this seventh international congress.[3][1]

The week-long meetings were held in the Hall of Honor of the Palace of the Academy of Sciences to consider a four-fold agenda, reduced now to sixteen main questions. The matter of the indeterminate sentence was noticeably absent, where it had been the main focus of debate at Brussels only five years before. "Moral classification" and the rights of prisoners were contained in two separate resolutions: "Accused persons should not be compelled to work while awaiting trial, even in cases where they have previously served a sentence of imprisonment. The reduction of the term of the sentence by detention pending trial should not depend upon the voluntary acceptance of work while awaiting trial." A second recommendation specified that "in case of accidents incurred during prison labor, indemnity should be awarded to prisoners or to their heirs dependent upon them for subsistence, on condition that the incapacity continues after release."

Once again the collection of "careful statistics" of crime and criminals was urged in order that the relationship of alcoholism to crime might be more definitely ascertained.

Strict separation of young prisoners from adults was endorsed, and "the cellular system is to be recommended only with reference to those sentenced for a very short period—one month, for example, for those under 16 years of age; three months for those above that age. As to those serving longer sentences, the execution of the sentence should follow the principles of the progressive stage system."

The innovation of the specialized court for children, first established in Chicago six years earlier, was praised by one delegate as "a new stage in the development of prison science and in the methods of reformation and education." In its official proceedings, the congress resolved that "The Seventh International Prison Congress while recognizing the efforts made in different countries of Europe to withdraw children arraigned in court from the dangers of publicity and association which the procedure commonly used implies, and in view of the results already partly obtained by the committees of defense and protection in Belgium and France, commends to the governments the study of judicial organization especially adapted to children and the extension of systems similar to that of probation officers applied in the United States."

An innovation at this congress was the dissatisfaction expressed by a number of prison chaplains and others at the absence of attention to the contribution which religion could make to the reformation of prisoners, resulting in the formation of the International Chaplain's Association.

Washington — 1910

Just forty years after the idea had been advanced in Cincinnati, the first international crime gathering to be held in the United States was convened in the Pan-American Union, presided over by Charles R. Henderson of Chicago.[32] It was perhaps most fitting, therefore, that this Congress should have been dominated once again by debate over the indeterminate sentence, but the lively discussion on three successive days resulted in approval of it only as a "scientific principle," including its application to "moral and mental defectives." It was recommended that it "be applied as an important part of the reformatory system to criminals, particularly young offenders, who require reformation and whose offenses are due chiefly to circumstances of an individual character."

Four conditions for its adoption were suggested: "a) that the prevailing conceptions of guilt and punishment be compatible with the principle of the indeterminate sentence; b) that an individualized treatment of the offender be assured; c) that the board of parole or conditional release be so constituted as to exclude all outside influences, and d) that this board should consist of a commission made up of at least one representative of the magistracy, at least one representative of the prison administration, and at least one representative of medical science."

Serious differences of opinion were expressed as to the significance of this principle of indeterminacy for the field of criminal law, however. Some claimed for it only a very limited advance over what had been said at Brussels ten years earlier. Sir Evelyn Ruggles-Brise of Great Britain reported that "the endorsement of the principle of the 'indeterminate' sentence in the general assembly of the Congress was loudly acclaimed and described in the American press as a triumph over European ideas. The resolution affirming the principle was carefully framed and was, in fact, a compromise between conflicting opinion. It did not do more than affirm the value of the principle for reformatory purposes, and restricted its application to 'moral and mental defectives'. . . . For such a moral defective as I have said, the Americans have invented the 'indeterminate sentence' and the Congress has approved the proposal. Logically, this means that where a prisoner is declared by competent authority to be a 'moral defective,' he shall not be released from prison."[33]

The view of Count Wenzel Gleispach of Prague, a key figure in the compromise solution, was completely opposite. In his estimate, the final resolution was practically equivalent to a recommendation that the indeterminate sentence be applied to all classes of criminals. Acceptance of the principle evidently varied by the degree to which a delegate's philosophy committed him to it. In actual application there were some delegates who would use it to keep prisoners in, while others saw it as a way of enabling them to release prisoners sooner than they might otherwise have been.

New items considered at this congress included the death penalty, and the differentiation of treatment between normal and abnormal children. For the first time in these international gatherings, parole was officially endorsed by name.

"Lively interest" was expressed by delegates during the discussion of the agenda item on special courts for minors. The first question: "Should young offenders be subject to the same proceedings as adults?" won a unanimously negative response. But some degree of diversity arose with regard to the second: "What should be the guiding principles in proceedings against children and young persons?"

The text of the resolution adopted in reply to that question included the following: that magistrates for children be selected for their special skill, understanding and knowledge of children—as well as of the social and behavioral sciences; that they be assisted by probation officers; that inquiries be made into the background of children coming before the courts; that information so gathered not be made public; that arrests of children should be avoided, warrants to be issued only in exceptional cases; that when detained, children "must not be placed in the adults' quarters"; that sittings of the court on children's cases be separate and apart from adult proceedings; and, finally, "It is desirable that, in young offenders' cases, the procedure should be a discussion in the child's interest rather than a trial."

Probation was also fully approved both as a term and as a specific concept, in the following words:

The effects of probation are beneficial when applied with due regard to the protection of the community, and to persons who may reasonably be expected to reform without resorting to imprisonment; and when the probationers are placed for a reasonable time under the supervision of probation officers. The effects of suspended sentence, without probation oversight, are difficult, if not impossible, to ascertain. It is desirable to introduce and extend laws providing for probation, and to establish in each country some central authority which will exercise general supervision over probation work.

During the following summer the first International Congress of Children's Courts was held in Paris, which led to the passage of two laws establishing children's courts—in Belgium under the law of May 15, 1912, and in France under the law of July 22nd of the same year.

The British Government extended an official invitation to the IPC to meet in London in 1915. The invitation was accepted, but the outbreak of World War I four years later forced the congress to be cancelled. It would not meet again for fifteen years.

Notes

1. A great deal has been written about the London Congress of 1872. The basic document to consult is International Prison Commission [*see under* International Penal and Penitentiary Commission], *Prisons and Reformatories at Home and Abroad—Being the Transactions of the International Penitentiary Congress Held in London, July 3-13, 1872*, ed. Edwin Pears. (Hereafter referred to as *London Transactions.*) For a recent summary and commentary on the London Congress, as well as the succeeding eleven congresses, see Negley K. Teeters, *Deliberations of the International Penal and Penitentiary Congresses*, pp. 13-39. For earlier discussions, see Howard Association, *The Prison Congress of London, July 1872*; Sir Hugh Evelyn Ruggles-Brise, *Prison Reform at Home and Abroad*, pp. 1-34; William Tallack, "Influence of the Great Prison Congress of 1872," pp. 174-84; and Enoch C. Wines, "International Prison Congresses," pp. 31-52. Also included in this last volume are the several accounts of meetings of the then new IPC held in Bruschal in August 1875. For additional background material on events leading up to the London Congress and the Congress itself, see E.C. Wines, *International Congress on the Prevention and Repression of Crime, Including Penal and Reformatory Treatment.*

2. Tallack, "Influence of Congress of 1872," pp. 175-76.

3. Pears, ed., *London Transactions*, p. xiii.

4. Ibid., p. xv.

5. Martino Beltrani-Scalia, "Historical Sketch of National and International Penitentiary Congresses in Europe and America," p. 275.

6. Ibid. The motivation for this unanimous decision may well stem from the fact that "France was the first country in the world to initiate the regular publication of statistics. It began in 1827, bringing together and analyzing the figures for the year 1825." Leon Radzinowicz, *In Search of Criminology*, p. 64.

7. Tallack, "Influence of Congress of 1872," p. 180.

8. Ibid., p. 183.

9. Enoch C. Wines, *State of Prisons and of Child-Saving Institutions in the Civilized World*, p. 56.

10. Free schools for destitute English young, first established by John Pounds (1766-1839).

11. See his discussion of the results of the London Congress in Enoch C. Wines, ed., *Transactions of the Fourth National Prison Congress Held in New York*, June 6-9, 1876, pp. 38-46 (hereafter cited as *New York Transactions*); and Tallack, "Influence of Congress of 1872," p. 180.

12. Wines, ed., *New York Transactions*, pp. 38-46.

13. Thorsten Sellin, "Lionel Fox and the International Penal and Penitentiary Commission," p. 195.

14. For information on and accounts of the Stockholm Congress, see Teeters, *Deliberations of IPPC*, pp. 40-49; Ruggles-Brise, *Prison Reform*, pp. 35-55; Enoch C. Wines, *Actual State of Prison Reform Throughout the Civilized World*. See the Bibliography under IPPC for a list of official publications of all the Congresses.

15. Wines had, three days before his death, completed the preface to his historic *State of Prisons*. This monumental work, which is without parallel in our times, is an interesting compendium of penal history and philosophy, together with accounts and detailed reports of the state of prisons in every part of the world.

16. Teeters, *Deliberations of IPPC*, p. 50. In addition, see Teeters, pp. 50-61; and Ruggles-Brise, *Prison Reform*, pp. 35-55 for accounts of the Rome Congress.

17. Teeters, *Deliberations of IPPC*, p. 24.

18. See pp. 47-55 below.

19. Roland P. Faulkner, "International Criminal Law Association," p. 1.

20. Radzinowicz, *In Search of Criminology*, esp. pp. 40-51.

21. For information on and accounts of the St. Petersburg Congress, see Teeters, *Deliberations of IPPC*, pp. 62-82; Ruggles-Brise, *Prison Reform*, pp. 35-55; and C.D. Randall, *The Fourth International Prison Congress, St. Petersburg, Russia*, 1891. The reader should also consult the Bibliography under IPPC for a list of the *Proceedings*.

22. The 250th anniversary of John Howard's birth will be celebrated in 1976.

23. John Augustus, *A Report of the Labors of John Augustus for the Last Ten Years in the Aid of the Unfortunate*.

24. For information on and accounts of the Paris Congress, see Teeters, *Deliberations of IPPC*, pp. 83-102; Ruggles-Brise, *Prison Reform*, pp. 56-88; and Samuel J. Barrows, *Report of the Delegates of the United States to the Fifth International Prison Congress*.

25. Barrows, *Report of Delegates*, p. 21.

26. Ibid., p. 40.

27. Ibid., p. 57.

28. Ibid., p. 6.

29. On the Brussels Congress, see Teeters, *Deliberations of IPPC*, pp. 103-14; Ruggles-Brise, *Prison Reform*, pp. 89-121; and Samuel J. Barrows, *Sixth International Prison Congress Held in Brussels, Belgium, August, 1900*.

30. Quoted in Teeters, *Deliberations of IPPC*, p. 107.

31. On the Budapest Congress, see Teeters, ibid., pp. 115-29; and Ruggles-Brise, *Prison Reform*, pp. 122-51.

32. On the Washington Congress, see Teeters, *Deliberations of IPPC*, pp. 130-52; Ruggles-Brise, *Prison Reform*, pp. 152-200; Samuel J. Barrows, *International Prison Congress, Washington*; and Charles R. Henderson, "The Resolutions of the 1910 International Prison Congress in Their Application to the United States," pp. 23-30.

33. Ruggles-Brise, *Prison Reform*, pp. 162-63.

4 The International Society of Criminal Anthropology

This interlude may serve as an appropriate point at which to introduce the work of another international group of scholars, research workers, and practitioners, the International Society of Criminal Anthropology. Their interests paralleled at many points those of the participants in IPC congresses. The Society held its own meetings over a period of twenty-five years, half of them in the closing years of the 19th century, and the second half in the beginning years of the 20th.[1] Their adherents were drawn chiefly from Italy and France and are best known as the Positive School of Criminology.

The influence of Lombroso and Ferri resulted in the formation of the Society and the convening thereafter of no less than seven international conferences of criminal anthropology. The first was held in Rome in 1885, the second in Paris in 1889, and the third in Brussels in August of 1892. The last was attended by representatives of all the countries of Europe, as well as of China and Japan.

The resolutions which emerged from the Paris meeting reflect the influence of the anthropological approach and placed emphasis, for the first time, on the study and understanding of the individual offender, an approach which was to exert so profound an influence long after the last of these conferences had adjourned. These resolutions recommended:

1. Courses in criminal anthropology should be required in medical and law faculties of universities.

2. All countries should be urged to adopt a system of measuring and recording anthropological measurements of criminals.

3. Encourage the establishment of special asylums, distinct from existing prisons and mental hospitals *(asiles d' aliénes)* which would be administered under a medical rather than a penal standpoint.

4. Considered it desirable that the medical inspection service characteristic of the Belgian prison system should be organized in other countries.

5. Urged governments to gather reports of criminal statistics, together with those indicating economic fluctuations.

6. Urged the inclusion in criminal and correctional dossiers—in addition to the data currently gathered—of data related to the physiology, psychology and morality of the personality, in order to provide judges and lawyers with medical expertise in these items.[2]

A score of years would have to pass before Goring's "The English Convict"[3] would disprove—at least to some—the validity of Lombroso's findings with regard to criminal anthropology. But it would be unfair, both to the ideas represented by these resolutions and to the participants who discussed and acted on them, to pass over their import, however tangential or delayed, for the understanding and treatment of antisocial conduct.

The sense of what was embodied in these acts of the delegates was, after all, not wholly irrelevant. Their discussions and resolves are perhaps most accurately seen against the spirit of the time, which was marked by beginning attempts to measure and quantify as many as possible of the sectors of the human endowment. Alphonse Bertillon, basing his work on the hypothesis of Adolphe Quetelet that no two human beings embodied precisely the same measurements, was to give to the world a system of identification of the individual criminal, based on fourteen accurate recordings of his anthropometric measurements, notes of deformities, color, scars, impression of thumb lines and other measurable bodily characteristics. Although "Bertillonage," as it was called, was to enjoy a relatively short-lived period of acceptance, its author did give to the world as well the *"portrait parle,"* a system of standardized photography of the subject in both full face and profile, used almost universally for criminal identification by both police and corrections departments today.

From this same anthropometric approach derived the discovery of the idiocyncrasy of the human finger identification. Recognition of the uniqueness of the print of the finger is ascribed by some to ancient Chinese references to "finger-marks" though the claim remains debatable to this day. Its application to criminalistics was the result of an extensive international chain of collaboration starting with two Englishmen, Henry Faulds, associated at the time with a hospital in Tokyo, and William J. Herschel, an Indian civil servant in Bengal. Both of these men, working independently, and widely separated, published letters in the latter part of 1880 in the British scientific journal *Nature*. Sir Francis Galton of England later verified the validity of the findings of these two as to the uniqueness and permanence of fingerprints through lengthy scientific observations. His work served as the technical basis for the fingerprint classification systems later developed by Sir Edward R. Henry, Commissioner of the London Metropolitan Police, and Juan Vucetich, a police official in the province of Buenos Aires. Except that the latter's work achieved acceptance in Latin American and other Spanish-speaking countries, Henry's system is today universal.[4]

The work of Alfred Binet and Thomas Simon of France on the measurement of the intelligence of children and the creation of a scale based on the "Intelligence Quotient" took place during this same period and contributed greatly to the understanding of the characteristics of delinquents. Nor can we leave this period without some reference to another scientist, working in his clinic and private office in Vienna, whose basic aim was to formulate a conceptual framework which would help to explain the dynamics of the individual psychotic or neurotic patient. It is fair to say that the later applications of the "individualization" of the offender (both before and after sentence by a court) stems from these two late 19th and early 20th century approaches: the anthropological of Lombroso and the psychoanalytic of Freud.

The child-guidance movement, and its rise as a diagnostic and therapeutic adjunct to the juvenile court, as a result of William Healy's pioneering work on the individual delinquent:[5] physical, psychological, psychiatric and social, derives basically from these two great seminal thinkers. It was more than a chance coincidence that the establishment in Chicago of the first clinic to specialize in the problems of children—the Juvenile Psychopathic Institute—took place in 1909, one year after Freud had delivered at Clark University in Worcester, Massachusetts (at the invitation of G. Stanley Hall), his first lectures in psychoanalysis in the United States.[6] And who can gauge the benefits which this same clinical and dynamic approach has wrought for an understanding of other emotionally disturbed persons—children as well as adults—the pre-delinquent as well as the convicted?

The intellectual history of mankind is replete with instances of great explosive ideas launched by brilliant men, to whose original work was ascribed an exaggerated significance and importance beyond what they had ever anticipated. In time the innovative settles down, the man and his idea are cut down to size, and both—diminished by subsequent research and experiment—finally take their proper and proportionate place in the long and exciting history of ideas. Thus we tend to forget the origins of ideas whose currency in the market place was not always universal. The influence of Darwin for the nineteenth century, for example, was manifested all the way up to World War I, in the until then prevailing notion of the infinite perfectability of man and his works. Psychiatry derives from hypnotism, or Mesmerism in the same sense that chemistry owes its origins to alchemy. Today's use of the encephalogram owes its beginnings to early nineteenth century experiments in hypnotism, as this was developed by Charcot, Janet and the later psychoanalysts, and to that pseudo-science—phrenology, much as today's sophisticated electronics stems from Volta, Faraday and Franklin.

Geneva in 1896, Amsterdam in 1901, Turin in 1906, were hosts to the 4th, 5th and 6th conferences on criminal anthropology. The last, the 7th, was held at Cologne in 1911, two years after Cesare Lombroso had died at the age of 73. Almost 40 countries were represented by the 280 participants.

As might be expected, the high point of the conference was the tribute to Lombroso. Delivered by Dr. Kurella of Bonn, the review and appreciation of his life's work brought a standing ovation. The conference ended with a speech by his daughter, Dr. Gina Lombroso Ferrero of Turin, who claimed for her father and his contributions to criminology, the new idea of the juvenile court (established first in Cook County, Illinois, in 1899); the growth of probation for both adult and juvenile offenders; the use of examinations for detection of possible epilepsy (forerunner of the experiments in the use of the electro-encephalogram, of dilantin for hyper-aggressive children, and of other pharmaco-therapeutic measures); the indeterminate sentence; the laws for control of alcohol; and the extension of statutes covering pardons.

After citing as further examples of the extent of the influence of her father's work (in addition to the above), the Elmira Reformatory, the Framingham Reformatory for Women in Massachusetts and the George Junior Republic in New York, as well as advanced penal institutions and methods in Brazil, her address concluded with a passage whose eloquence merits full and direct quotation:

> Voilá pourtant comment cette symbiose que mon pére avait preconisée pour le crime, commence à fructifier parmi les étudiants du crime.
>
> C'est ainsi que la société moderne, s'unissant d'un commun élan, a réussi a dominer la foudre et la tempête en profitant des

études des uns et des tentatives des autres, arrivera a tirer de la lie de sa population tous les avantages possibles—en composant de la ceindre de sa société des légers tissus incandescents dont le leur l'éclairera le long des routes de l'avenir.[7]

Narration of the contribution made to criminology by the "anthropological" approach would be incomplete without inclusion of two brief revivals of international effort in that field. As a result of the efforts of Professor A. Lenz of Austria and Dr. Viernstein of Germany, the moribund International Society of Criminal Anthropologists was revived. *Die Kriminalbiologische Gesellschaft*, an international organization, was the result, whose purpose was to secure collaboration of persons concerned with the criminal aspects of sociology and biology. The society convened congresses in Vienna in 1927, Dresden in 1928, Munich in 1930 and Hamburg in 1933. Their proceedings, together with reports and discussions, are available in four published volumes.[8] In Rome in 1938, one year before the outbreak of war, the first meeting of an Italian congress of criminology was held, whose five volume report was published the next year.[9] Deliberations of the delegates at Rome reflect the continued influence of the Positivist School. The International Society of Criminology continues to concern itself largely with many of the same agenda questions to this day.[10]

Notes

1. This section is based largely on the *Proceedings* of the respective conferences published in seven separate volumes, all in French with the exception of the final conference held at Cologne, which is in German. A list of the *Proceedings* is contained in the Bibliography under International Society of Criminal Anthropology.

2. Translated and summarized from *Actes du deuxième Congrès international d'anthropologie criminelle, Paris, août, 1889.*

3. Charles Goring, *The English Convict.*

4. *Encyclopedia Britannica* (New York: Benton Publishers, 1970), 9:270-9.

5. William Healy, *The Individual Delinquent.*

6. For an excellent resumé of the development of the child guidance movement, see Helen Wittmer, *Psychiatric Clinics for Children* (New York: Commonwealth Fund, 1940), esp. Ch. 3.

7. *Bericht über der VII International Kongress für kriminalanthropologie, Köln a Rhein, 9-13 Oktober, 1911,* p. 137.

8. All in German, and titled *Mitteilungen der kriminalbiologischen Gesellschaft.*

9. *Atti del I Congresso internazionale di Criminologia: Relazioni generali e discussion*, 5 vols. (Rome: Tippografia delle mantellate, 1939).

10. See pages 130-32 below.

Between the
World Wars

5   The League of Nations

Little did Mme. Lombroso-Ferrero sense in 1911, from anything that can be read into her then-hopeful challenge to the future, that three years later World War I would involve all of the major nations which had been represented at the Cologne meeting and that at least a decade would have to elapse before the world, devastated by that war, could turn its attention again to international efforts in the field of crime. World War I came and went, changing the entire fabric of society to a degree and in a fashion more wide-spread, more fundamentally, than any preceding single event in human history.

Before the IPC could convene its first post-war congress in 1925, a new area of work and effort had begun—this time by the newly and hopefully created League of Nations. Under its aegis in the imposing new Palais des Nations at Geneva, the League took up some of the proud boasts of Lombroso's daughter and began to direct international attention and impetus to two of the areas she had emphasized: probation and the juvenile court. The League was to give leadership in these and related areas, right up to the start of World War II, although participation in its activities tended to be limited to the British Commonwealth countries, the nations of Europe, and to a relatively small number of Asian and Latin American states.

The Child Welfare Committee

The idea of an international association for the protection of children was first put forward officially in 1911, and led in 1913 to an international congress summoned in Brussels by the Belgian government. National organizations of children's agencies had long existed; it was the expectation of this congress that these would now come together for mutual cooperation and exchange of information, and that the support of governments to these ends would also be forthcoming. This congress, having established an office, drafted and submitted through diplomatic channels to the various governments a constitution for their approval.

The outbreak of World War I one year later postponed further consideration, but soon after the end of hostilities the Belgian government summoned a second congress at Brussels. Official representation came from thirty-three countries and a large number of voluntary child welfare organizations as well. Despite the desire of some delegates that Brussels be made the headquarters of the new organization, the lure of Geneva and the bright expectations held for the newly formed League of Nations, resulted in the International Association for the Protection of Children being placed under the direction of the League, under Article 24 of its Covenant which specified such auspices for organizations established by general treaties.

At the Fourth Assembly of the League in 1923, the Association was reconstituted as a coordinating link between national private child welfare associations. The Social Section in the League secretariat was strengthened and enlarged to take on the new responsibility and its Advisory Commission made provision for liaison with international organizations concerned with matters of health and labor.

Thereafter the Child Welfare Committee concerned itself with, or expressed interest in, such problems as prevention of blindness, moral and social dangers besetting children, illegitimacy, legal age of marriage and consent, employment, health, repatriation of children and young people stranded abroad, and the influence of the cinema on child welfare. These were among the matters indirectly related to juvenile delinquency. Direct areas of concern included the juvenile court and the provision of probation and other services auxiliary to that court. Concern with questions of traffic in women and children, and in obscene publications, were directed to a separate committee, the two committees forming the composite Advisory Commission on Social Questions.

In all these matters, the League undertook to assist governments in four ways: by providing an "action center" to secure the cooperation of governments; by the preparation of conventions, agreements and conferences as well as through the cooperation of voluntary associations; by creating a "study center" which would direct and carry out investigations by means of its own members and "assessors," special experts, subcommittees or through other organizations; and by serving as a "world documentation center" designed to facilitate the exchange of information between governments and private bodies on such matters as conventions, agreements, laws, regulations, institutions, statistics, and the publication of a review.

It is pertinent to note here that questions relating to delinquency of children and the juvenile court were to remain matters of continuous concern to the League right up to 1937. Thereafter, the reorganized Advisory Commission on Social Questions turned its interest to the broader implications of the situation of children, especially concern for the "normal" child.

While admitting that the welfare of the young was a broad subject, the committee chose not to limit its concern to such matters as the health of infants and very young children, but to extend its conception of the term to include not only minors of all ages, but the wide field of family welfare, as well as the training of social workers. During the dozen years of the committee's work, six of its excellent publications were published by the League.[1]

One of the most significant of these League reports described the Scandinavian Child Welfare Councils (known today as Child Welfare Boards).[2] These Councils, composed of professionals as well as of citizens from the community, persons without technical training in problems of children and youth assume responsibility for the actions and conditions of young persons which in other parts of the world are handed over to the jurisdiction of the juvenile court. The historic exemption of children from the kind of punishments meted out to adults, incorporated in the Swedish Penal Code as early as 1734, and which found expression in the Swedish Act of 1902 which created the Child Welfare Councils, had derived from the "old Nordic tradition which entrusts child care to special ... local boards."[3] The League report on the subject received wide circulation and had far-reaching influence on the entire delinquency field. It came to attention at a time when the juvenile court was beginning to be viewed as perhaps not the optimum instrumentality for handling children charged with offences, or who, by reason of neglect, dependency, or other family difficulty, stood in need of the "aid, encouragement and guidance" promised in the pioneering juvenile court acts.

Thirty-five years have passed since this report was issued. Today, in many places, impatience with the shortcomings of the juvenile court is being manifested, at the same time that curbs are being placed on a procedure which, while presumed not to be criminal, may nevertheless have the same effect on the child as would his appearance in an adult criminal court. The term "juvenile delinquency" was coined originally in the hope that it would not convey the same stigma as "criminal." But the coin is tarnished—and today the need for a new euphemism may be at hand. Or something more drastic even than a change of label, such as a court procedure which with proper safeguards for legal rights will deal only with the type of offenses which, if committed by an adult, would be labelled crimes. All other conditions of childhood would be diverted from the juvenile court process and cared for in non-court, non-punitive, non-stigmatizing agencies. The Scandinavian countries had showed the way, and the League broadcast their message. Today, 35 years later, that message begins to be heard—and to be applied in practice. Scotland, for example, is not alone in its recent scrapping of the traditional juvenile court system in favor of a procedure more closely akin to that embodied in the Swedish Child Welfare Boards.[4]

With the rapid urbanization and industrialization of countries newly come to statehood (if not independence), the problem of how to deal with the increasing burden of maladjustment and criminality becomes a matter of grave importance. Seemingly part of the price which must be paid for "development," such countries now seek help from those places where special measures for dealing with delinquency are thought to be advanced. The questions which such newly developing nations now face is whether they will go the road of court and judicial dealing with their children and young people, or whether they will opt for the more socialized, non-court procedures suggested by the Scandinavian experience. There is a limit to the reliance that may be placed on the law for the solution of social ills. In no area is this more true than in matters relating to the conduct and the training of the young.[5]

The Child Welfare Committee began cooperation with the International Prison Commission very early in its work, their mutual interest in the issue of the juvenile court having first brought them together in 1926.[6] Joint concern in this and related matters was to continue almost up to the outbreak of war in 1939.

As one of its first acts, the committee in 1932 instructed the Secretary General to request the IPC and other international bodies concerned with penal and penitentiary questions to submit annual reports to the League. The initial responses were brief and nonspecific, but as the Secretary General's requests became more urgent, valuable materials in the way of reports and research were submitted to Geneva and found their way into their growing library of information on these questions.

From these data, the Child Welfare Committee drew the conclusion that probation officers should be required to have had extensive experience with children, to have some training in the social sciences, as well as being "fond of children and capable of exercising a strong moral influence over them."[7]

A search of the social documentation of the League from 1920 to

1939 turns up no significant further references or reports on the single topic of probation, although it may be recalled that this was indicated as an area of interest at the outset of their work. However, the Child Welfare Committee's interest in the question of juvenile courts extended to so-called "Auxiliary Services" of such courts, which included probation in passing. The importance attached to the duties of probation officers in the investigation and supervision of children, placed in their care by the court, implied a high degree of dependence on such officers within the tribunal for children.

The frequently arbitrary or accidental determination of the delinquency of some children whose background suggests many parallels to the condition of others who may not have been apprehended for commission of an offense, is reflected in the findings of the committee at its spring 1931 meeting. There exists a "close relationship of the problem of the child who is materially or morally abandoned with that of juvenile delinquency. This is one and the same social and educational problem, and for its practical solution, no distinction can be made between children in moral danger and juvenile delinquents."[8] The committee further stressed the importance of investigating the child's background, physical condition, and the need for observation centers (diagnostic clinics?) for examination and study.

The interest of the committee was now to be extended beyond the point of adjudication of delinquency to include concern for the kind of institutions to which such children were committed. The committee, at this same 1931 meeting, cited as "important ... the necessity for replacing penitentiary institutions—in particular, prisons—by homes or educational institutions," and the value of including women staff members "of every social class" into such institutions, including those for boys.[9]

During its 8th session in 1932, the Child Welfare Committee reaffirmed its declaration of the years before, that all confinement in prisons should be absolutely—and at once—excluded in the case of children, and that treatment applied to cases of delinquency should be prompted by a desire for the child's education and training and not for his punishment. As an example, the "so-called cottage system" was advocated because it "effectively minimizes the disadvantages of institutionalism and of artificial community life, and creates better educational conditions for developing the social sense of the inmates."[10]

The expressed concern of the Child Welfare Committee in institutions "for erring and delinquent minors," as it was phrased in one of their reports,[11] describes many findings that are valid today in some of the more advanced countries, and contains, as well, suggestions which have yet to be realized on any kind of universal scale. By "findings" are meant such conditions as the following: "allowing children, in certain cases, to be sentenced to imprisonment or to be kept in prison pending trial," and the fact that the age at which minors are regarded as criminally responsible does not "always correspond to the age at which a boy or girl is mentally altogether mature, and in many cases is several years below the age at which a child attains its civil majority."[1][2]

Suggestions included the creation of observation centers for study and diagnosis of children who come before the courts and that the commitment of children thus discovered to be in need of medico-psychological supervision be made to "establishments of a special character." Hostels "in which children live under a system of semi-liberty, enabling them to have independent work or training outside the hostel [affords] the inmates regular contact with normal, everyday life under the supervision of teachers. . . . "[1][3] Recent interest in community-dealing with offenders, whether in residential or nonresidential facilities, the development of the so-called halfway house, is thus seen to parallel, thirty years later, this early League of Nations recommendation.

The Borstal institutions of Great Britain were singled out for special endorsement as an alternative to "reformative institutions." The committee strongly advocated, in a separate subsection of its report, abolition of the names of institutions "which expressly imply that they are places for training delinquent minors," and the substitution, in their place, of the heading, "educational institutions."[1][4] Recent moves in some jurisdictions to place such institutions under departments of education, instead of corrections, welfare, or special youth services divisions, are belated responses to this earlier, forward-looking recommendation.

Of all the suggestions about the internal organization of such institutions—the value of case studies; specifications for the qualification of staff; educational, physical, and vocational training; maintenance of ties with the outside world, and length of stay—none is more euphemistic than the following with reference to disciplinary punishment, chiefly for what it indicates as to the disagreement that must have prevailed in committee before concensus was achieved: "Disciplinary punishment applied to children should not be prejudicial to their physical health or moral well-being, and should in particular, not be of such a kind as to weaken the child's sense of personal dignity." Indignation, tempered by chauvinism and diplomacy, one is tempted to observe.

The Child Welfare Committee was not unmindful of the necessity of accurate record-keeping "for judging the effectiveness of the various methods of treatment applied to such children; such records to contain basic data of his development during training." In the use of this material for followup purposes, after the child had left the institution, zealous researchers were warned "to proceed with the greatest discretion in order not to interfere in lives which may . . . have been reformed."

Coordinating Efforts of the League of Nations

Collaboration between nations in the holding of congresses on crime and the participation of their delegates in the discussions within such congresses did not, at this point, satisfy some of the private organizations, notably the Howard League for Penal Reform located in Britain. In 1929 it published a critical memorandum citing not only the inefficiency, but even the inhumanity, of the prison system of specific countries, and asking that the League of Nations place on its agenda the question of penal reform, and further that it elaborate and adapt prison codes which it would urge all member states to adopt. The shadow of John Howard, from which the society derived its name, could be sensed throughout the memorandum, which received wide attention in many countries. In January of the following year the initiative of Cuba succeeded in securing a place for the question on the agenda of the Council of the League.

A supplement to the 1932 report of the Secretary-General of the League drew the attention of member states to the common concern of the League and the IPC in such matters as international criminal and prison statistics; safeguards against the abuse of detention before trial; draft of a model treaty of extradition; repatriation after release of prisoners sentenced in foreign countries; the scientific examination of prisoners; and a survey of the prison systems of member nations. Concern for problems of prison labor was scheduled to be shared with the International Labour Organisation. The report also made reference to the Standard Minimum Rules for the Treatment of Prisoners, referred to it, after 1926, by the IPC. By a resolution of 26 September 1934 the Assembly of the League endorsed the Rules.

In that same year the Assembly of the League had instructed the Secretary-General to secure information from several "technical" organizations concerned with penal and criminal law problems and to make this information available. The seven organizations were: the International Penal Law Association, the International Bureau for the Unification of Penal Law, the International Criminal Police Commission, the International Penal Commission, the Howard League for Penal Reform, the International Law Association, and the International Penal Law Union. In May 1932 these organizations affixed their signature to a joint memorandum which formalized their intent to collaborate with the League in problems of mutual concern. Reports of the League's continued interest in penal matters from this time forward were thereafter regularly reported in its *Journal*.[15] It may be noted here that this interest was never reflected in the creation of a special organ within the League to deal directly with such questions.

An inquiry was undertaken to determine the total number of prisoners over the age of 18—both men and women—who, as of December 31, 1936 were deprived of their liberty (excluding persons in medical and mental hospitals) because they were: 1) awaiting trial, or on appeal; 2) under judicial sentence; or 3) were "detained and not included in the above categories." The implication was clear that the League Assembly was, in this third category, seeking to determine the number of persons—political prisoners, for example—who might be confined for other than criminal activities, or outside of the normal judicial channels. The questionnaire concluded with a request for information on "the measures taken in different countries during recent years with the object of reducing the number of prisoners."

This is the first instance of an international organization actually taking steps toward undertaking a world-wide statistical survey, although the idea had been bruited for at least sixty years. Two years later the onset of World War II made the inquiry, in more ways than one, purely academic.

As a result of the communication of the substance of the reports from these organizations, the League Assembly in 1934 urged the widest possible publicity for the Standard Minimum Rules and cited the following as among those abuses which were "contrary to the principles of rational treatment of prisoners":

a)   deprivation of opportunity for religious worship;
b)   use of violence and other physical restraints for the extortion of evidence or confessions;
c)   employment of prisoners gangs under conditions akin to slavery;
d)   protracted underfeeding;
e)   detention of women without supervision by women officers.

The attention of the League Assembly having been drawn to these "various reprehensible practices," it concluded its resolution with the "hope that such practices, where they exist, will be abandoned." The Standard Minimum Rules, at this point, totalled fifty-four articles.

The League should also be credited with the preparation of several significant draft conventions: for the international prevention and repression of terrorism; for the suppression of the illicit traffic in dangerous drugs; and for the suppression of the exploitation of prostitution. Additional subjects prepared for international acceptance and agreement included: slavery, traffic in obscene publications, as well as the suppression of counterfeiting of national currencies. A final draft convention was prophetically entitled "For the Creation of an International Criminal Court."

But this last may be giving the Secretary-General, or his staff, credit for too great prescience. Surely no one could foresee the convening of the International Allied Tribunal on War Crimes at Nuremberg just ten years later which, for the first time in history, was to hold persons individually responsible for acts which constitute a crime under international law whether such acts were committed by a head of state, a responsible government official, or were carried out by others under the direct command of their superiors.

One of the very last acts of the League relative to the criminal field was the convening of a small meeting of representatives of the technical organizations which had been furnishing the League with information. The meeting was charged with drawing up a joint memorandum on the subject of measures for preventing violence or other constraints against witnesses and persons being held for trial, and the question of guarantees against the abuse of preventive detention.

Whatever the results of this meeting, they were overshadowed two months later by the outbreak of World War II. The subject of "abuse of preventive detention," however, this time without accompanying "guarantees," would again appear in the public arena thirty years later.

Notes

1. These were *Auxiliary Services of Juvenile Courts* (1931); *Organisation of Juvenile Courts and the Results Attained Hitherto* (1932); *Institutions for Erring and Delinquent Minors* (1934); *Child Welfare Councils* (1937); *The Placing of Children in Families*, 2 vols. (1938); and *Study on the Legal Position of the Illegitimate Child* (1939).

2. See Child Welfare Committee, *Child Welfare Councils*.

3. *Social Work and Legislation in Sweden* (Stockholm: Tryckeriaktiebolaget Tiden, 1938), p. 223. We are indebted to Thorsten Sellin for his assistance in matters pertaining to the Scandinavian countries.

4. See Benedict S. Alper, "The Juvenile Court at Three Score and Ten: Will It Survive *Gault*?" *Albany Law Review* 34 (Fall 1969): 62-7.

5. See ed., "Crime Prevention in the Context of National Development."

6. In addition to the publications already referred to, primary sources for the work of the League in this area are League of Nations, Advisory Commission for the Protection of Children and Young People, Child Welfare Committee, *Minutes, 1925-1936* (Geneva, 1937); and *Monthly Summary of the League of Nations, 1921-1938*.

7. Child Welfare Committee, *Minutes*, 25 April 1935, p. 8.

8. Ibid., p. 9.

9. Ibid., p. 8.

10. Ibid., p. 6.

11. Child Welfare Committee, *Institutions for Erring and Delinquent Minors.*

12. Ibid., *Minutes*, 25 April 1935, p. 5.

13. Ibid., p. 7.

14. Ibid.

15. Its title was *Penal and Penitentiary Questions*, and it frequently carried the subtitle *Improvements in Penal Administration.*

6   The IPC Between
       the Wars

London — 1925

The Armistice which brought World War I to an end found the countries which had engaged in it confronting serious social problems. The result was a revival of interest in a meeting which would discuss those problems, leading to the convening of the 9th International Penitentiary Congress in London in 1925.[1] In his inaugural address, President Sir Evelyn Ruggles-Brise reflected upon the impatience which the war and the early post-war years had engendered: "The whole tendency of the international movement since 1872 has been a revolt, and a very strong and determined revolt, not only against the use and abuse of prisons, as the one and only means of punishing offenses against the law, but against the popular conception of prisons as gloomy strongholds, in which it is sufficient that a man should be locked up for so many weeks, or months, or years—if not literally 'branded,' as in old days, yet with the *fletrissure* or mark against his name, which would render almost impossible his re-instatement into honest life."

The war had also brought a rise in delinquency, which moved the president to remark, in words which are perhaps more striking today than when he delivered them:

No truth has been more clearly grasped by former Congresses, notably at Paris and Brussels in 1895 and 1900, than that the state which took the best care of its children was likely to be the most free from crime.

65

Crediting the recent past for some progress, he observed that "the two principal inventions of the last half century have been 1) conditional conviction—in its two forms, *sursis* on the continent of Europe, and probation in English-speaking countries; 2) the indeterminate sentence, with its double aspect as a measure of reform and as a measure of security." Thereafter he paid tribute to the devotion of the IPC Secretary-General Professor Simon van der Aa of the Netherlands but for whose "working quietly and unostentatiously in his bureau at Groningen, we should not have survived the dark and difficult days of the Great War."

The major recommendations to the Congress followed. The first affirmed "that all the States who are represented here officially today should arrive at a common agreement to come to the financial rescue of our Central Bureau . . . with sufficient resources to carry on its work with dignity and efficiency." The second recommendation went to the matter of an international criminal statistic which "would greatly stimulate activity in adopting in all States the best penal and preventive measures."

The major agenda items were legislation, administration and prevention. The failure to include a section on children and delinquency was due neither to neglect nor oversight, but was rather the result of the League of Nations assuming responsibility for this area. The major addresses delivered at the general assemblies of conference delegates were concerned with issues of punishment, flexibility on the part of those who prescribe and administer it, and on the individualization of punishment.

Additional topics included differentiation of the criminal and the insane; the "boarding out" of children; and the recommended reliance on prisoner's aid societies rather than on the police for the supervision of parolees. The question of Standard Minimum Rules for Prisoners was again put forth, to be endorsed nine years later by the League of Nations.

"The Meaning of Punishment," by the Rt. Hon. Viscount Haldane of Cloan, departed somewhat from the agenda with a plea for the total abolition of punishment, a possibility which he advocated as in keeping with recent psychological definitions of the nature of conscience. Perhaps his plea did not go totally unheeded, for among the congress resolutions was one which advocated "that every endeavor be made to substitute in suitable cases other methods in place of imprisonment: in particular that: 1) the system of probation should be extended to the utmost extent; 2) the power of the court to impose fines should be extended and the machinery for payment of fines should be developed so as to eliminate as far as possible imprisonment in default of payment." This was followed by a lengthy resolution on the value of individualization of punishment by judges in the sentencing process.

Approximately six hundred persons participated in the 1925 London

Congress, of whom slightly less than half were from other than the host country. The fifty-five governments represented marked a new high in the international crime meetings, and for the first time their proceedings were published both in French and in English.

In the year after London, the IPC met and voted to transform its secretariat into a permanent bureau for documentation and information and to move the headquarters to Berne, a more central location than Groningen. As one of its first undertakings, the IPC undertook to prepare, for consideration by member governments, the first preliminary draft of the Standard Minimum Rules for the Treatment of Prisoners, "a set of general rules designed to assure suitable treatment for all those who are deprived of their liberty by a decision of the competent judicial authorities in their different courts." These are the words of its initiator, Sir Arthur Waller, chairman at the time of the Prison Commission for England and Wales. Sir Arthur, Lord Polworth (Chairman of the Scottish Prison Commission) and Mr. (afterwards Sir Alexander) Paterson, the internationally respected penologist, composed the first draft. Thereafter the Minimum Rules were to be a recurrent subject on the agenda of almost every succeeding international crime gathering, whether or not formally acknowledged as such. The draft represented the first promulgation of the notion of internationally acceptable standards, although historically it may be seen to derive from the sense of the London Congress of 1872.

Prague — 1930

The then president of the IPC, Dr. August Miricka, professor of law at Charles University, served as presiding officer of the 1930 Prague Congress which held its sessions in the Palace of Parliament. The four-part agenda again included the question of child delinquents and the law.[2]

One important adopted resolution called for the unification of the fundamental principles of penal law on an international basis. The necessity for heeding the individual differences of member states was reflected in the caveat that "the effort of unification must be limited at that point where [there] is danger of depriving penal law in the various countries of the indispensable strength which accrues from the historical development of each country and from the ideas deeply rooted in the mind of the people."

Questions concerning the training of prison personnel, previously raised at London and again at Stockholm, were here again considered. The progress that had been made since may be gauged by the detailed resolution passed on this basic question:

All officials of the prison administration must be specially instructed and formed for their function, a higher scientific education being requisite for the superior positions.

It is indispensable to have special schools and courses for the instruction of the directing and supervising personnel. The establishment of an institute of penal science and criminology seems to be necessary in each country. . . .

The candidates for penitentiary service must prove their ability for practical and judicious fulfillment of their duties . . . and their aptitude for the scientific treatment of problems concerning the application of penalties by submitting to an examination and to a period of practical service.

No candidates should be definitely accepted unless they have shown during a specified period that they possess, besides the necessary practical and scientific knowledge, a personal interest in their profession, an honourable character, human sympathy and knowledge, and the ability to treat abnormals physically, intellectually, and morally.

The social and economic implications of these high standards moved the congress to recommend that "it is necessary to grant to the various grades of officials, taking into account their duty, a salary assuring their economic position. It seems desirable to grant to penitentiary personnel a special place in the hierarchy of public servants, according it the advantages generally granted to public servants in various countries."

The IPC was charged with responsibility for initiating a scientific study for the purpose of determining "the causes of fluctuations in criminality," a reminder of their historic interest in international crime statistics. Other subjects discussed included the children's courts, probation and parole, and cellular as against congregate regimes. The last had been the continuing object of heated debate at previous congresses, and at least one returning delegate later reported that a bitter battle had taken place in the section meetings between the proponents of the two rival systems. They seem to have divided into the two camps largely on the basis of national differences in their historic legal backgrounds.

The resolution that emerged is worthy of extensive quotation because it reflects the division of opinion that marked the debates which preceded it, and indicates, as well, a serious attempt both to express these diverse points of view as well as the areas where attempts at compromise could, at least, be proffered.

1)   Solitary or cellular confinement must be considered as an organic part of a progressive system.

2)   As for prisoners awaiting trial, the system of solitary confinement should in principle apply.

3)   Solitary confinement in the case of sentences of short duration, has advantages but also certain inconveniences. It is possible to realize the advantages and avoid the inconveniences by adequate medical service and a system of classification of prisoners.

4)   In the case of sentences of long duration, as a general rule, progressive regimes of community [i.e., congregate] treatment should be substituted for solitary confinement. . . .

5)   When feasible, at the request of the prisoner, solitary confinement may be continued if the prisoner has shown good conduct and if for physical or moral reasons he is entitled to special consideration.

6)   In general, isolation for the night must be considered as an essential element of modern prison administration, although there may arise in some countries certain exceptional circumstances which require a system of dormitories or community rooms properly supervised.

It is in relation to issues such as this that one may retrace the gradual evolution of an international consciousness, down a road marked initially by conflict, leading slowly to compromise, and finally to a degree of agreement, if not complete consensus. Erratic, frequently exasperating, dominated by considerations of nationalism, this resolution both exemplifies and epitomizes the process of developing cooperation in the international sphere.

As its final act, the Prague Congress approved the inclusion of the word "Penal" in the official name of the Commission, so that thereafter it was to be known as the International Penal and Penitentiary Commission, or IPPC. A review of the proceedings gives no hint of the dire events which would transpire in the latter years of the decade. No prophetic voice was to point out that Prague and Berlin, sites of the penultimate and the last congress to be held under IPC auspices, would soon confront one another in fateful fashion.

Berlin — 1935

Dr. Erwin Bumke presided over what was to be the last in the prewar series of these historic congresses under IPPC auspices, the 1935 Berlin Congress.[3] Officially representing fifty governments, the gathering included over seven hundred individual members, of whom just under one-half came from countries other than Germany. An unprecedently large number of preparatory papers had been submitted in advance, which were to serve as the basis for congress discussion.

Germany was at the time in the throes of a political upheaval which had its effect on the congress, as it was later to have on the whole world. Some indication of this effect may be gained from the portion of the published *Proceedings* which reports the Secretary-General of the IPPC as saying:

> The last Congress, pursuing the long series of the large international gatherings of this kind, which had been started more than sixty years ago, presents a general resemblance to the former and, in particular, to the two preceding ones. . . . There is however, a special feature that should be referred to. For the first time at the London Congress in 1925 and again at the Prague Congress in 1930, the agenda of the general assemblies included an address delivered by one of the most prominent men of the country on some topic in the field of penal and penitentiary science and practice which was not directly connected with any of the questions to be discussed by the Congress according to the program. In a similar way the plenary meetings at Berlin have had the advantage of beginning with addresses delivered by some of the highest and most competent authorities, but these addresses were not confined within the same cadre. The political and social revolution which occurred in Germany in the interval between the Congress of 1930 and that of 1935, having produced a change of fundamental conceptions also in the field of the criminal law and the prison system, these official orators have wanted to expose on this occasion to the members of the Congress, assembled from so many parts of the world, particularly important ideas and the main principles which are at the bottom of the new German penal law and its application, as also the spirit and the aims of the new regime as a whole.[4]

These remarks showed amazing restraint compared, for example, with those of a delegate from abroad:

> The reaction to the delineation of Nazi penal philosophy by its exponents who attended the Congress was intense. At no previous Congress was there so much hostility manifested among the delegates. Those from abroad could not endure the many drastic opinions voiced by the German spokesman. This Congress was later labeled 'A Congress in Chains' by the British delegate Geoffrey Bing.[5]

Major differences of opinion centered around considerations of the humane treatment of prisoners, sterilization and castration of criminals, and the rights of the accused in criminal trials. Although the German delegates outnumbered those from abroad, the former voted *en bloc* on nearly every issue, and succeeded in preventing a formal vote on the question,

"Are the methods applied in the execution of penalties with a view to educating and reforming criminals (intensive humanization, favors granted, considerable relaxation of coercion in the execution of penalties by degrees) calculated to bring about the effects aimed at and are these tendencies generally advisable?"[6]

The German delegation succeeded, however, in obtaining passage of a resolution favoring castration and sterilization in order to achieve "favorable preventive-therapeutic results."[7]

Excerpts from a speech by Dr. Goebbels, Reichs Minister for Propaganda, are revealing:

Behind every revolution there is an idea, and it is the object of the revolution that this idea should win the day in all domains of public and private life. Revolutions which merely exhaust their strength in the domain of the policy of power are generally only of short duration. It is true that they put new men in positions of responsibility, but the coming of these new men does not mean that any new ideas are evolved. It is only a policy of power which is felt to be a means for a higher purpose and whose real object is regarded as the transference of the ideology behind it, which set in motion from the realm of theories to that of realities, that gives the revolution an importance which continues to take effect beyond its own time.[8]

Implications of the projected German philosophy of penology and criminal law are further exemplified in the following passage from Goebbels:

The classical characteristic of the system that we overcame was liberalism. While liberalism started with the individual and made the individual the center of all things, we have replaced the individual by the nation and the man by the community. It must be admitted that in doing so the liberty of the individual had to be restricted in so far as it collided or was incompatible with the liberty of the nation. That is no limitation of the idea of liberty as such; for to overdo it for the individual means risking or even seriously endangering the liberty of the people. The limits of the individual idea of liberty therefore coincide with those of the national idea of liberty. No individual, however high or low his position, can have the right to make use of his liberty at the expense of the national idea of liberty, for it is only the security of the national idea of liberty that guarantees him personal liberty too in the long run.[9]

Reaction to ideas such as these, from correctional people who had spent their lives in attempts to extend the frontiers of individualization of punishment, ran very deep and very strong.

The agenda consisted of the familiar four sections: penal legislation, prison administration, crime prevention, and juvenile delinquency. Other questions discussed included the provision of homes for discharged prisoners, prison labor, and the problems of children and youth in moral danger.

No single item on the agenda aroused as much discussion and disagreement as the subject of *ex post facto* laws—punishment for acts which at the time of their commission had not been prohibited or were not punishable by law. This was the subject of a speech by Dr. Franz Gürtner, Minister of Justice, which opened the 1935 Berlin Congress. Entitled "The Idea of Justice in the German Penal Reform," it described in detail how the new government of Germany was revising the old penal code. The practical result of the lack of *ex post facto* laws, was that

> If the judge finds no penalty prescribed by the law for the case which he has to decide, he must acquit the accused, however deserving of punishment he may consider him to be, and, further, even if he is firmly convinced that the legislator wished to punish this case, and would have provided a punishment if he had included a case of this kind among the matters of consideration. . . It is at this point that the criticism of the National Socialist view of the law and the State begins. It makes the serious claim that *all* behavior deserving punishment shall meet with its just reward, that no one shall succeed in slipping through the meshes of the law, and that, on the contrary, everyone who commits an act deserving of punishment shall receive due punishment regardless of the incompleteness of the law. The maxim *'nulla poena sine lege'* is therefore contrasted to the maxim *'nullum crimen sine poena.'*[10]

The impact of this retrograde view of the power of the state to punish, its emphasis on the unlimited and completely arbitrary exercise of state authority, the move to reverse the long historic struggle to win respect for the rights of the individual, deeply disturbed visitors from abroad. Some of these demanded and received permission to visit well-known political opponents of the regime who were confined in German prisons, and made known to the outside world the fact and the conditions of their incarceration.

As a result, there emerged a movement on the part of some of the delegates to withdraw from the IPPC following the close of the Berlin Congress, though no immediate action was forthcoming. Rome was selected for the next Congress in 1940. It was never convened. The next—and final—congress of the IPPC would not be held until 1950. Fifteen years of war and post-war upheaval would first intervene.

The decade preceding that war had seen the involvement of the IPPC in more than the convening of congresses.[11] In 1927 it had concerned itself with courts for children, and in 1928 with review of the guarantees against the abuses of preventive detention. In 1935 it presented to its member governments a proposal for a treaty to cover extradition. Between 1935 and 1937 it published an account of penitentiary systems in various countries,[12] and within the next two years an account of the number of prisoners in confinement, proposing measures for the reduction of that number. A directive for the establishment of crime statistics, which had for some years prior been studied by a subcommittee, was issued in 1937.[13] In that same year the IPPC prepared a model format for the scientific examination of prisoners, including the anthropological and "criminal biological." In 1938, the last year before the war, two final reports were released, one on the repatriation of foreign prisoners discharged from custody,[14] and another presenting a suggested program for training of correctional personnel, and the encouragement of their international interchange between the administrators of various member states.[15]

Shortly thereafter the IPPC turned its attention to the last series of tasks it was to assume under its original name and format. It first undertook a fresh examination of the penal systems of member governments, and appointed a number of committees, each to undertake a specific study into such problems as the treatment of habitual criminals, the effect of war on criminality, penal aspects of the death penalty, measures of security in prisons, and the mentally abnormal offender. In 1949 it undertook to revise once again the Standard Minimum Rules, which was completed within the next two years by a committee appointed to that purpose. When completed, the revision was transmitted to the United Nations, upon their request, as the latter had meanwhile elected to initiate action toward gaining international accord for the Minimum Rules, for so long a central concern of the IPPC (see Exhibit 7 at the end of this book).

The IPPC had for better than seventy-five years worked for the improvement of the lot of the offender. The eventual assumption by the United Nations of their role and functions, due largely to partisanship toward the Axis powers during World War II, will be briefly recounted in the following chapter.

Notes

1. This section is based primarily on the English translation of *Proceedings of the IXth International Penitentiary Congress, Held in London, August 1925*, ed. Sir Jan Simon Van Der Aa. See also Negley K. Teeters,

Deliberations of the International Penal and Penitentiary Congresses, pp. 153-64; and American Prison Association, *Proceedings of the 55th Annual Congress of the American Prison Association, Jackson, Mississippi, November 7 to 14, 1925*, pp. 144-69 and 207-33. See the Bibliography for a complete list of *Proceedings*.

2. See Teeters, *Deliberations of IPPC*, pp. 165-76; Sanford Bates, "Report on the International Prison Congress," pp. 308-20; and Sheldon Glueck, "International Prison Congress of 1930," pp. 775-90.

3. This section is based primarily on the English translation of the *Proceedings of the XIth International Penal and Penitentiary Congress, Held in Berlin, August 1935*, ed. Sir Jan Simon Van Der Aa. See also Teeters, *Deliberations of IPPC*, pp. 177-90.

4. Van Der Aa, ed., *Proceedings of the XIth Congress, Berlin*, p. 4.

5. Quoted in Teeters, *Deliberations of IPPC*, p. 178.

6. For the final Resolution, see Van Der Aa, ed., *Proceedings of the XIth Congress, Berlin*, pp. 575-76; for the full discussion, see pp. 168-235 of those *Proceedings*.

7. Ibid., pp. 579-81 for the final Resolution, and pp. 293-386 for a full discussion of this question.

8. Ibid., pp. 444-45.

9. Ibid., p. 449.

10. Ibid., pp. 7 and 9.

11. For a discussion of the work of the IPPC during this period, see Leon Radzinowicz, "International Collaboration in Criminal Science," in Leon Radzinowicz and J.W.C. Turner, eds., *Modern Approach to Criminal Law*, pp. 486-91.

12. *Recueil de Documents en Matiere Pénal et Pénitentiaire*, 7:362-450.

13. Ibid., 5:490-505.

14. Ibid., 6:480-505.

15. Ibid., 7:258-71.

The Last Quarter Century

7   The United Nations

While World War II was still in progress (although its final outcome was no longer in doubt), the leaders of the Allied nations had already met and laid plans for an international organization which would both consolidate their ultimate victory and attempt to control the outbreak of new wars. The dropping of two atomic bombs on Japan not only signalled the final days of the war, but warned against the potential danger of a similar fate for all mankind.

Into the Preamble to the Charter of the new United Nations were written specific commitments for correction of the economic and social conditions which help to breed war:

> to reaffirm faith in fundamental human rights, in the dignity and worth of the human person . . . , to promote social progress and better standards of life in larger freedom, and for these ends . . . to employ international machinery for the promotion of the economic and social advancement of all peoples.

These broad social and economic objectives are further specified in Article I of the United Nations Charter in which one of its four basic purposes is stated as being

> To achieve international cooperation in solving international problems of an economic, social, cultural, or humanitarian character, and in promoting and encouraging respect for human rights and for fundamental freedoms for all without distinction as to race, sex, language or religion.

Deriving from this commitment, the Economic and Social Council (ECOSOC) was assigned a position on the table of organization which made it one of the major organs of the United Nations under the authority of the General Assembly, along with the Security Council and the Trusteeship Council. As its name indicates, ECOSOC was allotted two main areas of responsibility: for economic questions and for social questions. Among the latter were included prevention of crime and treatment of offenders, housing, human rights, the status of women, as well as traffic in women and children and in obscene publications. Some of these problems were, in turn, given over to the jurisdiction of the Temporary Social Commission, itself a subsidiary body of ECOSOC, having as its corresponding number an Economic Commission, which was later to proliferate into various Regional Economic Commissions. Within the United Nations Secretariat were created two distinct staffing units to serve, respectively, the Economic Commission and the Temporary Social Commission.[1]

The Temporary Social Commission, at its first session in February 1946, directed the United Nations toward the view that it should consider assuming responsibility for international cooperation in the field of prevention of crime and treatment of offenders on a worldwide basis. Pronounced interest was to be devoted, the implication ran, to the lesser developed areas of the world, including politically dependent areas. This was in marked contrast to its predecessor organizations, notably the League of Nations and the IPPC. So it was that the first meeting of the Social Commission in January 1947 at Lake Success, New York, confronted the problem of what to do with the heritage from both of these international entities. The Social Commission recognized that diplomacy and good will would be required in order both to continue this lengthy and worthy tradition and still to begin something new and constructively functional. As we have seen, a century of international cooperation had preceded the efforts of the United Nations in this area—and a great amount of results of this work was still very much alive as the new machinery was being designed to carry it forward. It would be an integral part of a broader program directed at the promotion of human welfare in general, of the relevant specific fields of standards of living, social security and social welfare; housing and town planning, physical and mental health; educational, scientific and cultural advancement; and human rights.

Furthermore, no less than eleven international organizations were at the time working in the field: the IPPC, and ten private organizations. Once ECOSOC had formally decided that the United Nations should assume international leadership in this field,[2] the first and immediate problem became one of coordination—how to avoid duplication and at the same time achieve maximum cooperation. The problem was technical and administrative as well as diplomatic. The one existing intergovernmental organization in the field—the IPPC—represented a long tradition with substantial achievements. Thus, as might be expected, the IPPC in 1946 and again in 1950 suggested that it be authorized to serve the United Nations "as an international body of experts in the field of prevention of crime and treatment of offenders."[3]

The Demise of the IPPC

The newly expressed concern of the United Nations toward the field of crime and punishment made it immediately apparent to many of its member governments that the possibility of a dualism of effort now existed, and that two intergovernmental organizations could not be encouraged to operate in identical areas.

But the IPPC, for all its pioneering work during the preceding 75 years and its rightful claim to expert technical and administrative experience, was now confronted with its record of association with the Axis powers during World War II. The account of those years was laid before the first meeting of the Social Commission in January of 1947. Headquartered in presumably neutral Switzerland, the IPPC was reported to have received the greatest proportion of its financial support from Germany, Italy, and Japan, as well as from Spain and Finland, between 1939 and 1945. It had also served to publish to the outside world the repressive acts and regulations promulgated by these countries, which might otherwise have had little access to the media of world communication. Many of these laws were—on their very face—contrary to the spirit of the kind of concerns and actions sponsored by the membership of the IPPC during the prewar years.

A new world and a new age was being born: for governments there existed the opportunity, and among peoples the desire, for the leadership of the United Nations to make a fresh start in the realm of international cooperation. The problem was met in traditionally diplomatic style but in unmistakeable language: "The resolution of the IPPC envisages the adaptation of its constitution to maintaining in existence an organization which has proved its usefulness, whereas the resolution of the Economic and Social Council envisages the eventual integration of the IPPC within the U.N. It appears to the Secretary-General that this can only be effected by the taking over by the U.N. of the major functions of the IPPC and the eventual winding up of that organization as an inter-governmental body."[4]

By a General Assembly Resolution adopted on 1 December 1950, the transfer of the functions of the IPPC to the United Nations, as negotiated and accepted by both organizations in advance, was approved.[5] A time limit of one year was established and the complete transfer of IPPC functions to the United Nations was to be accomplished before 31 December 1951. The United Nations, for its part, had agreed to appoint consultative groups of experts, composed of persons designated by governments which were members of either organization. The first such group was to include delegates from the IPPC.

The Section of Social Defence

Anticipating the entrance of the United Nations into a program for the prevention of crime and treatment of offenders, a "Section of Social Defence" had been created within the Department of Social Affairs in the Secretariat, the administrative or "civil service" counterpart of the deliberative or policy-making organs of the United Nations.

"Social Defence" is a concept best known on the Continent, dating from the 19th century. "It consists of the movement of ideas which would substitute the idea of rehabilitative justice for penal justice. It derives from, as it embodies, the precepts of the Positivist School of criminology first formulated by Garofalo and Ferri in Italy. These precepts prevailed up until the period between the two World Wars, when several trends became evident: the humanizing of the criminal law and the gradual diminution of notions restrictive of the rights of the individual, at the same time that developments in the behavioral sciences pointed to the possibility of redeeming the offender."[6] Both prevention and treatment, under this concept, are viewed as matters properly within the concern and powers of the state, which must needs "defend" itself against antisocial conduct. In its most positive sense, social defence regards the measures and approaches which it subsumes, to constitute the best protection of the society.

Selection of the term to entitle the new Section of Social Defence reflects, perhaps, the domination of the social side of the United Nations Secretariat at that time by personnel drawn largely from the Continent. From the outset, the Section of Social Defence was charged by the Social Commission, which was the source of its mandate and the guide to the areas in which it was to assume responsibility, with a four-fold program in the field of the prevention of crime and treatment of offenders. First, "a deliberate attempt is being made to establish a programme of international cooperation in the field on *a world-wide geographic basis*" (original emphasis). Secondly, the effort "is an integral part of a broader international programme directed at the promotion of human welfare in general." Third, "the emphasis on *operational functions*, and particularly on direct technical assistance, represents a new departure in the history of international cooperation. . . . " Fourth, "the U.N. has the unprecedented advantage of being able to avail itself to the full extent of the accumulated organizational and technical experience of other international organizations with special interest and competence in the field. This advantage derives both from the fact that the U.N. has become heir to the traditions and experience of the IPPC, and from the fact that the principal international non-governmental organizations in the field have pledged their cooperation to the U.N."[7]

The United Nations thus undertook to carry forward the tradition of the IPPC in the setting of standards—by governments, individual experts, governmental and nongovernmental representatives, of scientific workers and professionals. It was expected that these would undertake a new level of study and action to help understand, and hopefully to resolve, the unprecedented volume of crime which was now challenging every nation.

Note should be taken at this point of a major difference between the relationship of the U.N. to nongovernmental organizations in this field, and that of the League of Nations. The latter did not set up its own permanent secretariat to carry on research or convene meetings, but rather farmed out most of the work in this area to the various "technical" bodies which were qualified in the relevant topics. Thus, seven of the eleven international organizations in the field served the League in some capacity or in connection with a special problem at one time or another during the course of its existence.

The newly formed Section of Social Defence, thereafter to come under a succession of chiefs, was located within the Division of Social Activities (later called the Division of Social Welfare, itself a unit of the Department of Social Affairs). In addition to its own specially recruited staff, Social Defence established, and drew upon, outside groups of professionals in the field as well as individual experts, both from regional and national sources. As one of its first activities, Social Defence at once set about its initial undertaking—the gathering and compilation of official crime statistics. Questionnaires sent to all member states were returned by thirty-seven of them. Its results demonstrated that the postwar years saw a universal rise in rates of reported offenses, a decrease in the age of persons involved in the commission of these offenses, and a greater degree of violence and of the involvement of females in crime than had been manifest before World War II. A considerable amount of time on the elaboration of plans for the continuation of work on this question was devoted by the International Group of Experts convened by the United Nations in 1950.

The Annex to a Resolution adopted on December 1 of that year invited all member governments of the U.N. and IPPC "to appoint one or more representatives of expert qualifications or experience, professional or scientific, in the field of the prevention of crime and the treatment of offenders . . . to act in the first instance as individual correspondents with the U.N. Department of Social Affairs."[8]

These correspondents become key figures in the new United Nations program. They composed the membership of the regional consultative groups, played a role in naming the members of the *Ad Hoc* Advisory Committee of Experts, and figured prominently in the initiation and carrying out of technical assistance programs, both in the selection of national projects, and service on such projects as technical experts or advisors. They helped to man the U.N. Regional Seminars held preparatory to the quinquennial congresses. These national correspondents were originally charged "to meet biennially or more often if required," in addition to their continuing responsibility to furnish United Nations headquarters with reports on significant developments in the field.

A continuing tally of the names of these correspondents in member countries is recorded in the *International Review of Criminal Policy*, the United Nations' official publication in the social defence field, together with brief reports from them on current activities and accomplishments in their countries.[9]

During 1952, eleven additional governments appointed correspondents bringing the total number of countries participating to 38 (32 members and 6 non-members). By 1954 this had grown to 78 correspondents in 40 countries—by 1967, to 168 from 64 countries.

The European Consultative Group held several meetings up to 1959, when it was redesignated the U.N. Consultative Group on the Prevention of Crime and Treatment of Offenders, which has met twice in Geneva, most recently in August of 1968. In attendance at these meetings have been representatives of specialized agencies, intergovernmental agencies, nongovernmental organizations and representation from the United Nations Secretariat. The 1968 meeting helped to plan the Fourth Quinquennial Crime Congress at Kyoto in 1970, as well as considering four main substantial questions: the prevention of delinquency in the context of national development; the economics of staff training for corrections; implementation of the Standard Minimum Rules for the Treatment of Prisoners (once again); as well as an item on the abolition of the death penalty.

The Advisory Committee of Experts

This last constitutes an interesting example of the unobtrusive—almost accidental—fashion in which important decisions are sometimes arrived at in the course of international gatherings of government representatives. The question of the abolition of the death penalty had been placed on the agenda of the General Assembly at its 14th session in the fall of 1959.[10] The Assembly passed the subject to the Economic and Social Council, which referred it, in turn, to the Advisory Committee of Experts on the Prevention of Crime and Treatment of Offenders. Three years later the General Assembly adopted a second resolution requesting the Economic and Social Council to invite the Commission on Human Rights to make such recommendations on the subject as it deemed appropriate.[11] A 1962 survey of capital punishment[12] was supplemented by a second survey completed in 1967[13] which brought the subject up to date. At this point, it was not for want of basic information that the matter had not yet been resolved.[14]

As a consequence, the Consultative Group of Experts had before it, at its August 1968 meeting in Geneva, these three studies when it took the matter up for consideration as one of the main items on its four-point agenda. In its draft report to the final plenary meeting of the group, the section on capital punishment recommended that concerning the abolition of the death penalty, "almost every government approved." When this point in the review of the draft report of the section was reached, a section member proffered the suggestion that *no* government had, in fact, objected to the concept of abolition of the death penalty. There followed no demurrer on the part of any of his fellow section-members, nor objection from the body as a whole. Consequently the record stands that the latest United Nations body to consider the question of capital punishment up to 1968 did, in fact, *unanimously* favor its abolition. This action was, in due course, referred to the General Assembly at its 23rd session in the fall of 1968.

At its 26 November meeting in that year, the General Assembly adopted a resolution which, after taking note of the preceding steps taken both by itself and the subsidiary bodies to which it had referred the matter, invited the governments of the member states to safeguard the rights of accused persons in capital cases where the death penalty prevailed by providing that

    i)   A person condemned to death shall not be deprived of the right to appeal to a higher judicial authority or, as the case may be, to petition for pardon or reprieve;

    ii)   A death sentence shall not be carried out until the procedures of appeal or, as the case may be, of petition for pardon or reprieve have been terminated;

    iii)   Special attention be given in the case of indigent persons by the provision of adequate legal assistance at all stages of the proceedings. . . .[15]

The Secretary-General was thereafter requested to invite from U.N. member states information regarding possible further restriction on the use of the death penalty or its total abolition, and to inform him of any changes which had taken place since the last survey was concluded in 1965.

As this book goes to press it is understood that replies have been received from more than 50 countries. These are being compiled for consideration by the Economic and Social Council. Thus in characteristically slow and ponderous fashion does the complex machinery of the United Nations exert the weight of its influence in the direction of the protection of human rights and the extension of individual freedom.

An additional resource, authorized by ECOSOC, not long after the Section of Social Defence was organized, was the Advisory Committee of Experts, made up of seven internationally recognized authorities in the field, and selected by the Secretary-General as an advisory body to the Social Commission "in devising and formulating policies and programmes appropriate to: (a) The study on an international basis of the problem of prevention of crime and the treatment of offenders; and (b) International action in this field."[16]

This group of experts held their first meeting at Lake Success, New York, August 1949, their second meeting in December 1950. Thereafter they were convened at least five more times between that date and January 1963. In July 1965 the committee membership was increased from seven to ten and their appointment made for three years.

The first meeting of the enlarged committee in Geneva in December of 1965 emphasized that any programs for the prevention and treatment of crime should be more closely linked to general economic and social planning, and set in the broader context of national development plans. "In terms of crime prevention one strategy would be to take cognizance of prevailing conditions and seek to counteract or neutralize whatever criminogenic effects they might have."[17] This was a direct reflection of the advent into United Nations membership of several new nations, many of them struggling with problems of economic and social development. This recommendation was also properly within the spirit of the "Decade of Development" which had been declared by the United Nations for 1960-1970.

Significant developments arising from this broadened emphasis included the establishment of a Social Defence Trust Fund, to which governments and private sources would be asked to contribute directly for the expanded social defense program, and the creation in Rome in 1968 of the United Nations Social Defence Research Institute.[18]

In order to draw on, and to coordinate, the competence of the many organizations which had an interest in some aspect of the problem of crime and delinquency, the United Nations had called a meeting in October 1948 at the Palais de Chaillot, Paris. "Representatives invited to attend for the principal organizations concerned and of interested specialized agencies" were drawn from the International Labour Organisation, World Health, UNESCO, IPPC, Howard League, International Association of Penal Law, International Bureau for the Unification of Penal Law, INTERPOL, International Law Association, International Statistical Institute, International Union for Child Welfare, and the Nordic Association of Criminalists.[19] Out of this meeting came three results: a resolution to cooperate fully with the U.N.; the establishment of a permanent coordinating committee; and the appointment of resident representatives to United Nations headquarters in New York from each constituent organization, to maintain close contact with the Section of Social Defence. Accordingly, the Permanent Coordinating Committee held its first meeting in May 1950, in Geneva.

Since the inception of the United Nations Social Defence program, great emphasis seems to have been placed—as in the old League of Nations days—on problems of juvenile delinquency and probation. Certainly within the past decade, juvenile and youth problems have received more attention, at all levels, than any other single issue. This is manifest in the publications which Social Defence has published or commissioned from experts outside of its own staff, as well as in the contents of its journal, the *International Review of Criminal Policy*, which published its first issue in January 1952.

The basic approach of the *Review* was clearly set forth in the resolution authorizing its creation—it was to include, *inter alia*, the recommendations and findings of the Consultative and Advisory Group of Experts. Thereafter the *Review* appeared twice yearly. Originally published in separate editions by language, it began with the fifth number to include complete sections in English, French, and Spanish, with at least one article in each language, and summaries in the other two. Since 1963, with issue number 21, the *Review* has been published annually in separate-language editions and continues to present information from national correspondents and specialized agencies, including accounts of activities taking place in specific countries; announcements of congresses to be held or summaries of those already held by the numerous national, regional and international bodies in this field; and a listing of changes in legislation. Prior to 1963 each issue included an extensive bibliography of technical literature in the field, but since that date the bibliography has been published separately as a supplement.[20]

The *Review* often provides a wider forum for papers than that offered by the United Nations crime congresses, while its content tends to reflect the concern currently being emphasized by the U.N. programs. A typical issue of the *Review* will include from three to five articles. While originally these might have been related to two or more topics, more recent issues have been devoted to a single area. Over the years the topic of juvenile delinquency has been the one most frequently appearing in its pages, followed by research and the training of correctional personnel. Issues 23 and 28, published in 1965 and 1970 respectively, were devoted to research, while issues 22 and 24 concerned themselves with the training of personnel. Special issues in earlier years took up the medico-psychological and social examination of offenders (No. 3, 1958); and prostitution (No. 13, 1958). Thus the *Review* serves as an important international forum for ideas, as well as a definitive source of basic information regarding the work of the United Nations in the prevention of crime and treatment of offenders.

The libraries of the world are crowded with the results of surveys and research, some of the best of which are there as the result of the efforts of international gatherings and inquiries over the past century and a half, as herein described. There is no lack of recommendations, exhortation, suggestions and even ukases as to how governments might best proceed to prevent criminal behavior among their citizens, and how effectively to treat what was not prevented. If words were the measure, the entire world might today be almost free of crime.

The Technical Assistance Program

But much less effort has been expended by these international bodies and agencies to help put the fine words into practice. In this respect, the initial work of the United Nations in the social defence field has been noteworthy. The United Nations Technical Assistance Program has made possible for the first time, on a voluntary basis, and through international auspices rather than from a single government, provision of experts to a requesting government in connection with a specific need; subsidizing of a fellowship program for the training of professionals in other countries; and the furnishing of equipment. So far as can be determined, while no equipment in the field of prevention of crime and treatment of offenders has actually been furnished by the U.N. to any nation under the Technical Assistance program, a wide variety of immediately applicable assistance has indeed been extended in this area. Direct aid was granted to 49 governments for the first six years of the Technical Assistance Program between 1947 and 1953. This consisted of 130 fellowship grants and 18 scholarships in the social defense field, of which two-thirds were for workers in the area of juvenile delinquency, and the balance was related to adult criminality.[21]

With the growth of the Technical Assistance Program into its expanded phase in the mid-fifties, the statistics on just how many persons in the field of crime prevention and correction were given advanced training, or how many experts were sent out in response to the request of governments, are not readily accessible. But during the decade from 1956 on, it appears that 182 Fellowships were granted for advanced study abroad, while the services of 148 experts were made available to countries requesting them, for a total of 330 grants.

The number of developing countries which are members of the United Nations is no less than 80, with perhaps another score of member nations which can be regarded as lying somewhere between the level of "developed" and "underdeveloped." The gap between the two groups has not been diminished perceptibly in recent years. Only limited efforts have been made on the part of the United Nations and its programs to extend assistance of a technical nature in the area of social problems, including crime.

It must be regretfully reported here that the extent of technical assistance rendered by the United Nations in the field of crime prevention and treatment seems to have tapered off seriously in recent years. With the exception of two interregional advisers in social defense appointed after the 1970 Kyoto Congress, apathy seems to characterize the present level of technical assistance for which such promise was held out when it was first begun by the United Nations.

However, a recent appraisal of the present status and immediate future of the United Nations as a peace-keeping organization dominated by the victorious Allied powers of World War II—the super-powers—may serve, at this point, to illuminate the importance of such measures as those just enumerated. A recognized authority on U.N. affairs, Elizabeth M. Borgese, has written:

> Paralyzed in its principal decision-making organ, the Security Council, and immobilized in its primary area of operation, international politics, the U.N. began to throw its prime resources into the area of social, economic and cultural activities. By 1965, 85 percent of U.N. personnel and resources were dedicated to these activities. This was still a small fraction of what the super-powers were investing in bilateral aid in developing countries whose feudal allegiance they were courting in the exercise of old-fashioned power politics. Nevertheless, if one remembers that the League of Nations, whose Covenant was the model for the U.N. Charter, spent practically nothing on these activities, the shift is significant.[2,2]

It remains now to describe the four United Nations crime congresses which have been held since 1955. It may be recalled that the IPPC had established a pattern of such conferences at five-year intervals, and that this schedule had been maintained with fair regularity in the years between 1872 and 1935. The responsibilities for international action in the field of prevention of crime and treatment of offenders assumed by the United Nations, when it supplanted the IPPC, included a commitment to organize biennial regional sessions to discuss professional problems, as well as to continue the tradition of quinquennial international conferences on crime matters.

First United Nations Crime Congress, Geneva, 1955

Under United Nations auspices, the First United Nations Crime Congress met in Geneva between 22 August and 3 September 1955.[23] It had been preceded by extensive preparation, including two sessions by the *Ad Hoc* Advisory Committee of Experts devoted to planning and preparation in June 1953 and again in August 1955. The Permanent Committee of Specialized Agencies and Organizations, concerned with problems of crime, also met twice in Geneva, once in December 1952 and again in September 1954. Additionally, four regional seminars designed to prepare for the 1955 Geneva Congress were conducted: the First Latin American Seminar in Rio de Janeiro in 1953; the First Mid-East Seminar in Cairo in December 1953; the European Regional Consultative Group had met in December of 1952 and was to meet again in the late summer of 1954 in Geneva; the First Asia and Far Eastern Seminar met in Rangoon in the fall of 1954.

Additional U.N.-sponsored (in whole or part) seminars which preceded Geneva include: 1) On Probation—London, 1952; 2) European Social Welfare Seminar—Paris, 1949; 3) On Juvenile Delinquency—Rome, 1950; 4) On the Medical, Psychological and Social Examination of Delinquents—Brussels, December 1951; 5) On the Institutional Treatment of Juvenile Offenders—Vienna, September-October 1954.

Attendance at the 1955 Geneva Congress is summarized as follows in the final report:

A total of 191 delegates representing fifty-one Governments participated in the Congress. The International Labour Organisation, the World Health Organisation, the United Nations Educational, Scientific and Cultural Organisation, the Council of Europe, and the League of Arab States sent ten observers in all. Forty-three non-governmental organisations accepted invitations and sent a total of 101 representatives. Lastly, 235 persons attended the Congress as individuals, some of them from countries which were not officially represented at the Congress, or from Trust Territories or Non-Self-Governing Territories. In all 512 persons from 61 countries and territories took part in the Congress.

Five major items composed the agenda: 1) Standard Minimum Rules for the Treatment of Prisoners; 2) selection, training and status of prison personnel; 3) open penal and correctional institutions; 4) prison labor; and 5) prevention of juvenile delinquency. "The Congress also heard five general lectures by eminent experts from Latin America, North America, Asia and the Far East, Europe and the Middle East, respectively, on the main trends in the field of prevention of crime and the treatment of offenders in their 'regions.' "

It has been noted at several points in this book that the Standard Minimum Rules for the Treatment of Prisoners have a long history, notably since 1926 when they were first formulated by the IPC, which revised them again in 1933. In that year the League of Nations had taken note of the Minimum Rules. Almost twenty years later, in July 1951, the IPPC approved a second revision of the Minimum Rules as one of its final official acts. One of the first recommendations of the United Nations *Ad Hoc* Committee of Experts meeting in 1949 was that the Social Commission should undertake a further revision of the Minimum Rules, using the IPPC draft as its working paper. The 1955 Geneva Congress adopted a final revision of the Minimum Rules at its closing plenary meeting. It also adopted a set of recommendations on the selection and training of personnel for penal and correctional institutions, and another set of recommendations on open penal and correctional institutions. The resolution, embodying the three sets of recommendations, invited member governments to give favorable consideration to the Minimum Rules and to take the latter two groups of recommendations as fully as possible into account in the administration of their penal stations. Two years later the United Nations, as a result of the passage of a resolution[24] by the Economic and Social Council at its Meeting on 31 July 1957, officially invited governments to give favorable consideration to the adoption and application of the Standard Minimum Rules in the administration of their respective penal and correctional institutions.[25]

Neither of the two succeeding congresses on crime called by the United Nations considered, with any specificity, a followup of either the degree or the extent to which the Minimum Rules had been implemented in member countries. Delegates on both occasions concerned themselves rather with discussion of more specialized measures of treatment for various categories of accused and convicted offenders. Eleven years after the

ECOSOC resolution had been adopted on the subject, such an appraisal of the extent of implementation of the Minimum Rules was made public, this time by a nongovernmental organization, the International Prisoners Aid Association. In August 1970, at Kyoto, the subject again won acceptance on the agenda of, and received extensive consideration by, United Nations Crime Congress participants.[2 6]

Second United Nations Crime Congress,
London — 1960

Attendance at the Second U.N. Crime Congress in London in 1960 was double that of the first congress—1,131 persons, representing 70 governments. Nongovernmental organizations represented totalled 50.[2 7]

Six major items composed the agenda: 1) new forms of juvenile delinquency: their origin, prevention and treatment; 2) special police services for the prevention of juvenile delinquency; 3) prevention of types of criminality resulting from social changes and accompanying economic development in less-developed countries; 4) short-term imprisonment; 5) the integration of prison labor with the national economy, including the remuneration of prisoners; 6) pre-release treatment and after-care, as well as assistance to dependents of prisoners. The pattern of scheduling major addresses by a representative of a government from each of the major areas of the world was repeated in London.

The basic perspective at London in 1960 was the clear recognition of crime as a social problem within a particular social context, which stressed the interdependence of crime and its treatment within the broader socio-cultural milieu. In a speech describing United Nations activities in this field, the chief of the Section of Social Defence, representing the Secretary-General, suggested that much of the progress made in the preceding twenty years was more apparent than real. "Two main explanations might be given for this phenomenon; one was the growing tendency to imitate and transplant criminological theories, programmes and policies from one country to another, which implied a disregard for national reality and needs; the other was the subordination of the term 'prison' to the criminological cult of the personality of the offender."

Concerning the topic of special police services for the prevention of juvenile delinquency, the police were admonished, in effect, to stay out of the social service field and to concentrate their efforts within traditional areas. "The Congress considers that the police . . . should pay particular attention to the prevention of 'new' forms of juvenile delinquency. They should not, however, go so far as to assume specialized functions more appropriately within the field of work of social, educational and other services."

Growing awareness of the relationship between rapid social change and criminality in less-developed countries, considered under item three, aroused the greatest interest of any of the agenda topics. The participants raised more questions with regard to this topic than the congress was prepared to answer. The interest expressed helped to alert the Section of Social Defence to the need for further exploration of the matter, one of special concern to the suddenly increased number of newly independent nations which were beginning to confront a challenge brought about by profound and rapid industrial and urban change. The complexity of the causation question led the 1960 London Congress to call for extensive research on this subject with the result that this question was placed on the agenda of the Third U.N. Congress on Crime at Stockholm.

As summarized in their conclusions and recommendations, discussions by congress participants were characterized by a keen awareness of the problem of cultural relativity or national differences, which warned against any tendency to seek universal standardization in either the delineation of the common problems of crime, or in their solution.

Third United Nations Crime Congress, Stockholm — 1965

The Third U.N. Crime Congress, held from 8 to 18 August 1965 in Stockholm, drew representation from 74 governments and 39 nongovernmental organizations, with a total of 1,083 persons in attendance.[28]

The general theme of the congress was centered primarily on the topic, "Prevention of Criminality," under an agenda which included six major items: 1) social change and criminality; 2) social forces and the prevention of criminality (with particular reference to the public, the family, educational facilities and occupational opportunities); 3) community preventive action (with particular reference to the planning and implementation of medical, police and social programs); 4) measures to combat recidivism (with particular reference to adverse conditions of detention pending trial and inequality in the administration of justice; 5) probation (especially adult probation) and other noninstitutional measures; and 6) special preventive and treatment measures for young adults.

Secondary emphasis was placed on research, to which a special plenary meeting was devoted preceding the section meetings.

At the close of the conference, the representative of the United Nations Secretary-General, in his summation, noted that the congress had been characterized by two major trends: "On the one hand, a growing emphasis on the need for more technical knowledge as a basis for the development of social defence policy and, on the other hand, an interest in more imaginative approaches to the prevention of crime and the treatment of offenders, such innovations calling for support by government and other agencies. The important role that the public could play in this field had been defined."

The final report of the 1965 Stockholm Congress contains, in place of the usual conclusion and recommendations for each of the agenda items, a single resolution couched in general terms. The new emphasis on the total socio-cultural context within which crime should be viewed is reflected in the following extract from that resolution:

> It was agreed that economic explanations of crime are not fully satisfactory in all countries. While developing countries are likely to attribute their crime and delinquency rates exclusively to poverty and unemployment, and while certain developed countries are likely to attribute some of their crime to poverty in slum areas, the incidence of crime and delinquency appears to be extensive in countries which are economically highly developed. Such a situation is confusing and in a sense discouraging to developing countries. It appears that in both highly industrialized and developing countries the answers may well lie primarily in factors other than economic, namely, in organization, in new values and norms and in changes in social control.
>
> While there was some dissent, the consensus was that the factors in causes of delinquency and crime must be sought not so much in the individual or in his family as in the broader social and political changes taking place in his environment. Consequently, in formulating measures of social defence, this approach must be taken into consideration.

Consistent with this perspective was a call for research into agencies of socialization other than the family, such as the school, employment and leisure time.

More strongly and persistently than they had done in the preceding London Congress, representatives from the underdeveloped countries (though many delegates from such lands disliked the term, while some of those who came from so-called "developed countries" were not certain that their countries deserved to be so described) in both public and private discussions, challenged the advanced industrial nations to help them achieve the benefits of the new technology without at the same time extracting a toll in human dislocation, in the destruction of traditional norms and values, and the very basis of their social fabric. In the formulation of answers to such a formidable challenge, the so-called advanced societies might, in the process, bring forward solutions which could help them to meet the growing burden of antisocial conduct.

As reported by the delegates at Stockholm, an increase in crime in their countries was the one factor shared in common by all those in attendance. Uniformity in the gathering of international statistics of crime—one of the original purposes for convening the first congress in 1872—had not yet been achieved. The increase in reported crime was all too uniform; the need seemed greater than ever for a concerted international effort to cope with it. Selection by the delegates of Japan as the site of the next congress, the first to be held in Asia, may have been based partly on the desire of Asians for attention to their special needs. The fact that EXPO '70 was to be produced in Osaka was, to be sure, an additional inducement to convene in nearby Kyoto.

Fourth United Nations Crime Congress, Kyoto — 1970

The Fourth United Nations Crime Congress, held in Kyoto in 1970, was the first to be held in Asia. It was convened in the new International Conference Hall in the ancient capital of Japan, between 17 and 26 August,[29] under the presidency of Yoshitsugu Baba, former chief prosecutor of the Japanese Ministry of Justice and recognized for his interest in international penal affairs. The oustanding British criminologist Professor Hermann Mannheim, Emeritus from the University of London, was honored by unanimous election as Honorary Vice-Chairman of the Congress. The 1,200 participants from 85 countries were welcomed by the Emperor's brother, Prince Takamatsu.

At the same time that EXPO '70, attended by over 55 million visitors, was showing the world (especially the Asian world) the progress which Japan had made technically and industrially in the past quarter century, the Japanese Government wanted to show the conferees the advances in court-correctional programs which had been introduced under the new Constitution of Japan adopted at the end of World War II.[30] While the prisons of the country were still operating under prison regulations drawn up in 1908, recent innovations, especially in civil liberties, probation, clinical services and provision for juveniles, had brought the country to the level of advanced countries in other parts of the world. Those persons in the centralized Ministry of Justice who continued to strive for reform of the 1908 prison regulations were heartened by the support they received from the speeches delivered by, and the private conversations held with, other participants. Additionally, the schedule of visits made available to congress participants was both lavish and well-organized: fourteen tours were offered to a total of thirty nearby institutions: juvenile training schools, hostels and rehabilitation centers, adult prisons, hospitals for mentally disturbed and for the retarded.

Four main topics shared the official agenda: 1) prevention of crime; 2) public participation by citizens in crime prevention and control (both of these within the context of development planning); 3) research programs into both causation and the effectiveness of social defence measures; and finally, 4) that hoary perennial entry, Standard Minimum Rules for the Treatment of Prisoners.

These main topics were discussed in four separate sessions, the total body assembling only twice—in the opening and the closing plenary meetings. A distinctive feature of the Kyoto Congress was the provision of facilities for meetings of small groups of participants with common interests. Official United Nations gatherings are required, by their rules of procedure, to provide services of interpretation, translation and documentation, which precludes the holding of any but large, formal gatherings, characterized by individual statements by delegates of governments and other participants. Sometimes informative, frequently repetitious, predictably chauvinistic, these sessions are seldom conducive to true discussion or anything that could be described as "a meeting of the minds." It was therefore noteworthy that such topics as probation and parole, the problems of the families of prisoners, the teaching of criminology, the role of the police in crime prevention were provided a forum within the larger, more restricted framework of the congress. Approximately one-fifth of the total participants shared in these small group meetings, without any supportive services, and providing their own interpreters from among themselves.

The substance of a congress discussion is expected to hew to the professional and eschew the political. But the United Nations being, by its format and membership, a political body, the passions of the day cannot always be excluded. Thus it was that such matters were brought onto the floor as: the exclusion by the congress of representation from certain socialist regimes—particularly those in divided countries; charges by the Arab states of mistreatment of their nationals and of prisoners in the Mid-East war; and veiled, but nevertheless understandable, allegations that certain larger countries could limit criminal activity in other countries if the former were to control—or completely forbid—the export of arms and of narcotic drugs. Such allegations were seldom rebutted—or refuted. They hung above the other relatively milder and less controversial speeches as a reminder that political realities will insist on being heard, despite all efforts to treat them as if they did not exist simply because they did not win a place on the official program.

The fact that the 1970 congress met in Asia set the tone of the discussion of several agenda topics. This helped to focus on the special concerns of the overwhelming majority of the peoples of Asia, given their relatively undeveloped economic and social condition. The "Declaration of Social Progress and Development," which had been "adopted and solemnly proclaimed" by the General Assembly in its 24th session in the fall of 1969, had in one of its 27 Articles specified "the adoption of measures to ensure the effective participation, as appropriate, of all the elements of society in the preparation and execution of national plans and programs of economic and social development."[31]

It is therefore interesting that the session on participation of the public in crime prevention and treatment drew the largest number of participants. The ample documentation on this subject, provided both by the United Nations Secretariat and by individual governments and international organizations, helped to focus attention on what is generally regarded today as one of the most hopeful areas within the total field of crime. The use of volunteers and para-professionls, the potential contribution that may be expected of ex-offenders—as ex-addicts have become an important resource in dealing with the victims of drug abuse—introduced new information on a topic which had not appeared so prominently in previous international gatherings.

The last item on the agenda, Standard Minimum Rules for the Treatment of Prisoners, received extensive attention. The participants had been informed that since the Third United Nations Crime Congress in Stockholm, the Secretary-General of the U.N. had, on 6 November 1967, "addressed a *note verbale* to all Member States of the Organization, requesting a report on the implementation of the Standard Minimum Rules for the Treatment of Prisoners. He sought information on three main aspects of the implementation: the extent to which [they] had been incorporated in national legislation; a review of the implementation of the Rules and progress achieved; and difficulties encountered. Forty-four countries replied to this inquiry. . . ."[32]

The results, most briefly summarized, were that "the Rules had not been formally embodied into national laws, though they had influenced, the regulations and practice in half the countries reporting. Five countries were beyond the Rules in their law and practice. Implementation had depended upon the extent to which the Rules accorded with existing practice, the number of experts and specialists needed and available resources. However, some 60 percent of the countries replying claimed that they were applying the Rules to some extent." Such difficulties as had arisen were ascribed by the countries which reported as including "lack of funds, lack of trained or specialist personnel, inadequate physical facilities, complication of ensuring uniformity of standards throughout a country (especially in federal systems), legal and administrative rigidities or inertia."[33]

The section of the Kyoto Congress which considered the Minimum Rules concluded its lively examination of the subject by recommending that the congress' plenary session endorse its conclusions: that the General Assembly should approve and recommend implementation of the Rules to U.N. member states; that an adequately staffed Section of Social Defence should undertake research and develop technical assistance for promotion of the Minimum Rules, in particular by the establishment of a working party which would undertake an international evaluation of needs, means and results, specifically through periodic inquiries addressed to member states with regard to the Minimum Rules. Consideration of the item ended with the recommendation that the Fifth United Nations Crime Congress should receive a report on the action taken in the interim on these recommendations.

Amnesty International, an international and nongovermental organization with consultative status at the United Nations, distributed a series of proposals. These urged amendment of the Minimum Rules "to cover treatment of all categories of prisoners and detainees, including political prisoners and prisoners of conscience, whether detained by police, military or prison authorities," and amendment of the Minimum Rules to provide for a reporting system to a special United Nations committee or to the U.N. High Commission for Human Rights.[34]

Headquartered in London, Amnesty International has national sections in 22 countries and is financed by 850 groups. It works for the release of prisoners from different parts of the world and of differing religious and/ or political views. Its work parallels, in many aspects, that of the International Commission of Jurists, whose Secretary-General serves also as chairman of the International Executive Committee of Amnesty International.

A resolution was also introduced by the representative of the International Programme for Prisoners' Children, a joint effort on the part of 22 nongovernmental organizations, which urged that the Minimum Rules, numbered 79 and 80, be studied with a view to including a provision that more attention be paid to the family situation of persons arrested, detained or imprisoned. The resolution concluded with the further recommendation that at the moment of arrest or imprisonment, a social service office should be notified of the fact so that it might concern itself with the family situation resulting from such arrest.

It was left to the Rapporteur General in his general report to the closing plenary session of the Kyoto Congress to express the conviction that "the adoption of the Standard Rules was never more urgent than now." Reviewing the history of the Standard Minimum Rules since their inception as a vague ideal at the First Crime Congress in London in 1872, he briefly traced their growth from the 55 articles in 1932 when they were endorsed by the League of Nations, to the 94 which they total today. "Have we now at last reached the end of the road, or are we going to go on like this forever?" he asked, which he followed with a second question: "Will the Rules be buried or cremated with full military honours and made into a worthy subject of pedantic doctoral dissertations?" Rules were as essential for prison staff as for the prisoners themselves. He further argued that the Advisory Committee of Experts should be expanded into a Commission on the Prevention of Crime and Treatment of Offenders within the United Nations framework in order to bring to the problem of crime the recognition it deserved, and as a means of meeting the rising challenge of crime in every nation.

Toward the close of the proceedings, a rash of international incidents of sky-jacking of airplanes took place, including one belonging to the airline of the host country, prompting several delegates to publicly condemn the practice and to urge the congress to take some strong steps toward outlawing it.

While no resolutions were formally adopted by the body, it did give its assent to a closing declaration which expressed the concern of the participants over "the effect that urbanization, industrialization and the technological revolution may have upon the quality of life and the human environment." The congress was moved to this expression of concern because of its stated belief that "the problem of crime in many countries in its new dimensions is far more serious now than at any other time in the long history of these Congresses," a belief which was reported by all of the participating countries but one—the host country, Japan.

After alerting the world to the serious consequences to society of the inadequate attention being given to both prevention and treatment of crime, the Kyoto Congress Declaration then proceeded to call upon governments to intensify their crime preventive efforts and to urge the United Nations and other international organizations to give high priority to the "strengthening of international cooperation in crime prevention, and in particular, to . . . effective technical aid. . . ."

This declaration was considered, ten months later, by the Economic and Social Council at its 50th session in June of 1971. Not only did ECOSOC endorse that Kyoto Declaration but it took extraordinary steps to implement its recommendations, calling upon the Secretary-General to "intensify . . . international efforts to advance knowledge, exchange experience and develop policy, practice and public participation in crime prevention. . . ."[35]

Exhibit 4
Declaration of the Fourth United Nations Congress on the Prevention of Crime and the Treatment of Offenders, 26 August 1970

The Fourth United Nations Congress on the Prevention of Crime and the Treatment of Offenders, meeting at Kyoto, Japan, in August 1970, attended by participants from eighty-five countries representing all regions of the world,

Being deeply concerned with the increasing urgency of the need for the world community of nations to improve its planning for economic and social development by taking fuller account of the effects of urbanization, industrialization and the technological revolution upon the quality of life and the human environment,

Affirming that inadequacies in the attention paid to the quality of life in the process of development are manifest in the increasing seriousness and proportions of the problem of crime in many countries.

Observing that the world-wide crime problem has many ramifications, covering the range of conventional crime as well as the more subtle and sophisticated types of organized crime and corruption, and subsuming the violence of protest and the danger of increasing escapism through the abuse of drugs and narcotics, and that crime in all its forms saps the energies of a nation and undermines its efforts to achieve a more wholesome environment and a better life for its people,

Believing that the problem of crime in the world in its new dimensions is far more serious now than at any other time in the long history of these Congresses, and

Feeling an inescapable obligation to alert the world to the serious consequences for society of the insufficient attention which is now being given to measures of crime prevention, which by definition include the treatment of offenders,

1. *Calls upon* all Governments to take effective steps to coordinate and intensify their crime prevention efforts within the context of economic and social development which each country envisages for itself;

2. *Urges* the United Nations and other international organizations to give high priority to the strengthening of international cooperation in crime prevention and, in particular, to ensure the availability of effective technical aid to countries desiring such assistance for the development of action programmes for the prevention and control of crime and delinquency;

3. *Recommends* that special attention be given to the administrative, professional and technical structure necessary for more effective action to be taken to move more directly and purposefully into the area of crime prevention.

In detailed fashion the ECOSOC resolution went on to urge direct aid to governments, through technical assistance, the use of advisors at all levels, and the distribution of needed information. Research of "an action-oriented character" was advocated, together with a wide variety of related measures; seminars, training courses, workshops and meetings, to involve governments, universities and nongovernmental organizations.

The Consultative Group, a carry-over from the old IPPC days, was terminated, and the Advisory Committee, expanded to 15 members, re-named "The Committee on Crime Prevention and Control," with a man-date to report to the Commission for Social Development, and, where appropriate, to the Commission on Human Rights as well as to the Commis-sion on Narcotic Drugs. Its final request was that an item be included on the agenda of the 1971 session of the General Assembly on "Criminality and Social Change," in view of "the situations arising from increasing criminality."

The Kyoto Declaration closed with the recommendation "that special attention be given to the administrative, professional and technical struc-ture necessary for more effective action to be taken." Now that the General Assembly is to be seized, directly and forcefully, with the problem which ECOSOC has laid before it, a vigorous international program of action may be expected from the United Nations organization as it ends its first quarter-century of involvement in the problems of crime.

During the final minutes of the Kyoto Congress, a member of the Canadian delegation offered, and the congress members accepted, an invita-tion to convene in Toronto in 1975. One item which may well appear on its agenda is consideration of the most appropriate manner in which to cele-brate—in the following year—the 250th anniversary of the birth of John Howard, pioneer prison reformer. If the world has as much assurance that it will manage to hold together until that year as it has that crime will con-tinue to be a matter of serious social concern, then the Sixth United Nations Crime Congress will undoubtedly be held in 1980—in either Africa or Latin America—the only continents which so far have not hosted inter-national congresses concerned with the prevention of crime and treatment of offenders (see Exhibit 4).

United Nations Specialized Agencies

It remains now to describe briefly the contributions made to the field of crime prevention and treatment by the specialized agencies of the United Nations—the satellites which seem at times to cast more light into the darkened corners of the world's ills than the international stellar body around which they pivot, itself noted more often for the generation of heat than light.

Representatives of these specialized agencies which have at least a tangential interest in the subject of crime are, of course, in attendance at all the sessions of all the international meetings concerned with it. Their direct involvement in the proceedings is often of value, even if it is not always possible to single them out for special note.

World Health Organization (WHO), Geneva

The World Health Organization was first established in 1946. During the brief period thereafter (before twenty-six members of the United Nations ratified the WHO constitution), an interim commission was formed to prepare for the First World Health Assembly. At one of its early meetings, this commission undertook a preliminary study of crime prevention and the treatment of offenders at the request of the Social Commission of the Economic and Social Council with a view to the inclusion of these matters in the organization's first program of work. The subject has, however, never risen high on the new organization's list of priorities. Given the vastness of the international problems of physical and mental health which WHO confronted, this becomes understandable.

The records of WHO reveal only one WHO Assembly decision and one board resolution directly related to the prevention of crime and the treatment of offenders. In July of 1948 "The First World Health Assembly agreed that cooperation with the Economic and Social Council on the prevention of crime and the treatment of offenders should be continued."[36] At its second session, the Executive Board in November of the same year

> noted the relevant decisions of the ECOSOC, which had been presented for the information of members. With regard to the report of the WHO expert on prevention of crime and the treatment of offenders, the Director-General stated that this report would be included in the one being prepared by the United Nations, in consultation with interested non-governmental organizations and specialised agencies, and would also be considered for publication by WHO.[37]

Reporting on the first decade of its work, WHO had this to say with regard to its concern in this area:

> If what is now known about preventive treatment of the mental health problems of childhood and youth is properly applied, it should

help to reduce the amount and importance of juvenile delinquency. Most of WHO's work on this question has been in connection with the United Nations' program on the prevention of crime and the treatment of offenders. As a contribution to that program, a WHO consultant made a study (published in 1951) of the etiology, prevention and treatment of juvenile delinquency, in the course of which he visited some sixty institutions in Europe and the United States and conferred with more than 150 specialists in juvenile delinquency. WHO consultants have also discussed the psychiatric aspects of the problem at seminars and congresses organised by the United Nations.[38]

From all available data, it would appear that WHO activity in this area was strongest during the early 1950s and had declined since the early 1960s. It is clear that the emphasis has been on delinquency and the psychiatric examination of offenders. Nor does it appear that WHO has concerned itself with problems of environmental health, notably sanitation, in penal establishments.

WHO was instrumental in setting up two seminars related to the general field. The first was on the "Medical, Psychological and Social Examination of Delinquents," organized at the invitation of the Belgian government by the United Nations in collaboration with WHO, and was held in Brussels in December 1951. The second was the WHO Seminar on Psychiatric Treatment of Criminals and Delinquents, held in Copenhagen for the European Region in April-May of 1958.

The concern of WHO in this area was further displayed when it convened under its auspices a meeting of experts on forensic psychiatry in Rome at the United Nations Social Defence Research Institute, from 6 to 12 December 1969.[39] The major purposes of this meeting were to review the mental health aspects of social defence as well as the extent of, and the possibilities for, international collaboration in this area. Of particular concern was the potential for close cooperation in the field of research between WHO and the Social Defence Research Institute in Rome. The participants agreed upon four areas in which this collaboration could and should take place: diagnosis and classification, psychiatric treatment of offenders, legislation and the abnormal offender, and the psychiatry of adolescence.

The meeting concluded with several recommendations, including one for the appointment of a full-time psychiatrist to the Institute who would be charged with transmission of the knowledge available within WHO to the research program of the Institute. This meeting and its outcome represent an important step in the continuing effort by WHO to improve the quality of relevant research and to expand knowledge in this area.

*United Nations Educational, Scientific and Cultural
Organization (UNESCO), Paris*

A review of United Nations Educational, Scientific
and Cultural Organization (UNESCO) annual reports reveals some expressed interest in international law, but otherwise little direct concern with the field of prevention of crime and treatment of offenders.[40]

As of December 1968 several related international nongovernmental organizations were listed as among those having consultative relations with UNESCO. These were the International Law Association, the International Society of Criminology, and the International Union of Child Welfare. The International Law Association is the oldest of all the international bodies admitted to consultative status, having been established in 1873.

UNESCO has published two excellent books: *Selected Documentation on Criminology*, compiled by the International Society of Criminology at the request of UNESCO in 1961, appearing as Number 14 of Reports and Papers in the Social Sciences published by UNESCO. Its preface sets out the purpose:

> to offer to teachers and research workers in different countries a list
> of 'classics'—using this term in its double sense, to include both the
> older but still important works of the founders of criminology in dif-
> ferent linguistic or national settings, and some of the new works
> which, by virtue of their contents or their new methodological ap-
> proach, have come to be regarded as essential reading. It has been
> thought opportune to complete each selective bibliography with a
> summary survey of statistical source material and of institutions—
> penitentiary, clinical, and academic—which have specialized in the
> study of criminal phenomena or their prevention. Though this issue
> presents only part of the documentation which is of international
> value in the field of criminology, and is still to be followed by a sec-
> ond containing further data on Eastern Europe, Asia and Africa, the
> Secretariat believes that this first collection will be a useful comple-
> ment to existing social science bibliographies and directories.

An earlier UNESCO publication, *The Teaching of the Social Sciences: Criminology*, provides an excellent guide to the academic offerings available to persons interested in pursuing a career in criminology and penology. Under UNESCO sponsorship, one teaching fellow was appointed under the Technical Assistance Program, in the field of international law.

International Labour Organisation (ILO), Geneva

A significant International Labour Organisation publication dealing with crime, "Juvenile Delinquency Viewed as a Labour Problem," a report prepared by the ILO for presentation to the First United Nations Crime Congress in Geneva in 1955, appears to be one of the few excursions—by this specialized agency—into this field.[41] The report confined its attention to delinquency prevention, and made no reference to treatment.

> The contention in this report will be that proper attention to labour conditions affecting all youth will help to eradicate certain forms of vocational service, e.g., vocational guidance, vocational training and placement in employment, which are becoming increasingly necessary for the social adjustment of all youth, and that they must therefore, as a minimum, be made available for those groups of young people and individuals who can be singled out as pre-delinquents.

The ILO also published a survey of prison labor in two parts, based on data drawn from seventeen countries, which was released in two separate issues of *International Labour Review.*[42]

ILO conventions dealing with forced labor specifically exclude prison labor from their coverage, nor have they made any recommendation about payment of wages to persons in confinement by reason of a court commitment.

United Nations Children's Fund (UNICEF), New York

While the United Nations Children's Fund is noted primarily for its contribution to the health and educational needs of disadvantaged youth throughout the world, it has also made a significant and distinctive contribution to the prevention of juvenile delinquency. UNICEF was founded in 1946 to meet the postwar needs of children. It has since become a development-centered agency which attempts to assist governments within the context of their national plans in behalf of childhood.

UNICEF funds find their way into a variety of institutions affecting the health and welfare of youth, including those for young offenders. Related research and training programs are likewise assisted. The voluntary contributions of 127 national governments and of numerous private donors presently provide continuing assistance in 111 countries.

United Nations Institutes

United Nations Asia and Far East Institute
(UNAFEI), Fuchu

In addition to the regional seminars conducted from time to time under United Nations auspices for the training of workers in the correctional and allied fields, provision by the United Nations of technical assistance has also made possible advanced study and training for professional personnel. Furthermore, the United Nations had, since a resolution adopted in 1954, been committed to the idea of establishing regional institutes in the social defence field. To date only two are in operation. South America, the Mid-East and Africa continue to wait and to exert what pressures they can in behalf of an institute for each of these three regions.

The United Nations Asia and Far East Institute was originally slated for Pakistan as the host country, but due to political changes in that area it was decided to locate it instead in Japan, although Australia had put in a strong bid for it as well. In 1961, a treaty signed between the government of Japan and the United Nations set forth the obligations and expectations of the two parties with regard to its establishment and operation.[43]

The regional Training Institute to serve Asia and the Far Eastern countries was established in 1962 in Fuchu, nearby one of the largest of Japan's prisons. The Institute provides living and dining quarters, classrooms, library and administrative offices in its own modern, four-story building only thirty minutes from downtown Tokyo. The Institute in 1971 will have completed nine years of service. During this period, the Japanese Government assumed the cost of constructing and maintaining the building and facilities, while the United Nations has provided the director and the cost of fellowships.

Its function is four-fold:

1)   to provide training courses for officials in the Region;
2)   to pursue research into techniques of treating crime and juvenile delinquency, concentrating on problems in the Region;
3)   to disseminate information concerning correctional practices throughout the Region;
4)   to provide advisory service to Governments.

The first international training course was begun in September of 1962, with twenty trainees from twelve separate countries, ten of them under fellowship grants. In inaugurating the Institute's first course, His Imperial Highness Prince Takamatsu said, in the course of his address:

Crime is one of the great human problems common to all countries, and the processes of cultural interchange are so intimate that it may not be too much to say that the problems in the field of the prevention of crime and the treatment of offenders can no longer be regarded as the particular burden of each separate country. Rather, the solution of such problems has to be regarded as one of the most urgent tasks facing the totality of countries in the region. . . .[4] [4]

The curriculum included nine class topics: Law and Society; Comparative Survey of Correctional Practices; Criminology and Juvenile Delinquency; Institutional Treatment; Correctional Administration; Social Case Work; Psychology; Psychiatry; and Clinical Criminology, taught by twelve faculty members in addition to guest lecturers. The method of instruction was largely by means of discussion, in which the role of teacher and student was frequently reversed. Class content of the curriculum was supplemented by fieldwork one day a week, with a three-week intensive period in the field at the end of the course.

In 1963, three training courses were conducted, of one-, three-, and six-months duration, respectively. The experience of these first two years showed that while Asian countries had many correctional problems in common, these were not greatly dissimilar to those confronted in Europe and America. The problems included: shortage of trained personnel; overcrowding; excess of short-term offenders; archaic and repressive penal laws; unimaginative prison regulations; lack of psychiatric facilities for treatment of mentally disturbed offenders; and inadequate parole and after-care programs.

This second year of the Institute's operation saw increased emphasis on fieldwork placement in Thailand and Malaysia. At the same time, these countries were selected as sites for new courses, many of which were given from Institute headquarters. The governments of Australia, Malaysia and the United States made fellowships available as well as assignments of senior correctional personnel to the teaching staff. Relevant research projects, totalling five, were initiated during the year, as well as the extension of consultant services to the local (Fuchu) area crime prevention project.

The opening of the 1964 session was highlighted by an expansion of the Institute library and housing facilities and increased cooperation with international and other organizations interested in social defence, human rights, and the administration of justice. At the same time the Institute began to confront a shortage of funds needed to expand the extensive and varied research program for which the first two years had indicated a need.

By the time the fourth year opened, 137 trainees had been graduated, representing a wide spectrum of related disciplines including judges and other court personnel, juvenile and adult correction, police, probation and parole, welfare services, training and research.

The social defence needs of the region were now clearly seen to include trained personnel at the executive, managerial and custodial level; understanding of the extent of crime and delinquency problems; and on-the-spot advisory services to help correctional administrators resolve their problems. Recognition by the government of Japan of these needs was expressed in their official invitation to the United Nations to hold the Fourth International Crime Congress in 1970 in Kyoto, the ancient capital of Japan.

The fifth session of UNAFEI was opened by a second address by Prince Takamatsu, who welcomed the new students by saying:

> I am most pleased to note that this Institute, since it was established a few years ago, has become an important center for the encouragement of studies and research, and for the exchange of ideas and experiences, so that the countries of Asia could be prepared to meet the increasingly difficult and serious problems that confront them. . . .[45]

The Institute began to become involved more broadly than ever in the region with the holding of the Seminar on Crime Prevention and Treatment in the Philippines, as well as a participatory representation in a parole conference in Australia, a research meeting in Copenhagen, and the Third United Nations Crime Congress in Stockholm.

At the same time, the Institute's 1966 *Annual Report* reflected the diversity of professional interests represented by its participants:

Judicial Administration (planning and research)	11
Judges	14
Public Prosecutors	21
Correctional Administration	18
Adult Correctional Institute	30
Juvenile Correctional Institute	20
Probation, Parole, and After-Care Services	30
Police Services	20
Family and Child Welfare	8
Social Welfare	7
Medico-Correctional Services	11
Training and Research	13
	203

The first year's courses had emphasized open and short-term institutions; prevention of delinquency was the main concern of the second session; planning and implementation of penal policies in developing countries occupied the third year; probation, parole and after-care were the central feature of the fourth.

Lack of funds to carry on needed research projects continued to limit the effectiveness of the Institute. Faculty and students began to call attention to the dearth of teaching in the role of psychiatry in both diagnostic and treatment services within the training programs.

The year 1967, the Institute's sixth, saw the formation of an Alumni Association and of a pilot project in group training for human rights. The Institute was now capable of conducting a three-month course relying entirely on its own resources, and without the need to call in outside experts.

The 1968 sessions saw the end of the grants to be provided by the United Nations to fellowships at the Institute. By the end of the year, 22 countries had sent 381 of their court-correctional personnel to attend the 20 sessions of the Institute. The following year continued the tradition of earlier training courses, but the structure of the Institute began to change in anticipation of the expected changeover in auspices.

A "Refresher-Evaluation Course," conducted in the summer of 1970, was given to invited former participants of previous training courses. Participants discussed the difficulties they had confronted after they had graduated and returned to their home countries and to their daily duties.[46] Out of these discussions flowed evaluations of the effectiveness of UNAFEI training based on these experiences, which will be applied in the design of subsequent curricula. Items on the agenda of the then-upcoming United Nations Crime Congress in Kyoto were discussed in advance by these post graduate students in class sessions, after which the participants went on to Kyoto to observe the proceedings there.

A meeting of the Third UNAFEI *Ad Hoc* Advisory Committee, held at the conclusion of the Kyoto Congress, summed up the consensus of the intent of the two contracting parties with regard to the future of the Institute "that it was vital to the continued success of the Institute that its international character should be preserved not only by continuing the present policy of selection of trainees, but also in the appointment of visiting experts."[47] For the first time, the Institute was to operate under a single Japanese director.

On 31 August 1970 an agreement between the United Nations and the government of Japan was implemented. This agreement provided for the taking over by Japan of the facilities and maintenance of the Institute, the provision of a director, faculty and other staff, and the implementation of the training program. The agreement carried the very clear implication that while the United Nations was handing over the major responsibility of the Institute to the Japanese government, it was by no means withdrawing its interest—or its support in the form of consultants, teaching experts and fellowships for trainees. The auspices of the Institute would continue to be joint, though in somewhat modified form.

The Alumni Association now totals over 500 graduates from more than a score of countries. An innovation in training programs, it presents, for the first time, an opportunity for the creation of a diversity of correctional and rehabilitative programs throughout all of Asia. As these alumni increase their contacts within their own countries and throughout the region, they may be expected to constitute an important source of new institution formation—the creation of special training centers or university-based programs.

The role of UNAFEI as a model training scheme on the international level has been no small accomplishment. Its ability to attract trainees from twenty-two countries; the steady flow of suggestions for courses from participating countries, and its ability to consistently recruit the services of an international elite in the field of criminology and related disciplines is testimony not only to the needs that exist, but to the vital role that UNAFEI has played throughout Asia and the Far East. It has served as a means of disseminating ideas, theories, and programs from all over the world, while processing them for application to the peno-correctional institutions of the entire region.

While UNAFEI acknowledges that it may be limited in the kind of original research which it may initiate, there is no doubt as to the need within the region for the continuing education of practitioners in the field— an area in which the Institute has excelled. It is to be expected that on the basis of this experience, the United Nations might be moved to postpone no longer the creation of similar training institutes for professional correctional personnel in other regions, especially Latin America and Africa, which have long pressed for it.

United Nations Social Defence Research Institute (UNSDRI), Rome

For many years, the resolutions adopted at international gatherings had reflected concern for the inadequacy of crime statistics. Furthermore, there was a need for more extensive and intensive research into the results of innovative programs in order to evaluate their long-range effect and implications. Yet relatively little has actually been done at the international level to ensure that these kinds of information would be gathered.

It was at the Stockholm Congress in 1965 that the topic of research first received major emphasis in the proceedings. Thereafter, on 8 May 1968, a special agreement between the United Nations and the government of Italy established the United Nations Social Defence Research Institute. Although located in Europe, the Defence Institute at Rome was to have its primary focus "on problems of special concern to the countries of the developing world," through both action research and policy-oriented research.[48]

Its aim was to seek "to develop research skills and to encourage research in various countries. It was endeavouring to develop comprehensive information services which would assist Governments and their specialists in their research work. In this sense, the Institute would become an international clearing-house for data and findings gathered in various countries. These findings would be widely disseminated so as to be of maximum benefit, particularly as to developing countrie . The Institute was expected to render significant assistance in the area of social defence training through the development of suitable training materials. There was general agreement on the potential ability of the Institute to meet social defence needs and to coordinate research efforts at the international and regional levels."[49]

The Defence Institute is not financed through the regular budget of the United Nations but from a trust fund which receives contributions from U.N. member governments, nongovernmental organizations and private sources. In this regard, the Italian government has been signally generous in providing the Institute with an historic palazzo, modernized and fully equipped, together with an annual cash grant in support of its activities. By the spring of 1969, twenty-one governments had made contributions to the trust fund and a number of others had indicated their intent to do likewise.

While administratively the Institute is attached to the office of the director-general of the United Nations office in Geneva, it receives its policy guidelines from the Commission for Social Development of the Economic and Social Council. In addition it benefits from the regular advice of the United Nations Advisory Committee on the Prevention of Crime and the Treatment of Offenders. The basic elements of the Defence Institute's research tasks occupy much of the effort of its staff. There is at the same time an extensive effort underway to establish an international network of national and regional research institutes with the Rome Defence Institute at the center.

The publication program of the Institute includes an annual catalog of current research throughout the world as well as publication of the findings of research projects sponsored by the Institute itself. It houses a library and a documentation center and has organized and played host to a number of meetings and seminars for research specialists in the field. To date, the countries of Uganda, Tunisia and Venezuela have been the major beneficiaries of the Institute's efforts. Visiting fellows, scholars and students have taken advantage of the Institute's facilities for conferences with its staff or to pursue projects of their own.

The first director of the Institute has recently resigned to accept a post as one of the two interregional advisors in social defence. Thus the program of the United Nations in the field of crime appears to reach out in active fashion: in addition to its established program of congresses, publications, correspondents, fellowships and regional institutes, it now makes outstanding experts available for direct involvement with national social defence programmers and workers at both the policy and operational levels.

Notes

1. Information in this chapter derives largely from official United Nations materials. Symbols of U.N. documents are composed of capital letters combined with figures, e.g., E/CN.5/AC.6/L.4. The capital letters which begin the citation specify the organ or subsidiary body from which the document emanates. In the above example, E/CN refers to the Economic and Social Council (ECOSOC), while AC indicates an Advisory Committee. All resolutions are those of the General Assembly unless otherwise indicated.

For a detailed description of the various U.N. organs, bodies and subordinate organizational entities, see L. Larry Leonard, *International Organization*, esp. chs. 4, 20-24.

2. ECOSOC Resolution 155C (VIII), 13 August 1948.

3. E/CN.5/AC.6/L.4.

4. Ibid.

5. Resolution 415 (V), 1 December 1950.

6. Freely translated from the introductory remarks of Professor Marc Ancel, Président de Chambre à la Cour de Cassation, Paris, and President of the International Society for Social Defence, at a meeting of the Society and its Japanese affiliates held during the course of the Fourth United Nations Crime Congress, Kyoto, 20 August 1970.

7. *International Review of Criminal Policy*, no. 1 (January 1952), pp. 16-17.

8. Annex to Resolution 415 (V), 1 December 1950, para. a.

9. Through 1970, a total of 28 numbers had been issued.

10. Resolution 1396 (XIV), 20 November 1959.

11. Resolution 1918 (XVIII), 5 December 1963.

12. *Capital Punishment*, U.N. Publication ST/SOA/SD/9, sales no. 62.IV2.

13. *Capital Punishment*, U.N. Publication ST/SOA/SD/10, sales no. E/7.IV.15.

14. See, for example, Marc Ancel, *The Death Penalty in European Countries.*

15. Resolution 2393 (XXIII), 26 November 1968.

16. ECOSOC Resolution 115C (VII), 13 August 1948.

17. E/CN.5/398.

18. See pp. 108-10 below.

19. *International Review of Criminal Policy*, no. 1 (January 1952), p. 11.

20. Beginning with number 21.

21. *International Review of Criminal Policy*, no. 5 (January 1954), pp. 83-89.

22. "Last Days of the Superpowers," *Center Magazine* 3 (July 1970):3.

23. *Report of the First United Nations Congress on the Prevention of Crime and the Treatment of Offenders, Geneva, 22 August-3 September 1955*, A/CONF.6/1.

24. Resolution 663 (XXIV), 31 July 1957.

25. See *Report of First Congress, Geneva,* for the report entitled "Standard Minimum Rules for the Treatment of Prisoners and Related Recommendations"; and, more recently, *Standard Minimum Rules for the Treatment of Prisoners in Light of Recent Developments in the Correctional Field.* See also Exhibit 7, above.

26. See "Provisional Draft of the Final Report of the Fourth United Nations Congress on the Prevention of Crime and the Treatment of Offenders," pp. 9-11.

27. See *Second United Nations Congress on the Prevention of Crime and the Treatment of Offenders, London, 8-20 August 1960*, A/CONF. 17/20.

28. See *Third United Nations Congress on the Prevention of Crime and the Treatment of Offenders, Stockholm, 8-18 August 1965*, A/CONF. 17/26.

29. See "Provisional Draft Report, Kyoto."

30. See Masaharu Yanagimoto, "Some Features of the Japanese Prison System," *British Journal of Criminology* 10 (July 1970):209-24.

31. Resolution 2542 (XXIV), 11 December 1969.

32. A/CONF.43/3, p. 3.

33. Ibid.

34. Amnesty International, *Proposals by Amnesty International to the U.N. Congress on the Prevention of Crime and Treatment of Offenders, Kyoto, August 1970* (London: T.B. Russell, n.d.).

35. ECOSOC Resolution 158 (L), 7 June 1971.

36. World Health Organization (WHO), *Handbook of Resolutions and Decisions of the World Health Organization and the Executive Board*, off. rec. 13, 321, p. 82.

37. Ibid., off. rec. 14, 18.

38. WHO, *First Ten Years of WHO*, pp. 332-33.

39. *International Review of Criminal Policy*, no. 28 (1970), pp. 120-22.

40. U.N. Educational, Scientific and Cultural Organization, *Report of the Director-General on the Activities of the Organization, 1947-1971* (Paris: Joseph Floch, 1971).

41. For basic information on the work and activities of the International Labour Organization, see their *Summary of Annual Reports* and *Index to Conventions and Recommendations Adopted by the International Labour Conferences, 1919-1966.*

42. These were "Prison Labour I" and "Prison Labour II," *International Labour Review* 25 (March 1932 & April 1932):311-31 & 499-524.

43. For an account of the first training program offered by the Institute, see UNAFEI: The First International Training Course, September-December 1962 (Fuchu: UNAFEI, 1963). Much of the information for this section was taken from the annual reports—1963-1970—prepared and published by the Institute entitled *UNAFEI: Report for [year]*.

44. *UNAFEI: First International Training Course*, p. 3.

45. *UNAFEI: Report for 1966*, p. 2.

46. *UNAFEI: Report for 1970.*

47. Ibid., p. 18.

48. See pamphlet, "United Nations Social Defence Research Institute (Rome, n.d.).

49. Ibid. See also *International Review of Criminal Policy*, no. 28 (1970), pp. 75-78.

8   Other International Organizations

Howard League for Penal Reform, London

Although the membership of the Howard League is confined to the British Isles, and the major impact of its program is directed nationally, its work, like that of its parent organizations, has been of international significance, constituting a long and distinguished history.[1]

The Howard League for Penal Reform assumed its present name in 1921 with the merger of two organizations—The Howard Association and the Penal Reform League, which date back to 1866 and 1907, respectively. The Howard League is a reform-oriented organization, consistently committed to the cause of penal reform and the principles of rehabilitation and progressivism. It maintains close relations with British governmental departments, committees and commissions, and makes available the latest criminal and penal information to policy-makers as well as to the general public.

From a lengthy list of the reforms in which the Howard League, or its parent societies, have played a significant role, only a few will be mentioned. The early Howard Association actively campaigned for the introduction of probation in Great Britain, and, much later, the establishment of children's courts. Between 1925 and 1939 the Howard League actively assisted in the work of the League of Nations by providing information and pressing for reforms. It was largely as a result of its unstinted efforts that the League of Nations ultimately endorsed the Standard Minimum Rules. Currently, the Howard League holds consultative status as a nongovernmental organization with the United Nations as well as with the Council of

113

Europe. Throughout the years it has taken leadership in campaigns to abolish capital punishment, and was largely instrumental in the suspension of the death penalty in Great Britain for a period of five years, starting with 1966.[2] Thereafter both Houses of Parliament voted against its re-introduction, a fit centennial commemoration of Portugal's initial action in outlawing capital punishment in 1867.[3]

On that occasion, Victor Hugo, on 15 July 1867 wrote to Brito Aranha a letter, from which the following is extracted:

> Le Portugal vient d'abolir la peine de mort.
>
> Accomplir ce progrès, c'est faire le grand pas de la civilisation.
>
> Vous n'avez pas cessé d'etre, vous portugais, des navigateurs intrépides. Vous allez en avant, autrefois dans l'océan, aujourd'hui dans la vérité. Proclamer des principes, c'est plus beau encore que de découvrir des mondes.[4]

The League's most recent effort has been the establishment of the Howard Centre of Penology, with the purpose of training probation officers in group-work techniques. In addition to maintaining its library of criminology and penology, the Howard League annually publishes the *Howard Journal of Penology and Crime Prevention*. It also organizes an extensive program of public lectures, summer schools and conferences.

International Association of Youth Magistrates, Brussels

The First International Congress of Children's Courts took place in 1911 in Paris—at the time that both France and Belgium were considering the introduction of specialized courts for children. The 350 participants, caught up in their enthusiasm for this new non-criminal instrumentality for dealing with young offenders, give the impression, when one reviews the record of their deliberations, that they believed they had indeed come upon a universal panacea. The good will and amity which marked this first congress is captured in the following words by its amiable President, M. Paul Wets, *juge des enfants à Bruxelles*:

> les premiers contacts furent marqués par cette affabilité souriante qui est la marque innée des hommes de bonne compagnie. Les débats s'ouvrirent et se poursuivirent dans la sérénité, dans cet espirit de cordialité conciliante, dans ce souci de bien faire, qui devrait toujours être l'atmosphère où agissent et s'expriment ceux qui, animés de préoccupations identiques et soucieux d'un même idéal, entendent le pousser toujours plus loin dans la voie de la prospérité et du progrès.

Before they departed the Paris Congress, the delegates adopted a constitution for their new international organization and elected a committee to prepare the second congress. It was not until 1928, however, that the Belgian government made possible the creation of the International Association of Youth Magistrates. It did so by offering the services of the Children's Court of Brussels as the secretariat, under the leadership of its president and founder, Paul Wets, the illustrious judge of that court. Its first congress convened in Brussels at the end of July 1930, in response to a call issued by the government of Belgium,[5] with Judge Henri Rollet of Paris as presiding officer.

Except for the usual run of speeches which are delivered at the launching of a new society—or publication—this first congress was not especially noteworthy. Two resolutions were passed: one relating to the repatriation of minors and the need for a convention to cover the necessary implementing procedures; and a second urging all governments to establish autonomous tribunals for children in criminal or moral danger, with appropriate competence to deal with them.

Five years later, again in Brussels, the Association met in its second congress. By this time, the political and economic plight of the world outside made its way into the conference halls, resulting in discussions and resolutions which touched again on the necessity for providing for repatriation of children, and for special efforts in behalf of young persons who were the victims of unemployment.

The third congress, held in Liege in 1950 after a lapse of fifteen years, seems to have attracted the largest attendance up to that time. It made up for lost time by reasserting in detailed and vigorous fashion a list of twenty principles for the guidance of those jurisdictions which had accepted the doctrine that juveniles charged with delinquency were to be considered not as persons who should be punished, but rather as persons in need of protection and correction. While the reassertion of these guiding principles was necessary, perhaps, to remind a world which had recently been at war of the duties of society toward its erring young, they contained little that was new and nothing that was startling. References to the newly formed International Union of Child Welfare, and to the World Health Organization and the United Nations, served as a reminder of the involvement of important recently organized international bodies in the field of child welfare and protection.

The United Nations in particular was asked to contribute to the solution of the problem by encouraging research into causation as well as into means for combating crime, through the gathering of comparative international statistics, by facilitating international exchange of juvenile court personnel, and finally by urging the expansion of programs of technical assistance to underdeveloped countries.

Nothing especially worthy of record appears in the proceedings of the fourth or fifth congresses held in Brussels, one in 1954 and the second in 1958, except for one resolution regarding "adult delinquent minors." This resolution called for the drawing up of special statutes to cover young people in the age group between "penal majority" and 25, who had not yet attained "biopsychic maturity." This concept applies to young persons whose physical, intellectual and emotional maturity does not parallel their chronological development.

For this age group the congress resolution recommended the organization of a "young adults chamber" or adolescent session within the judicial system, which would be presided over by judges chosen for their special competence in dealing with young persons. Facilities for observation and diagnosis of persons brought before the youth sessions of the courts were recommended, to the end that they might be reintegrated into society through the provisions of medical, psychological and psychiatric measures of treatment. Failure to respond to such corrective treatment, or "the seriousness of the offense," would justify the application of "adult delinquent procedures" in place of the special adolescent court. The idea of special courts for adolescents, based on the experience and principles of the children's tribunal, had been much emphasized in the decade prior to World War II. This action on the part of the International Association of Youth Magistrates to revive the adolescent court movement is the first evidence that the idea was not entirely dead, although since 1958 it has not been seriously proposed in the deliberations of any international organization concerned with juvenile delinquency.

The removing of the congress from Belgium, where the previous five congresses had been held, to Naples for the 6th in September of 1962, was followed by the convening of the 7th in Paris in June of 1966. Participants at this congress expressed their concern over the increasing involvement of younger children in criminality and the "hardening" of adolescent delinquency. In the face of these developments, the congress went on to warn of the dangers which would arise from the lack of welfare personnel and of institutional facilities.

The most recent congress of the Association, its 8th, was held in Geneva in mid-July of 1970, under the patronage of the Director-General of the United Nations European Office. The general theme of the Congress, "The Magistrate, the Child, the Family and the Community," was considered in three sections: 1) safeguarding the basic rights of the child and the family; 2) legislation for child welfare and the reintegration of the child into the family and into society; and 3) the youth magistrate's legal and social role in the community.

The congress took note of the 70th anniversary of the founding of the first court for children in Cook County, Illinois. It then proceeded to debate the seventeen resolutions brought forward for its consideration. Among them were "that the trend in future should be towards raising rather than lowering the age of criminal responsibility" (No. 13); that the training of lawyers in law schools should include courses in the administration of juvenile court law as well as "disciplines and methods connected with the treatment and rehabilitation of children in trouble" (No. 15); and (No. 17) that the Declaration of the Rights of the Child, first adopted in 1924 by the League of Nations and endorsed in modified form by the General Assembly of the United Nations in 1959, "should be embodied in the laws, procedures and practices of every country."

International Center for Clinical Criminology, Rome

The International Center for Clinical Criminology (ICCC) is the most recent echo of the faraway last meeting of the International Society of Criminal Anthropology, which did not survive beyond 1911. In 1970 the ICCC announced that its purpose was

> to favour the development of clinical criminological studies in as many countries as possible, because such studies appear to be increasingly important to the following aims: the development of an effective special preventive policy; the collaboration with judicial authorities in the study of the offender's personality, and specifically of his criminal potentialities and of his social dangerousness, to the purpose of individualizing and humanizing the penalty; the collaboration with correctional administrations towards the improvement of those treatment techniques which, in order to insure an effective social rehabilitation of the offender, must be based on more sound criminological diagnoses which are indispensable to the application of the specific medical-psychological-educational and social treatments, required in each individual case.[6]

As an additional aim, it called for the establishment of schools of clinical criminology, patterned after the school by that name founded in 1967 at the University of Rome. Like the Rome school, the International Center intends to train "physicians, judges, lawyers, police and correctional officers, whose criminological clinical training must be considered of fundamental importance for the functioning of penal justice really useful to the individual and society."[7]

In addition, the Center promises to serve as a collection point for documents as well as to publish the results of criminological research. As of this writing, only a prospectus—from which the above has been quoted—is available. Its call to action is reminiscent of all that the Italian School has given to the field, but only a future writer can measure what it will—hopefully—accomplish.

International Center for Comparative Criminology, Montreal

With the theme of research beginning to play a greater role at international gatherings, and with the establishment of the United Nations Social Defence Research Institute in Rome serving as a fresh model, it was only a matter of time before new efforts to coordinate and extend criminological knowledge would emerge on the international scene. This trend continues. The International Center for Comparative Criminology is the most recent example of this thrust. The Center was established in June 1969, and is headquartered at the University of Montreal, where it maintains a close working relationship with the department of criminology. An agreement between the University and the International Society for Criminology formalized the close affiliation between the two.

In general, the Center devotes itself to "the institutionalization of comparative research on a worldwide scale [as] the only alternative to the loss of data."[8] Its chief objectives are "the initiation of comparative research studies and the training of professional personnel and research workers in the field of criminal justice; the dissemination of cross-cultural experience and resources; and the exchange of information in research and penal reform among the western countries, Japan, the socialist countries and the Third World."[9] The Center seems particularly committed to the notion that the developing world can and must profit from mistakes made in the past by industrialized nations, and that scientific interchange between capitalist and socialist countries is of fundamental importance to the growth of knowledge in this field.

Research studies are undertaken, particularly concerning the adaptation of traditional crime prevention and treatment programs to the demands of developed and developing countries. The Center staff has been engaged in two rather unique research projects. One combines two basic goals: the attempt to determine primary trends in social reaction against crime, and thus of criminal law in the making; and to establish an International Lexicon of Criminological Terms. The second project, currently underway, is the creation of a bank of methodological instruments used by researchers in crime and related matters the world over.

Future research plans include such topics as socio-cultural indicators of crime and delinquency; the correlation of the phenomenon of violence with an armed or unarmed police force, and the incidence of mass violence.

Through training of research workers, and the interchange of projects and ideas, as well as by organization of refresher courses for experienced practitioners in the field, the Center hopes to extend the frontiers of knowledge in the social defence field. It intends to supplement, as well, the technical assistance program of the United Nations to countries requesting it. In this regard, the Center cooperates closely with UNESCO and the United Nations Social Defence Research Institute in Rome.

Annual symposia are planned, alternately in North America and Europe. The first, held in 1969, dealt with methodology and research in comparative criminology. In the following year the second symposium examined the cost of crime and the application of economics to problems of crime and criminal justice.

The basic budget of the Center is provided by the University of Montreal. Policy is determined, and administration guided, by a nine-member Board of Directors, supported by an Advisory Council of twenty-five. The latter consists of economists, administrators, and magistrates, in addition to several noted criminologists. Finally, several Fellows appointed from related disciplines serve as distinguished consultants to the overall research program of the Center.

International Commission of Jurists (ICJ), Geneva

A nongovernmental and nonpolitical body organized in 1952 to promote the rule of law and human rights in the world, the International Commission of Jurists (ICJ) has since its inception taken an active part in programs relating to some of the most basic aspects of the problem of crime. It has been involved in such matters as preventive detention, legal counsel, penal legislation, conditions within prisons, economic and social rights of prisoners, capital punishment and the Standard Minimum Rules for the Treatment of Prisoners. In 1968 it called, at Stockholm, a conference on "The Right to Privacy," a topic closely related to the field of crime detection and apprehension.

Its basic aim is furthered through a variety of activities: its publications, which include special studies and reports in addition to its quarterly *ICJ Review*;[10] the organization of seminars and congresses, and the initiation of international surveys and inquiries. In human rights matters of special gravity and importance, it dispatches observers to report on alleged violations of the rule of law, or to attend trials of major importance through missions and visits by officers of ICJ. It also renders technical legal assistance through international exchange of persons interested in problems related to the rule of law.

Collaboration between the ICJ and the United Nations has been expressed in attendance at, and participation in, United Nations conferences as well as by such direct action as the promotion and stimulation of interest in these topics among lawyers and jurists throughout the world who compose the ICJ membership within their national sections. The ICJ has maintained close contact with the United Nations Section of Social Defence, and has made its services and advice available to the recently established Social Defence Institute in Rome.

The ICJ has served both to inform the public and to arouse world indignation when notorious incidents contrary to the rule of law and human rights take place. Thus in 1969 it drew attention to the provisions of the Standard Minimum Rules when these were flagrantly disregarded in the prisons of South Africa. The ICJ was instrumental in exposing these conditions to the world.[11]

The ICJ has further exemplified its inclination to be active rather than hortative in areas of its concerns. For example, it has consistently pushed for the implementation of the Standard Minimum Rules by means of corresponding legal sanctions embodied in national legislation rather than leaving them to acts of "administrative generosity [which is] . . . at best arbitrary and subject to abuse. To this end, the ICJ suggests, the U.N. Section of Social Defence could make its services available, and should initiate consultation with governments to this end."[12]

Considering the length of time that the Standard Minimum Rules have been on the international agenda, it is refreshing to catch a sense of impatience on the part of the ICJ at the snail's pace with which decent international standards in the social field are applied by the governments who send the delegates who make speeches and pass resolutions which all too often are stillborn; as if delivery of a speech were somehow tantamount to "delivery" of the issue (which may have been talked to death!).

As an additional example, the ICJ has urged that the manner in which the Minimum Rules are applied should be internationally supervised under a covenant open to ratification by all states. It has also warned against lowering the standard set as a *minimum*, with the very clear implication that the Minimum Rules constitute a floor—and not a ceiling. Such a proposed covenant "should contain machinery for the regular reporting by governments as to the extent to which the Rules are being implemented."[13]

The next step proposed is that governments should present accurate statistics, on a regular basis, giving the number of prisoners held, the categories, the reason for confinement, and the accommodation available to them. The suggestion recalls one of the original reasons put forward by the proponents of the earliest international conferences in the field—that the gathering and dissemination of world-wide criminal statistics be the first order of business for international action. It is also reminiscent of the 1936 proposal of the League of Nations, although the latter did not go so far as the ICJ did when they called for inspection of all places of detention by an international body.

By reason of its nongovernmental status, or perhaps by reason of the dynamic leadership of its Secretary-General, the ICJ had rushed in openly and strongly in areas where other international bodies do not normally dare to tread. It has continued over the years to call international attention to the need to protect political prisoners and prisoners of conscience, hundreds of thousands of whom, it has claimed, are in confinement, frequently without trial, by reason of political or religious belief, race, or color. The ICJ has correctly pointed out that "often, [a] lower standard of treatment is applied to such prisoners than to the criminal offender."[14]

The need to protect the rights of such prisoners has led the ICJ to call attention to the special status of categories of prisoners known as "political," and to the pertinent provisions of United Nations resolutions, such as that of the International Conference on Human Rights convened at Teheran in May 1968, which as part of its Preamble, stated that it was:

> *Noting also* that minority racist or colonial regimes which refuse to comply with the decision of the United Nations and the principles of the Universal Declaration of Human Rights frequently resort to executions and inhuman treatment of those who struggle against such regimes,
>
> *and considering* that such persons should be protected against inhuman or brutal treatment and also that such persons if detained should be treated as prisoners of war or political prisoners under international law...."[15]

The ICJ has further called attention to the "torture, ill-treatment or inhuman treatment" to which prisoners, particularly political prisoners, are subject, and has urged as "desirable that specific provisions should be embodied in national and international legislation...," declaring such treatment to constitute a crime against humanity and making provisions for the trial of persons who torture or ill-treat prisoners.[16] In this connection, reference is made to Principle IV of the Nuremberg Principles, adopted by the International Law Commission in 1950, as pertinent:

The fact that a person acted pursuant to order of his Government or of a superior does not relieve him from responsibility under International Law, provided a moral choice was in fact possible to him.[1][7]

"The International Commission of Jurists has repeatedly drawn attention on the escalation in brutality and violence in the world and has pointed out that this was inevitably leading to the erosion of the moral standards upon which respect for the dignity of the human personality is founded. Unfortunately, often this brutality stems from the actions of governmental authorities. These acts of brutality inevitably erode human standards and are contagious; they are among the primary causes for the mounting violence and brutality and the spread of crimes of violence which disgrace this era. For these reasons, it is suggested that the 4th United Nations Congress on the Prevention of Crime and the Treatment of Offenders should":

(a)   invite governments to use their best endeavour to ensure the strict observance of the humanitarian laws in all armed conflicts and situations wherein force has to be used;

(b)   invite the leaders of all religious and ideological denominations to use their best influence to secure observance of humanitarian rules in all circumstances where force is used.[1][8]

International organizations in the field of crime, in both their deliberations and resolutions, have not been noted for speaking out against the inhumanity of man to man which is epitomized in the long and tortured history of penal treatment. The clarity and force of the statements uttered by the ICJ are to be commended, therefore, especially in today's world, where brutality, torture and inhumane treatment of people is known to be practiced. Recently reported allegations as to conditions at My Lai and Con Son in South Vietnam, at Attica Prison in New York and on the Arkansas prison farm, within the confines of South African and Greek jails, are indications of continuing concern with this problem of violations of human rights.

In a recent document the ICJ has performed a valuable service by comparing the Standard Minimum Rules for the Treatment of Prisoners with the text of the Rules Relating to Non-Delinquent Detainees as drafted by the Medico-Legal Commission of Monaco at the request of the International Committee of the Red Cross. In this comparative study, the ICJ has argued against what has been called "the principle of lesser eligibility," arguing that non-delinquent detainees were entitled to more generous, not less, provisions for their care than was the case for the regular run of prisoners: "While the security of the State may be an important consideration for the State itself in regard to political grounds, it is hardly appropriate that the Medico-Legal Commission should deal with detention in the same *optique.*"[19]

The ICJ is composed of thirty national sections which cooperate with the Commission, and a secretariat which, since 1959, has been headquartered at Geneva where it is incorporated under the laws of Switzerland. It is dependent for its financial support on contributions and gifts from members, societies, individuals and foundations.

International Criminal Police Organization
(INTERPOL), Paris

The International Criminal Police Organization (INTERPOL) is the direct successor of the International Criminal Police Commission which was established in Vienna in 1923. The stated aim of the Commission at that time was "to ensure and to develop the greatest possible measure of mutual assistance between all criminal police authorities acting within the framework of the laws existing in the various countries, and to establish and develop all agencies which may effectively contribute to the repression of offences other than political or military offences."[20]

Prior to the Second World War, the Commission's activities were restricted largely to Europe. During the war the Commission ceased to function, but in 1946 it was revived, sparked by the initiative of M.F.E. Louwage, Inspector-General of the Belgian Police. It was then that its headquarters were transferred to Paris. The reconstituted Commission was to operate for ten years, first in nineteen countries and eventually in fifty-five, with a new five-member executive committee, and a constitution. In 1956 a second series of major changes gave the organization its present structure and name.

INTERPOL is composed of persons officially designated by their governments; each country usually sends two representatives. The new constitution in 1956 embodied essentially the same purpose as the original. In brief it states the purpose of INTERPOL as "to enable police forces in different countries to co-ordinate their work effectively in the double aim of law enforcement and crime prevention."

The operating structure of INTERPOL is composed of the General Secretariat in Paris linked to a network of National Central Bureaus located in nearly every country of the world, the major exceptions being the Soviet Union, the People's Republic of China, and most of the Eastern European countries. These National Central Bureaus, in turn, are linked to each other and to local police departments. The General Secretariat provides a clearinghouse for theoretical and technical information, but, more importantly, serves to direct the attack on international criminals through the "exchange of police information; identification of wanted persons and suspects; arrest of individuals for whom the courts have issued warrants and, usually, extradition requests."

This task is largely made possible through an international radio network set up by INTERPOL, with its central station in Paris. In 1966, stations in thirty-four countries were tied in to this network.

The INTERPOL General Assembly, the policy-making body, meets annually. It plans the general program of the organization, which is implemented by the administrative and technical staff of the General Secretariat under the supervision of a thirteen-member executive committee. To further the attainment of its primary goal—the apprehension of international criminals—the organization sponsors three regular publications: *International Criminal Police Review; Counterfeits and Forgeries Review*, and *International Crime Statistics*. The last is issued biennially. In addition, since 1959, INTERPOL-sponsored symposia, conferences and seminars have been conducted in many parts of the world for specialists on topics ranging from road traffic offences to the use of electronics in police work.

INTERPOL works closely with the United Nations, particularly in the field of narcotics. The organization was granted consultative status, category B, with the Economic and Social Council in 1949. A measure of the degree of success of this organization can be inferred from its rapid growth. In 1946, at the time of its reconstitution, INTERPOL counted 19 sovereign states as members. By February 1970 this number had increased to 105.

International Penal and Penitentiary Foundation (IPPF), Berne

The development, achievements and eventual decline after World War II, of the International Penal and Penitentiary Commission has been earlier described in this book. In 1950, pursuant to the agreement reached between the United Nations and the IPPC, the latter ceded its pre-eminent position in the field to the newly organized U.N. Section of Social Defence. But prior to the entrance into effect of this agreement, the IPPC was to convene its twelfth and final international congress at the Hague, 13-19 August, 1950.[21] Thereafter the organization would be known as the International Penal and Penitentiary Foundation (IPPF).

Less than 400 delegates representing 32 countries participated, a 60 percent drop from the attendance reported for their eleventh congress in

Berlin 1935. In addition to a United Nations observer, one other representative of an international organization was present. Duties of presiding officer were shared between the president of IPPC, Sanford Bates of the United States, and Judge Hooykaas, delegate of the host country. The sessions were held in the Ridderzaal, the hall where the Queen of Holland opens Parliament. The tradition of a four-part agenda for section meetings and discussions was here, for the last time, honored. Questions included the pre-sentence report; psychiatry and individualization in treatment; classification; open versus traditional institutions; prison labor; short-term imprisonment and alternatives to it; recent developments in institutions for juvenile offenders; the juvenile court; the habitual offender; and extension of the methods employed for treating young offenders to the treatment of adults.

This professional bill of fare differed little from that of its predecessor congresses. It would be both heartening and dramatic to be able to report that the 80-year-old commission went out in a final burst of glorious pronouncements, but such was not the case. Among several of the more moderately novel resolutions were those recommending the use of prediction tables, the establishment of psychiatric centers in prisons, the protection of minors against arbitrary infringement of their rights before tribunals for juveniles (presaging the *Gault* decision in the United States in 1967?), and the condemnation of the "all too frequent indiscriminate use of short-term imprisonment." Such measures as conditional sentences, probation, fines and judicial reprimand were suggested as alternatives.

Finally, discussion of the capability of young adults to respond "to the kind of training and conditions which in several countries are applied only to juveniles," led to the suggestion that such young adults should, while undergoing imprisonment, be given "opportunities of education, training and reform."

A round of receptions and dinners in two countries, Holland as well as in three cities in Belgium, was tendered the delegates as befitted the final IPPC congress. Its president was soon thereafter to report that "there seemed to be little or no resentment at the proposed move" of the IPPC's functions to the United Nations, and expressed his belief that this amalgamation "should mean a greater influence and scope for the work of the IPPC in future years. . . ."[2 2]

The United Nations, for its part, had agreed to convene every five years an international congress similar to those previously organized by the IPPC, and to assume financial responsibility for all such meetings when they were held at U.N. Headquarters in New York. It also assumed responsibility for the publication of an international review.

Provision was also made to transfer to the United Nations Library in Geneva the collection of books which had been the property of the IPPC, and to make the latter's archives part of the U.N. library, where they would be available to interested parties. Further, the U.N. offered the two professional officers of the IPPC appointments on the staff of its Section of Social Defence.

The United Nations diplomatically invited the IPPC to turn over its property and other residual assets which had grown considerably during the war years when expenses were light and contributions from certain member governments generous. Any such funds or proceeds from the sale of IPPC properties would become part of the general revenue of the United Nations, or if the IPPC preferred, might be added to the library endowment fund to make the U.N. Library "one of the most complete and up-to-date libraries in the world in the field of social defence."

But the IPPC declined the proffered honor, because of the limitations imposed by its statutes of organization, and instead chose to remain master of its assets. On July 6, 1951, less than one month after their joint meeting with the United Nations, which saw the venerable organization stripped of its basic functions, library and staff, the newly elected IPPC Executive Council met at their headquarters in Berne to reconstitute itself anew as the International Penal and Penitentiary Foundation.[23]

Its stated aim was now to promote studies in the field of prevention of crime and the treatment of offenders, especially by scientific research, publication and teaching to be financed by income from its remaining assets (which totalled at the time over 600,000 Swiss francs). It pledged itself further "to ensure so far as possible that its activities shall not overlap the work of [U.N.] groups of the Social Commission. . . ," and fixed the date of its official dissolution as 1 October, 1951.[24]

Since its formation, the IPPF has been instrumental in convening a series of meetings on significant topics, including the following:

1959 — The Strasbourg Seminar on Three Aspects of Penal Treatment;
1962 — International Colloquium on New Psychological Methods for the Treatment of Prisoners—Brussels;
1964 — First International Meeting of Heads of Penitentiary Administrations—Rome;
1967 — International Colloquium on New Methods of Restriction of Liberty in the Penitentiary System—Ulm;
— Second International Meeting of Heads of Penitentiary Administrations—Paris;
1969 — Third International Meeting of Heads of Penitentiary Administrations—Lisbon;

and has published significant studies, largely devoted to penal problems.

Immediately after its inception, the IPPF undertook an inquiry into modern methods of penal treatment in twenty-five countries. The results were published in 1955 in a report which emphasized two main points, including

> the adoption, among penal methods, of scientific examination processes for the observation of delinquents; and at the same time, the great movement to humanize the prison regime which, whenever it is possible without danger to the social order, tends to break down punitive regulations and unnecessary physical restraints. Thanks to this twofold development, the conditions of prison life are improving, and the door is open for the elaboration of more precise and more scientific methods of treating difficult cases. Our efforts must be directed to this end.[25]

Five years later the IPPF issued a second report on "Three Aspects of Penal Treatment." These two inquiries were preparatory to the first important meeting sponsored by the IPPF at Strasbourg in September of 1959, with the assistance of the Council of Europe at whose headquarters it met. The seminar dealt with three aspects of penal treatment: 1) penal observation; 2) penal treatment; and 3) readapting prisoners to normal life. A two-volume summary of the proceedings of this seminar was prepared by the Criminal Law Section of the Institute of Comparative Law of the University of Paris. Several paragraphs from the preface by Paul Cornil, IPPF president, are worthy of quotation here.

> The prison is still, and will be for an appreciable time to come, an essential element in the repression of crime. But it is obvious that this institution is radically changing before our very eyes and breaking out of its too rigid frame. The prison system is gradually taking its place as part of something far wider in scope. The prison, according to M. Dupréel, is becoming a link in the chain of social institutions. But it is being necessarily changed in the process: loss of liberty today is rarely absolute. The "open" prison is no longer an object of curiosity, but has become a commonplace among penal institutions. In Sweden, already 40% of those sentenced to imprisonment are sent to open prisons (Goransson). There is no reason why other countries should not follow this example, and it is by no means certain that this percentage is to be regarded as an absolute maximum.
>
> In several countries, notably in the United Kingdom, work in conditions of semi-liberty and the granting of home-leave are being extended. Thus, little by little, loss of liberty is assuming forms and methods of much greater variety. Instead of radical isolation from the outside world, imprisonment now involves, in certain cases at least,

only a partial and intermittent incarceration, which is less spectacular than detention in its traditional form, but appears infinitely richer in its educative possibilities. And whatever the ill-informed may think, it is probable that these forms of detention, though apparently less severe, are yet harder to endure, precisely because of the prisoner's more frequent contacts with the outside world.[26]

The object of the 1962 Brussels Colloquium was to examine methods of group counselling and group psychotherapy as applied to the treatment of prisoners. The United Nations and the Council of Europe collaborated in this project, which also had representation from the International Criminal Law Association, the International Society of Criminology, and the International Society of Social Defence.

In the published proceedings it is stated that "this Colloquium is linked both substantively and in the minds of the participants with the United Nations Seminar in 1951 on the medical, psychological and social examination of delinquents."[27] The IPPF wanted it known that it was supplementing, and not duplicating, the work of the U.N. in the field.

The Second International Colloquium of the IPPF held in Ulm in 1967 was concerned with new methods of restricted liberty in prisons and places of detention, specifically conditions of semi-liberty, limited detention, weekend arrest, work-release homes for probationers who are in difficulty, and compulsory attendance centers. Although the United Nations was not represented, participants included the Howard League for Penal Reform, the National Centre for Prevention of Crime and Defence of Society (Milan), the International Criminal Law Association, the International Society of Criminology, and the International Society of Social Defence. The Third Colloquium, at this writing, will take place in 1972.

The IPPF continues to maintain close ties with the last three in the above list, the so-called "sister" associations. This relationship has been regularized through inter-associational colloquia which are held at five-year intervals in Bellagio, Italy. The third such meeting is scheduled for April 1973.

The Council of the IPPF held its regular quinquennial meeting in Kyoto during the Fourth United Nations Congress in August of 1970. A slate of officers was elected, and the work of the IPPF for the next five years agreed upon. The representative from Finland, more in hope than in expectation, introduced again the age-old search-question: that an inquiry be undertaken to determine the size, structure, and length of sentences being served by the prison populations of various countries. Nothing came of it.

In all, twenty-one countries, including forty-one representatives, constitute the present membership and the national correspondents of the IPPF, whose treasury appears to have increased by almost one-fourth since 1951.

Ten years after the reorganization of the IPPF, its outgoing president had this to say about its role in the international field in which it had for so many years predominated:

> The Foundation took the view that the decision of the United Nations to assume the leadership of international activities in the field of social defence obliged it to maintain a certain reserve and to limit itself to playing this modest complementary part. Nevertheless, it was implicitly agreed, in 1951, that if the United Nations—modifying the attitude adopted in 1950, which led to the disappearance of the International Penal and Penitentiary Commission—decided to cease or even to reduce their activity in this field, the Foundation should immediately declare its willingness, if it were provided with the necessary means, to take over the work given up by the United Nations.[28]

Certainly the field is challenging—and large—enough to accommodate the concern and the contributions of all persons and organized bodies which are interested in helping to advance the "art." While deprived in some measure of the unique stature of its predecessor organization, the pioneering IPPC, the IPPF seems to have carved out for itself a number of distinctive areas in which to continue to make its membership—and their efforts—productive.

International Prisoners Aid Association (IPAA), Milwaukee

Concern for the discharged prisoner has long been expressed by voluntary prisoner-aid societies, whose origins go back almost two hundred years, further perhaps than those of any other existing related agency. It was not until 1950, however, that this concern became the object of a world-wide association. The International Prisoners Aid Association (IPAA) is a federation of independent, voluntary organizations devoted to the rehabilitation of offenders, the after-care of prisoners and the prevention of crime. Its initial impetus derived from a regional North American organization which modestly began in 1950 with the issuing of a newsletter, thereafter distributing a directory of prisoners-aid agencies, and serving as a center of documentation and information.[29]

Its president and executive director participated in the first United Nations crime congress in London in 1960, and the IPAA has played an active role in all subsequent congresses through 1970. Its sessions precede the opening of the major United Nations affair, thus allowing its members to transact their own business before joining the subsequent deliberations of the crime congress itself. Its first such "world-wide membership meeting convened in Stockholm in August 1965 with representation from 24 national federations and individual societies."[30]

IPAA published an excellent and authoritative survey of the implementation of Standard Minimum Rules for the Treatment of Prisoners, which it distributed at the second session of the United Nations Consultative Group in Geneva in August 1968.[31] It has also issued reports on the use of volunteers in prisoner after-care, probation and parole, and a study of the loss and restoration of civil rights by convicted public offenders. The Association has compiled and distributed the most comprehensive worldwide directory of voluntary agencies specializing in services to ex-offenders, first published in 1951 and thereafter in revised form in 1962, 1968 and 1970.[32]

Also during 1968, as part of its contribution to the International Year for Human Rights, IPAA sponsored a comparative study by Dr. Mirjan Damaska, professor of law at Zagreb, titled "The Adverse Legal Consequences of Conviction and Their Removal."[33] The IPAA has taken an active role in encouraging the employment of volunteers in penal and aftercare programs, and has led the way in advocating the services of ex-offenders in the correctional process at all levels. Recently it has had referred to it the question of payment for prison labor at rates prevailing outside the prison.

Present objectives and programs include: to exchange information with interested organizations; to conduct seminars, institutes and conferences for the benefit of voluntary organizations for aid to offenders; to initiate and support research on related problems; to assist in the training and recruiting of personnel for after-care organizations; and to propagandize in behalf of enlightened public attitudes towards ex-offenders. Some of its affiliate organizations are local societies, others are regional and a few are national in scope and influence.

International Society of Criminology, Paris

International concern in the field of crime during the last decades of the 19th century and the first decades of the 20th century tended to center largely on the philosophical, legal and administrative aspects of the problem. Time and again such phrases as "too little is known about" and "more research is needed with regard to" are to be found in conference papers, committee reports and congress resolutions during those years.

Despite the early and continuing stress on the inadequacy or absence of international criminal statistics and other basic comparative data, as of the measures to remedy the situation, little was being done apart from the efforts of the Positivist School to develop the comparative study of criminology on a scientific basis. Theoretical perspectives continued to be more closely tied to philosophical considerations than to facts systematically collected and analyzed.

Against this background, the founding of the International Society of Criminology appeared particularly significant.[34] In 1934 its initiating sponsors decided upon the principles for the establishment of the Society, but it was not officially formed until its first international congress held in October 1938 in Rome. Over 1,000 persons from 46 countries participated in the proceedings.

Its statutes were approved more than a decade later, at an international meeting convened at Paris in 1949. The stated purpose of the Society was "to cooperate with existing specialized organizations with a view to the advancement of the application of the scientific method to criminal phenomena."[35] Both individuals and organizations were invited to join as members.

The Society seeks to establish scientific contacts among its members through the medium of congresses, conferences and publications, exchange of students and teachers of criminology, and the awarding of prizes and scholarships. In addition to holding quinquennial congresses, it has established the International Institute of Criminology as a center for study, research and documentation. It has served the United Nations Economic and Social Council and UNESCO in a consultative capacity since July 1949. It is also represented on the permanent committee of specialized agencies and international organizations concerned with the prevention of crime and treatment of offenders which was set up in 1949 by the United Nations. Its publications include original studies in addition to the proceedings of the congresses. Understandably, the Society draws heavily from the university community for leadership and participation, as well as from the fields of psychiatry and law. Its board of directors is elected by individual members meeting in general assembly. This board in turn elects their executive committee which is responsible for the affairs of the Society.

Ties with the United Nations are emphasized by the presence at each Society congress of an official representative from the United Nations, who usually addresses the opening session. Congress agendas are characterized by a concern with scientific method, the etiology of criminal behavior, the systematic evaluation of correctional programs, current research in the field, and contributions to the general body of theory relating to criminal behavior. Each congress is organized around a specific theme. At Paris the agenda of the second congress considered: 1) the role of the empirical sciences in the identification of the etiological factors in crime; 2) synthesis of the causes of crime in individual cases; and 3) methodology, and the future of criminological research.

In 1955 in London the third congress had as its theme "Recidivism." The fourth congress at The Hague in 1960 focused on mental abnormality and the psycho-pathological aspects of criminal behavior. Sexual offences and epilepsy as a factor in criminality were also discussed. The Montreal Congress, five years later, dealt with the treatment of adult and juvenile offenders, under the headings of prophylaxis and treatment, methods of treatment, and scientific research. The most recent congress in Madrid in September 1970 took as its theme "Scientific Research in Criminology— The Link Between Theory and Practice." Participants had before them several major reports, which were taken up in respective section meetings. These included general problems concerning scientific research in criminology; research in the area of probation, as well as of pre-trial detention and bail, and supervised liberty; and problems of methodology in criminological research. In addition to hearing reports on research in progress by invited participants, the Madrid Congress listened to lectures and engaged in round-table discussions.

At the conclusion of the congress it was voted to change the schedule of meetings from a five- to a three-year cycle, and Moscow was voted as the site for the gathering of the seventh congress of the Society to be convened in 1973.

International Society of Social Defence, Paris

The first international congress of Social Defence was organized by the International Institute for the Study of Social Defence in San Remo in 1947, where its theme was a critical examination of prevailing concepts of punishment and responsibility.[36] The second congress, called by the Institute two years later in Liége, discussed the individuality of the offender and of his rights. The International Society of Social Defence was officially established after the conclusion of this congress. Its president, the distinguished French jurist Marc Ancel, describes its *raison d'être* and its distinctive approach to problems of crime as one designed "to bring together all those who, in this difficult period of transition, would promote a policy . . . for the prevention of crime and the re-socialization of the offender which, in effect, serves in a manner rational and scientific—to assure both the protection of the individual and the community, and help to bring about a new, humanistic penology."[37]

The headquarters of the Society are in Paris; the Secretary-General is located in Rome. It is not by accident, but rather by the historical development of its distinctively Continental concept, that France and Italy presently give the Society a large part of its leadership—as they did its predecessor body—the International Society of Criminal Anthropology, whose last meeting, it may be recalled, took place in 1911. Thus the Society may be seen as the ideological descendant from, and the bearer of, a penal philosophy which derives directly from the Positivist School.

The Society's board of directors, a governing body of twenty-seven members, are drawn from sixteen countries, all but five of which are European, and are elected in a general assembly of the membership. The board of directors, in turn, elects an executive committee to carry on the work of the Society.

This is done largely through regional groups, by means of cooperation and collaboration with other associations, both national and international, by its publications, and through international conferences of social defense. Of these, there have been seven since 1947. A summary of the theme for each of the congresses may provide an overview of the areas of the Society's concern and action:

1. The transformation of existing penal and penitentiary systems into systems of education and treatment in accord with the personality of the individual delinquent. (San Remo, 1947.)
2. The human personality from the point of view of the rights of society and in accordance with the rights of man. (Liége and Spa, 1949.)
3. Individualization of sentences and of their execution (observation and re-socialization). (Antwerp, 1954.)
4. Prevention of measures against human life and physical inviolability. (Milan, 1956.)
5. Administrative and judicial intervention in regard to socially maladjusted children and youth. (Stockholm, 1958.)
6. How can the differences, in statutes and in treatment—as between offenders who are minors, young adults or adults—be justified? (Belgrade-Opatija, 1961.)
7. Professional interdictions and the interdiction to exercise certain activities. (Lecca, 1966.)[38]

In addition to its regularly organized meetings and conferences on various aspects of social defence, the Society of Social Defence annually awards prizes for outstanding original contributions on such subjects as philosophy, law and medicine in relation to the main thrust of the Society's interests. The first issue of its *Rivista di Difesa Sociale* appeared in 1947, and three years later was expanded to accommodate the *Bulletin de la Societé Internationale de Défense Sociale.*

The fifth congress of the Society held in 1958 at Stockholm paid tribute to the tenth anniversary of the adoption of the Universal Declaration on the Rights of Man, and to the memory of Margery Fry who had died in the preceding year. Among the more novel of the resolutions brought up for consideration by participants was one which specified that a special system should be created for young adults aged 18 to 25, a system distinct from that applied to younger persons as well as to adults. The discussions are evocative of those heated debates which accompanied the introduction of the reformatory idea 100 years before, when the age group 18 to 30 was singled out for special corrective treatment, for reasons of both its vulnerability to criminality and its potential for such less punitive approaches.

There was a time, not long before 1958, when hope was high in some quarters that findings of the child guidance movement and the special non-criminal procedures of the juvenile court would result in a socializing influence that one day might modify the adversary process, especially in judicial systems which derive from the Anglo-Saxon common law, as well as the rigors of the process as practiced in the adult criminal courts.[39] With this as historic (some might say, nostalgic) background, the resulting concensus on the part of the delegates is worthy of full quotation:

> The Congress, *considering that* the regime for minors indicates the future orientation of a modern system of criminal law based on the contributions of criminology and the doctrines of the new social defence,
>
> *expresses the belief* that the extension to adults of the principles of the regime for minors should be progressively studied with all the necessary adaptations.[40]

The conclusion is inescapable that some ideas never die.

Most of those in the leadership of the Society of Social Defence are judges, professors of law or criminology—or officers in their national ministries of justice. Given these professional backgrounds and affiliations, the academic and theoretical inclination of the Society's work may be readily comprehended. This is not to minimize in any way the contribution they have made over the past quarter century in carrying on, and extending, the traditional European concept of social defence, which regards concern for the individual offender and his scientific and humane treatment as the surest preventive of crime and recidivism, and at the same time the most effective protection of society.

The eighth conference of the Society was convened in Paris in November 1971, with the title, "The Technique of Individualizing the Judicial Process." This is a followup of the discussion on a related topic at the Antwerp Conference of 1954. The conference was divided along traditional lines into four sections: Juridical, Criminological, Penal and Biological-Medical.

International Union for Child Welfare, Geneva

The past 50 years of activity by the International Union for Child Welfare have been devoted chiefly in behalf of health, nutrition, and maternal and child welfare.[41] Nevertheless, this nongovernmental world-wide agency, the result of a merger in 1946 of the Save The Children International Union (created in Geneva in 1920) and the International Association for the Promotion of Child Welfare (founded in Brussels in 1921), has also made distinctive and valuable contributions to the understanding and treatment of delinquency among minors.

A major purpose of the Union is to make known to the world the principles of the "Declaration of the Rights of the Child," endorsed by the Assembly of the League of Nations on 26 September 1924. The United Nations General Assembly adopted the declaration in somewhat expanded and slightly revised form on 20 November 1959. Pertinent provisions of this declaration are Principle Number 5, which specifies special treatment, education and care required by the child with physical, mental or social handicaps; and Number 9, which specifies the protection of the child "against all forms of neglect, cruelty, and exploitation."

The Union, today an international federation of 111 member agencies in more than 50 countries, promotes, *inter alia*, child care, guardianship and placement services for minors, and special institutions for children committed by the courts by reason of delinquency, neglect and dependency. The federation has been closely associated with the work of the International Association of Youth Magistrates since its inception in 1928, and the Union's *Bulletin* served for many years thereafter to carry the reports of the Youth Magistrates congresses and other pertinent events.

The Union has published its *International Child Welfare Review* since 1947. The second issue, published that year, is devoted to the topic "The War and Juvenile Delinquency," a report on a conference convened in the spring of 1947 at its headquarters in Geneva. This appraisal of the effects of war on social maladjustment of children, including statistics on delinquency from eleven countries, represents one of the first attempts at such an appraisal to be made after the end of World War II.

For its part, the Union has held fourteen sessions of *Expert Groups for Delinquent and Socially Malajusted Children*—the 13th at Edinburgh in the summer of 1968 and the last at Rome in May 1970. At this time it prepared for submission to the United Nations Crime Congress at Kyoto a report, "Participation of the Public in the Prevention of Crime and the Fight Against Delinquency," which was the second item on the Kyoto Congress agenda.

This report by the Union was mainly directed toward treatment centers for delinquent children in the community, of both a residential and nonresidential nature. In this respect the thrust of its recommendations was in line with the current trend to locate treatment centers in the areas from which such children come, and to which they are destined ultimately to return. This development was endorsed by the Union's report, which stressed at the same time the need to integrate such centers with the community in order for them to be successful. In this process, it is imperative that the community be informed of plans to establish a center in its midst and thereafter to continue to draw the community into the program and the lives of the children served by such a neighborhood facility. While the report was mainly concerned with children who were socially disadvantaged by reason of court commitment, it had unmistakable implications for persons with other problems—the mentally disturbed, the alcoholic, and the narcotic addict, adult as well as juvenile.

Notes

1. A summary of the League's activities and accomplishments is available on request from its London office: "The Howard League for Penal Reform,"September 1967.

2. See Hugh J. Klare, ed., *Changing Concepts of Crime and its Treatment.*

3. See *Pena de Morte, Colóquio Internacional Comerativo do Centnário da Abolição da Pena de Morte em Portugal,* 2 vols. (Coimbra: Faculdade de Direito da Universidade de Coimbra, 1968).

4. "Liste des Participants," in ibid., 1:18.

5. Summaries of the *Proceedings* of each of the eight congresses are available on request from the Brussels office of the general secretary of the Association.

6. International Center for Criminology, *Prospectus* (Rome, July 1970).

7. Ibid.

8. Denis Szabo, exec. dir., *International Center for Comparative Criminology* (Montreal: the Center, n.d.—pamphlet).

9. Ibid.

10. *IJC Review*, published quarterly since March 1969; it combines the two publications it replaces: *Bulletin* and *Journal*.

11. See International Commission of Jurists, "Memorandum submitted by the International Commission of Jurists to the United Nations' Section of Social Defence," n.d. Available on request from IJC.

12. Ibid.

13. Ibid.

14. Ibid.

15. Taken from a mimeographed copy of the Teheran Resolution; available on request from the IJC.

16. International Commission of Jurists, "Memorandum to U.N."

17. Ibid.

18. Ibid.

19. "Comparison of the Standard Minimum Rules for the Treatment of Prisoners with the Text of the Rules Relating to Non-delinquent Detainees," report drafted by the Medico-Legal Commission of Monaco at the request of the International Red Cross. Annotated comparison prepared by the IJC, December 1969 (mimeographed). See also Exhibit 7.

20. *International Review of Criminal Policy*, no. 1 (January 1952), p. 32. This first issue contains basic information on a number of international organizations active in the field of crime prevention and the treatment of offenders at the time of the transfer of functions from the IPPC to the U.N. Information on the activities, accomplishments and organizational development of INTERPOL is available in pamphlet form from their Paris headquarters.

21. See Sanford Bates, "Report of the American Delegate to the Twelfth International Congress of the International Penal and Penitentiary Commission," pp. 41-51. For a list of the questions considered, see Negley K. Teeters, *Deliberations of the International Penal and Penitentiary Commission*, pp. 191-92. See the Bibliography for a list of *Proceedings*.

22. Bates, "Report of American Delegate," pp. 50-51.

23. For an account of this period, see Thorsten Sellin, "Lionel Fox and the International Penal and Penitentiary Commission."

24. From *Statutes of the International Penal and Penitentiary Foundation*, 1965 edition. Available from the Foundation on request.

25. International Penal and Penitentiary Foundation, *Modern Methods of Penal Treatment*, from the Preface by Paul Cornil, then president of IPPF.

26. Ibid., *Three Aspects of Penal Treatment*, 1:78.

27. Ibid., *New Psychological Methods for the Treatment of Prisoners*.

28. Ibid., *Three Aspects of Treatment*, 1:iii.

29. International Prisoners Aid Society, "IPAA: Past, Present and Future," pamphlet available from IPAA on request.

30. Ibid.

31. Badr-El-Din Ali, *International Survey on Standard Minimum Rules*.

32. IPAA, "IPAA: Past, Present and Future," p. 4.

33. Ibid., p. 5.

34. For basic information on this organization, see the booklet published in both French and English, *International Society of Criminology* (Paris: ISC, 1962).

35. *International Review of Criminology*, no. 1 (January 1952), p. 34.

36. See ibid., p. 35, for background information on the Society.

37. Freely translated from the introductory remarks of Professor Marc Ancel, President de Chambre à la Cour de Cassation, Paris, and President of the International Society for Social Defence, at a meeting of the Society and its Japanese affiliate, held during the course of the Fourth United Nations Crime Congress, Kyoto, August 1970.

38. From a leaflet printed by the Society, for the Eighth International Congress on Social Defence, Paris, 18-22 November 1971.

39. See Jeanette G. Brill and E. George Payne, *The Adolescent Court and Crime Prevention*; Benedict S. Alper, "Young People in the Courts of New York State," New York State Document 55 (1942); and Benedict S. Alper, "Youth Courts: Existing and Proposed," *Law and Contemporary Problems* (Autumn 1942), pp. 732-7.

40. International Society for Social Defence, *Actes du Cinquième Congrès, Stockholm, 1958*, p. 50.

41. See *International Review of Criminal Policy*, no. 1 (January 1952), pp. 38-39; and a special edition of *International Child Welfare Review*, no. 7 (June 1970), commemorating the 50th anniversary of the Union.

9 Regional Organizations

Benelux Penitentiary Commission

The Benelux Penitentiary Commission came into existence after World War II as one aspect of the larger aim of the governments of Belgium, the Netherlands and the Grand Duchy of Luxembourg. They wished to establish a union which would represent the common economic, cultural and social welfare interests of these three neighboring countries which had suffered and fought side-by-side during World War II.[1]

After preliminary discussions between representatives of the ministries of justice of each of the three countries, a convention among them was accepted and signed in November of 1950, forming the Benelux Penitentiary Commission. The purpose of the Commission was to contribute to the development of the penal system of the three member countries, and to facilitate the creation of new programs in the area of social defence.

This was to be accomplished by the formation of a professional association of prison personnel, the provision for exchange and visits between them, and the holding of training courses; and the establishment of a documentation and statistical center, with the interchange of information about programs and rules governing the penal stations in each of the member countries.

In the past twenty years the Benelux Penitentiary Commission has held forty meetings, in the course of which it has examined a great diversity of topics and suggestions introduced by the delegates, all of them officials of their respective ministries of justice. These have ranged from studies of causation of delinquency to the role of the open institution in a penitentiary system. In order of frequency of their occurrence on the agenda of the

Commission's meetings, the following items appear to have received the largest share of attention: 1) questions relating to young persons: age limits, preventive detention of juveniles, visits of children to their parents in confinement; 2) matters relating to prison personnel: training, exchange of personnel between the staffs of the member countries, the formation of a regional professional association.

Questions relating to institutional administration of prisons have covered such topics as: detention of persons awaiting trial; wages and conditions of labor of detainees; short-term and weekend detention; group counselling; correspondence courses; mail censorship; medico-psychological examination of delinquents; the special needs of the female offender; treatment of recidivists and conditional release.

Architectural designs and plans are exchanged among the administrators of the three penal systems, as well as documentation and statistics as to trends in prison populations. Vagabondism, for example, occupied the attention of the delegates at their 34th and 35th sessions.

Most recently, members of the Benelux Penitentiary Commission have turned their attention to the question of conjugal visits to prisoners, examining it from two opposing points of view, described by the Commission as the Swedish and the Italian, respectively—the permissive and the prohibitive. While the Commission, after examining the arguments for and against conjugal visits in prison, agreed that sexual privation was both a consequence of the penal sanction as well as a part of that sanction, they could not foresee any change in the ban on conjugal visits which presently prevails in the prisons of all three member countries.

The final item entered on the agenda for discussion at the last meeting of the Commission was the problem of drugs. The Commission agreed to consider at its next meeting the report of a Dutch psychiatrist specialized in narcotics, the relationship between narcotics and crime, and measures for treating drug-users in penal institutions.

The Commission has cooperated with the Council of Europe on the several conventions which that body has negotiated among its member states, as well as with the United Nations in its congresses, meetings of experts, and with the Section of Social Defence. In 1967 one of the most interesting results of this collaboration among penal experts in the three Benelux countries took place. This was the creation, in Zeeland, the Netherlands, of a special camp for young offenders called "The Corridor" (Passage). Here an intensive program has been introduced in which work, sports and socio-cultural training play equal parts. The camp is characterized by an intensity in its programming for the small groups—ten members each, into which the population is divided. Work is mostly in the nearby forests.[2] In the description of this experimental institution, its director ascribes its initial impetus to the ideas put forward by delegates to the Benelux Penitentiary Commission's meetings as presented in two of its publications. Credit is also given to Highfields (New Jersey) for the guided group interaction approach which has been introduced into "The Corridor's" treatment program.[3]

To honor its twenty years of work, the Benelux Penitentiary Commission issued, in November 1970, a retrospective commemorative booklet.[4] Three of the original commissioners, who formed one-half of the originating body, are among the eight members who presently constitute the Commission. This continuity of dedicated professional administrative service accounts in large measure for the excellent results obtained by the collaborative efforts of the Benelux countries in the area of penal reform and innovation.

The Council of Europe, Strasbourg

The years following World War II saw a remarkable increase in the formation and growth of international organizations. One of the most important of these, though interim, was the International Committee of Movements for European Unity. This group convened the "Congress of Europe" at The Hague in May 1948 with 713 delegates in attendance from 16 countries and observers from 10 others. "The purposes of the Congress were to demonstrate the wide support for the cause of European unity, to provide fresh impetus to the movement and to make practical recommendations for its accomplishment."[5]

On 5 May 1949 representatives of the governments of Belgium, Denmark, France, Ireland, Italy, Luxembourg, the Netherlands, Norway, Sweden and the United Kingdom signed the statute creating the Council of Europe, which entered into force on 3 August of that year. Its stated purpose was to reassert the "pursuit of peace [as] vital for the preservation of human society and civilization, . . . [to] reaffirm their devotion to spiritual and moral values . . . [to bring] closer unity between all like-minded countries of Europe . . . in the interests of economic and social progress," by the creation of an organization which would "bring European States into close association."[6] The statute makes it very clear that matters relating to national defense do not fall within the Council's competence.

Briefly, the structure of the Council of Europe consists of the Committee of Ministers—its executive body composed of the foreign ministers of each member state, which is assisted in its work by a deliberative body, the Consultative Assembly. This body, 135 in number, consists of representatives drawn from the parliaments of the 17 member states, the various political parties being proportionately represented. The Consultative Assembly deliberates on matters of greatest common concern and makes its recommendations to the Committee of Ministers. The Council is served by a secretariat, its administrative arm, in much the same way as the United Nations is served by its secretariat.

The Consultative Assembly is a political and not an intergovernmental body. "In the Council of Europe was realized for the first time the creation of an international parliamentary assembly, independent of governments, whose members have a mandate that is not national but European."[7]

For the first ten years after its inception in 1949, the Council of Europe does not appear to have much concerned itself with problems of crime and delinquency. However, as early as 1953 a member of the Council's Committee of Experts, charged with preparation of a European convention on extradition, had recommended to the Committee of Ministers the establishment of a committee to prepare a convention on mutual assistance in criminal matters. The committee was chosen by September 1956.

This new committee met twice in 1957 and once in 1958, concluded the convention and opened it for signature in April of the following year. It entered into force in June, 1962: "The Convention . . . deals with such matters as letters rogatory for the examination of witnesses or experts, service of official documents and judicial verdicts, summoning of witnesses, experts, or persons in custody and transmission of information from judicial records."[8]

It is interesting to record that the European Committee on Crime Problems (ECCP) grew out of discussions held from 1956 to 1958 between the Council of Europe and those United Nations bodies which were concerned with the prevention of crime and treatment of offenders:

> The United Nations was at the time trying to decentralise its work, and cut down its expenditure, on social defence; concurrently, the legal programme of the Council of Europe was expanding. The Ministers' resolution of June 1956 therefore instructed the Secretary-General to bring to the notice of Member Governments the conclusions and recommendations of the European Consultative Group of the United Nations, to request their comments thereon and then draw up for submission to the Committee of Ministers proposals for action which the Council of Europe might usefully take—without overlapping with the United Nations—relating to the prevention of crime and the treatment of offenders.[9]

The emerging Committee of Experts held its first meeting in mid-1958, adopted a program of six questions and appointed subcommittees to study them: 1) the problem of the death penalty in European countries;

2) civil and political rights of prisoners and discharged prisoners; 3) mutual assistance in after-care or post-penitentiary treatment; 4) cooperation between European states with regard to road traffic offences; 5) certain aspects of the question of juvenile delinquency; and 6) prisoners' wages and related questions.

An additional committee was appointed to draft the text of a European convention on the international validity of criminal judgements, which was to cover such matters as the conditions under which a state may request enforcement by another; when such an obligation may be accepted or refused; judgements *in absentia*; and measures of provisional detention. The Committee of Ministers approved the draft text in January 1970, and the convention itself was opened for signature by Council of Europe member states four months later.

These efforts of the ECCP stimulated their Sub-Committee of Penal Reform to propose in 1959 "that the Committee of Ministers should organize a system of interchange of prison staff (for example, deputy governors) between Member countries for [a] period of study of methods of prison administration."[10] In addition, the following far-reaching principles, enunciated by the Sub-Committee, were referred to the ECCP for further consideration, and provided:

(a)　that a first offender who has committed an offence punishable by imprisonment shall, unless a serious crime is involved, receive a suspended sentence or be placed on probation or accorded some similar treatment;

(b)　that no person shall be provisionally detained in prison without an order of a Court, and such provisional detention shall not be continued unless the Court shall certify that detention is strictly necessary and give its reason therefore;

(c)　that no person shall be imprisoned for inability to fulfill a contractual obligation;

(d)　that every prisoner suffering from a mental or physical ailment shall be given appropriate psychiatric or medical treatment.[11]

The ECCP has carried out and published an impressive number of excellent studies. These consist largely of descriptive reports on some aspect of crime or its treatment in member countries, based usually on replies received to questionnaires. The ECCP has served as a clearinghouse for ideas and programs throughout Europe and is now seeking to initiate programs and promote specific coordinated research.

Its publications are of various types: study and topical reports by consultants to provide information for committee members on the critical issues in a specific area (totalling 19 in 1970); research bulletins (8); conventions (6); resolutions (12) and conference reports (8).

The ECCP called the first European conference of directors of criminological institutes in 1963, which has since become an annual affair. It has also issued bulletins on current research ("International Exchange of Information on Current Criminological Research Projects in Member Countries") twice yearly since 1963. Addresses delivered at these sessions are available in a series of volumes entitled *Collected Studies in Criminological Research*. Recently a fellowship program was begun, with the aim to permit researchers to study methods and findings in other member states.

The Council of Europe has formal agreements of cooperation with the United Nations, The Hague Conference on Private International Law, and the International Institute for the Unification of Private Law, and makes regular reports to the Consultative Assembly on its activities:

> A formal agreement was concluded between the Council and the Rome Institute on January 12, 1954. This provides for the exchange of information on subjects of common interest and the exchange of observers at meetings at which such subjects will be discussed. It furnishes provisions that the Institute will assist the Council, at the latter's request, in the study of questions of comparative law or the unification of private law, by preparation of technical studies and preliminary draft conventions. In addition, the Institute is given the right to propose items for inclusion on the Agenda of the Committee of Ministers or the Consultative Assembly.[1][2]

The *Council of Europe Treaty Series* contains European conventions related to crime and treatment of offenders: 1) on extradition (1957); 2) on mutual assistance in criminal matters—opened for signature in 1959 and entered into force in 1962; 3) on supervision of conditionally released offenders—opened for signature 30 November 1964; 4) on punishment of road traffic offenses—opened for signature on 30 November 1964; 5) on the repatriation of minors; and 6) on the international validity of criminal judgements.

The chief of the division of crime problems within the directorate of legal affairs which serves the European Committee on Crime Problems is in attendance at international gatherings where questions of crime and delinquency are discussed. He consistently plays an active role, through his intervention in the debates, and by his personal influence on his fellow delegates and colleagues, who are not limited to representatives of the member states of the Council of Europe.

Through its European Committee on Crime Problems and the work of its secretariat in Strasbourg, the Council of Europe is the largest, as it is perhaps the most productive, of all the regional bodies concerned with problems of crime prevention and treatment. It nevertheless shares, with other regional bodies which have parallel involvement, a sense of urgency and of immediate applicability of its recommendations which may seem all too often to be lacking in the actions of the larger international bodies in the field. The extensive literature published by them conveys an impression, as well, of greater practicability, of less lofty aims, and an absence of the quality of "lowest-common-denominator" levels of penal practice which abounds in so many of the utterances of the global organizations. A proliferation of these positive regional accomplishments, for this among other reasons, may well be seen in the years which lie ahead.

Latin America

A recent United Nations survey states: "In Latin America, there exist very few national and no international criminological research institutes. The absence of any international facility impedes the incorporation of available data into the mainstream of world-wide research. When the Latin American investigator does expand his work beyond his national setting, he directs his attention, not towards another Latin American country but towards Europe or the United States of America. In Latin America libraries, with few exceptions, European and North American works predominate."[13]

It has been noted earlier that one of the first examples of international interchange, almost fifty years before the first international conference on crime was convened, was the forwarding from London to Buenos Aires of a tract which set out the precepts of penitentiary management current in Great Britain at that time. While representatives from some Latin American countries have been in attendance at most of the subsequent international gatherings, the region as a whole has not yet experienced the same degree of interchange which is characteristic of other geographical areas of the world, notably Europe.

Despite the gravity of the problem of crime, little organized effort has been expended in the area of criminological research in Central and South America, except between the years 1899 and 1912 under the leadership of an extraordinary man, José Ingenieros. In June of 1907, authorized by a decree of the Argentine government, Ingenieros established the Institute of Criminology in the National Penitentiary of Buenos Aires, the first clinic of its kind in the world. Studies conducted by the Institute covered three areas: criminal etiology, clinical criminology and criminal therapeutics. Ingenieros was a prolific contributor to the fields of psychiatry, psychology and criminology, with some 500 articles and monographs in leading reviews and journals. A professed socialist, he was profoundly influenced by Lombroso, Ferrero and Ferri, leaders of the Italian Positivist School.[14] Today there exist in seven Latin American countries—Argentina, Brazil, Chile, Columbia, Ecuador, Mexico and Venezuela—research institutes which are engaged in the study of crime in its various manifestations, and which publish professional journals.

Buenos Aires was the site of the first of three subsequent and significant regional crime congresses which had repercussions throughout Latin America. This congress was convened in 1938, shortly before the meetings of the First International Congress of Criminology in Rome that same year, likewise Positivist in outlook. Three years later the second Latin American Congress of Criminology was convened in Santiago de Chile. Interest engendered by these two assemblies was renewed by the First Pan-American Congress at Rio de Janeiro in 1947, the last meeting of consequence to be held in South America for some years to come.[15]

In addition, mention should be made of the groups of Latin American professionals which have come together on at least four occasions since the United Nations took leadership in this field. The first of these, organized by the United Nations, was the Latin American Seminar on Prevention of Crime and Treatment of Offenders, which met in Rio de Janeiro in April 1953. Ten years later, in La Guaira, Venezuela, the United Nations convened a Latin American Working Group of Experts on the same topic. Representatives of Argentina, Brazil and Chile also participated in the interregional seminar on Research in Criminology on the eve of the Stockholm Crime Congress of 1965. This seminar, meeting in Copenhagen had the collaboration of the governments of Denmark, Norway and Sweden. The record shows an International Seminar on Criminology in June 1969, organized by the Center for Criminological Studies of Mendoza, Argentina. At this time there was a proposal for the creation of a Latin-American Association for Criminological Research, which was accepted by the participants.

There have been additional interregional congresses on crime which were attended by Latin American criminologists and penologists. The first, under Catholic auspices, was established following the first Latin American Congress of Penitentiary Research and Action, held in Santiago de Chile in October 1958.[16] Basing itself on the words of Pope Pius XII that "Punishment has been created, in effect, not to deprive but to redeem," the Latin-American Penitentiary Movement has held a total of five international congresses up to 1970.[17] The theme of each of these serves to illustrate the areas of the organization's interest. The first was entitled, "Basis for a Christian Penology in Latin America," which carried forward into the second meeting at Bogotá under the title "The Christian Concept of Punishment." The third, fourth and fifth, held respectively in Lima, Buenos Aires and Caracas, have been more secular in their approach to such problems as juvenile delinquency, reintegration of the prisoner into society, considerations of post-commitment, and release. The *Movimiento Penitenciario Latino Americano*, as it calls itself, is represented at international crime gatherings by its executive secretary, based in Chile, who is also responsible for publishing occasional papers, under the title "Colección Pastoral Penitenciaria."[18]

The close relationship felt by Latin American nations for others which share a common cultural heritage, makes understandable their coming together under the auspices of an Ibero-American and Philippine Penal and Penitentiary Congress. Since the inception of the organization, five of these congresses have met: the first in Madrid-Salamanca in July 1952, the second in São Paulo in 1955, the third in Lisbon in 1960 and the fifth in La Coruña, Spain. This last had as its purpose consideration of the four main topics of the United Nations Crime Congress which was to take place the next month in Japan.[19]

After discussion of these items, and as its final act in plenary session, the La Coruña Congress unanimously adopted a resolution which took note of the increasing frequency of skyjacking. The resolution called on all states to acknowledge such acts as "common, non-political, international crimes," which should be dealt with on an international level, by courts having jurisdiction over such acts, and "determining the applicable penalties." Pending arrival at such an international agreement, the resolution acknowledged that any state where such aircraft might land should consider itself authorized to deal with "the crime of aircraft seizure" under its own law. Any state which gave protection or immunity to persons who unlawfully seized an aircraft was to run the risk of having the United Nations take "whatever measures it deemed appropriate, such as severance of diplomatic or economic relations, boycotting its shipping and airlines, etc."[20]

Discussion on the same topic, which later took place in August at the Fourth United Nations Crime Congress, led to no such drastic—or clearly articulated—response.

It is interesting at this point to take note that Argentina and Chile, the southernmost of South American countries, have taken the leadership in Latin America in promulgating the Standard Minimum Rules for the Treatment of Prisoners. The Argentine, particularly, has undertaken to distribute the Minimum Rules through the medium of the *Revista Penal y Penitenciaria* published by their National Prison Service, as well as to students in courses in its correctional training school. A year after the Fourth United Nations Crime Congress in Japan, an extensive article in the *Revista* appeared which discussed in detail the application of the Standard Minimum Rules to prisoners in Latin America, pointing out especially the difficulties in regard to prison labor, as well as the financial implications attendant upon the full application of these Rules.[21]

The conclusion, from this brief review of efforts by Latin American countries to establish regional relationships or the interchange of information, methods, and personnel among them, confirms the importance of establishing a United Nations-sponsored institute, along the lines of either Rome or Fuchu, or a combination of the two. Such an institute has been long proposed and longer postponed. Whether at Rio de Janiero, as originally scheduled, or at Caracas or some other central point which meets with the approval of the majority of the states concerned, the creation of such an institute would indeed be timely.

Pan-Arab Organization for Social Defence

The Pan-Arab Organization for Social Defence was created by the League of Arab States (which came into existence at the end of World War II) in March of 1965. The organization has four expressed purposes:

1. to study the criminal patterns existing in Arab society;
2. to work for the prevention of crime;
3. to guarantee suitable treatment of offenders in Arab member states; and
4. to achieve mutual cooperation between the criminal police and anti-narcotic organs of these states.[22]

A secretariat was established in Cairo, and thereafter three Pan-Arab bureaus were founded: in Baghdad for the prevention of crime; in Damascus for Criminal Police; in Cairo, a Pan-Arab Anti-Narcotic Bureau.

The executive council of the organization appoints the secretariat staff, which in turn services the council's semiannual meetings, undertakes technical consultations, cooperates with other international bodies and publishes and distributes a social defence journal, which contains the results of studies and research. Seminars have also been convened from time to time for the consideration of mutual problems of social defence in the Arab countries.

The most recent conference called by the Pan-Arab Organization of Social Defence was held in Kuwait in April 1970. Co-sponsored by the United Nations, this conference was preparatory, on the Mid-East regional level, for the Fourth United Nations Crime Congress scheduled to convene in Kyoto in August of that year. The conference passed two resolutions, both directed to the participants in that congress, calling attention to the condition of the Arab prisoners and detainees in occupied territories.

Nordic Association of Criminalists, and the Scandinavian Research Council of Criminology

A regional association, the Nordic Association of Criminalists has its antecedents in the national organization of criminalists founded by its member countries: the Norwegian in 1892, the Danish in 1899, the Swedish in 1911, the Finnish in 1934 and the Icelandic in 1949. Each has its own separate membership and executive board. The first three had been early associated with the International Union of Penal Law. Each of these national associations is composed of jurists, criminologists, sociologists, psychiatrists, psychologists, and social practitioners as well as research workers.[2 3]

Prior to 1936 the individual national associations published their own proceedings. In that year they began a cooperative enterprise with the issuance of the *Yearbook* of the Nordic Association, containing the proceedings of the separately held meetings of the constituent national groups as well as summaries of the papers given and the discussions held. In later years the *Yearbook* also contained summaries in French and English. A main point of interest of the meetings was concerned with projected penal and related legislation in the respective countries, which likewise appeared in their journal, *Nordisk Tidsskrift for Kriminalvidenskab*, along with articles in the field of criminology. The Nordic Association holds a joint congress of its five constituent national associations quinquennially.

After some years of experience in the development of this kind of cooperation during the period between the two world wars, the Nordic Association created an international commission for the purpose of coordinating their activities and of serving as a joint body to represent their national memberships.

This regional collaboration is also reflected in the formation of a Nordic Penal Law Committee, appointed as the result of a decision of the Danish, Finnish, Norwegian and Swedish ministers of justice. The committee was charged with problems of uniform legislation in the field of criminal law. Iceland joined the committee in 1963. Since then, their scope of interest has been broadened to include such questions as the enforcement of sanctions, confiscation, limitations of sentence, and conditional release, resulting in the passage of much uniform legislation among the constituent countries. Current concerns include questions regarding fines, the treatment of mentally abnormal offenders, and measures for deducting time spent in pre-trial custody from the imposed sentence.

Membership in the constituent national Nordic associations currently totals over 2,000 professionals and other interested persons in the five Scandinavian countries. Subscription from these members financed the activities of the national societies and of the larger regional group.

The Nordic Association was instrumental in the creation of the Scandinavian Research Council for Criminology, which became operational in 1963.[24] This council represents the formalization of several years of co-operation among members of the several national research institutes, and serves as a link between these bodies whose members continue to carry on the bulk of the research effort in this field.

The Research Council consists of thirteen members, with the four Scandinavian countries represented by three members each, and Iceland having one. Its purpose is "to work for the promotion of criminological research in Scandinavia and to assist the authorities of the Scandinavian countries in criminological matters."[25]

The Research Council sponsors annual research seminars, conducts surveys of ongoing research activities throughout its member countries, and is engaged in publishing a series entitled *Scandinavian Studies in Criminology*. Independent scientific interest rather than direct relevance to public policy seems to be the prime motivating force behind the Research Council's research activities.

Notes

1. For two accounts covering the first 15 years of the Benelux Penitentiary Commission, see their two booklets, published in French, *La Pénitentiaire Benelux*, 1, *1950-55*, 2, *1955-65* (Nivilles: BPC, 1956 & 1966).

2. A challenging obstacle course, requiring rope climbing, scaling of nets and walls, balancing skills, some of it at considerable heights, is one of the main features of the program. A recent addition is the requirement that certain tasks be done in groups rather than individually, such as carrying a heavy log up a ramp and across a trestle. Much of this is reminiscent of, as it is derivative from, the "Outward Bound" programs begun in England during World War II, and later introduced into the United States. Evening therapy sessions draw on the day's experience as material for their discussions.

3. Lloyd W. McCorkle, Albert Elias, and F. Lovell Bixby, *The Highfields Story* (New York: Henry Holt and Co., 1958). See also Jean Dupréel, "Régime applicable aux jeunes adultes condamnés à une peine privative de

liberté," report presented to the U.N. in the name of the Benelux Penitentiary Commission, 1962; and "Application des courtes peines privatives de liberté," report presented by the Commission to the European Committee on Crime Problems, Council of Europe, 1963.

4. *Commission Pénitentiaire Benelux: 1950-1970* (Le Haye: le service d'information du Ministère de la Justice, 1970).

5. A.H. Robertson, *Council of Europe*, p. 3.

6. Ibid., p. 10.

7. Ibid., p. xiii.

8. Ibid., p. 7.

9. Ibid., p. 199.

10. Ibid., p. 201.

11. Ibid.

12. Ibid., pp. 233-34.

13. *International Review of Criminal Policy*, no. 28 (1970), p. 108.

14. Ibid., no. 23 (1965), p. 26.

15. Ibid., p. 28.

16. Information concerning the Movimiento Penitenciario Latino Americano is available in mimeographed form from the office of the Executive Secretary in Santiago: "Estatutos Del Movimiento Penitenciario Latino Americano," August 1970.

17. Ibid.

18. Number 1 of this collection is "Documentos Penitenciarios Pontificios"; no. 2 is "Delincuencia"; no. 3 is "Recommendaciones para el Tratamiento Penitenciario" (all undated; all presumed to have been published in Santiago).

19. J. Carlos Garcia Basalo, *Introducción al estudio de la penología*, pp. 17-18.

20. Ibid. For a full discussion on this subject, see J.W.F. Lundberg, "La Piraterie Aérienne," *Revue Internationale de Droit Penal* 41 (1970): 165-78.

21. J. Carlos Garcia Basalo, "La Applicación de los Reglos Minimos para el Tratamiento de los Reclusos en America Latina," *Revista Penal y Penitenciaria* (1971).

22. Information in this section was drawn from "A Message to Kyoto Congress," published by the Secretariat of the Pan-Arab Organization just prior to the Fourth U.N. Congress on the Prevention of Crime and Treatment of Offenders, Kyoto, August 1970.

23. We are indebted to Thorsten Sellin for providing us with some of the information presented in this section in a personal letter dated 19 February 1971. See also *International Review of Criminal Policy*, no. 28 (1970), pp. 101-2.

24. *International Review of Criminal Policy*, no. 28 (1970), pp. 101-2.

25. Ibid., p. 101.

Conclusion

10   Retrospect and Prospect

While crime is the oldest social problem of international concern, development of changes within its ambit as well as changes in attitude toward the lawbreaker or criminal reflect—and incorporate—concomitant developments in related fields: law, psychiatry and psychotherapy, medicine, endocrinology and pharmacology, education and welfare, social work and social planning. Criminology and penology are not sciences which have a clearly or uniquely defined area of concern or application. The disciplines on which they draw are as extensive and varied as the potential—or perversity—of man himself.

It would be expecting too much, therefore, in reviewing the impact of the history of international concern and action in the field of crime, to be able to derive from all that has been set out in the preceding pages an unbroken series of successful breakthroughs in the search for the precise causes of crime, the effective prevention of delinquency, or successful methods of readjusting the acknowledged criminal to a law-abiding life in society.

For some, at this point of summation, the temptation may be strong to infer a note of pessimism. The scores of international gatherings, the reams of resolutions and exhortations, the torrent of words recorded on the miles of shelves which house the proceedings, may well be viewed by some as having been in vain. For all those who see progress as a result of all this effort, there may well be an equal number who see none. At least one observer has commented, for example, that the country with the highest reported crime rate in the world also leads in the number of criminologists and in the output of criminological research.

For despite the ideas so hopefully advanced from time to time during

155

the 150 years under review in this book, the history of penology by no means represents a constantly rising level of humane treatment. Even today, in the words of John Conrad,[1] the message of most of our places of confinement for convicted offenders—adult or juvenile throughout most of the globe—is punishment. What little progress has been made, as set down in these pages, has been over a long, slow and tortuous route. The pendulum may be, perhaps, a more accurate measure of penal progress than any other, as it swings alternately between rival philosophies and treatment methods within the ambit of a narrow number of modes, understandably limited by the human condition of those who are kept and those who keep.

If one is prompted, now and again, to put the best and most forward-looking construction on some of the proposals brought forward in the course of these international efforts, perhaps he seeks presages, however dim, of later concepts and bold new notions. For the opposite view there is ample testimony, dating from the dawn of history. The sculptures of ancient Assyria, the frescoes of Egypt and the triumphal arches of Rome bear timeless witness to man's consistent and never-ending inhumanity to his fellow man. The cruelties of yoke and torture which were imposed on prisoners of war were the same as were imposed upon the slaves or the nonmilitary offenders in those days—the prisoners of peace. From one point of view, many of the prisoners of our times may be seen as captives in a war which they are deemed to be waging against society.

The media daily report, from at least four widely separated fronts, wars in which the declarations of decency and humane treatment, which civilized nations have set out in charters and international accords, are regularly violated. Since 1914, it has been estimated, 100 million members of the human race have been slaughtered as a result of wars. The line between political prisoners and prisoners of war, if it exists at all, is seen to operate to the disadvantage of the former. As war becomes more vicious, the horrors it visits upon the total population draw no distinction between combatants and civilians. As civil wars erupt, dissidents are punished as much for their ideas as others for their acts against the prevailing regime.

Grotius, observing the conduct of his contemporaries 350 years ago, saw

> throughout the Christian World . . . a lack of restraint in relation to war, such as even barbarous races should be ashamed of; I observed that men rush to arms for slight causes, or no cause at all, and that when arms have once been taken up there is no longer any respect for law, divine or human; it is as if, in accordance with a general decree, frenzy had openly been let loose for the committing of all crimes.[2]

Given these proclivities of mankind embattled against itself, why should there be any grounds for expectation that the civil prisoner would be spared? If the Conventions of Geneva regarding limits on the use of gas and biological warfare, to assure decent regard for civilians, are daily outraged; if the principles of the Nuremberg Tribunal are applied only to the weak or vanquished and not to the aggressor; if disarmament continues to sit outside the doors where it is being debated; why should it be expected that international meetings of experts in penology—at Geneva or any where else—should succeed in tempering the plight of prisoners? If the rules governing the use of international waters are not universally regarded, why should it be expected that the Standard Minimum Rules for the Treatment of Prisoners should by now be in force universally?

The idea that crime represents the pathology of a given society is by no means new: "Every society gets the criminals it deserves," runs the old adage. It was Lacassagne who described society as the bouillion and the criminal as the bacterium. If there is validity in this view, then the extent of criminal behavior which characterizes every country which keeps any kind of statistics gives evidence that all our societies could benefit from serious examination of their basic values and forms of organization, if they are intent on dealing with the problem in fundamental fashion.

The oncoming generation, in its way, may be trying to tell us just exactly that. It is more than as a result of instant international interchange that there has arisen this new phenomenon of a world-wide youth culture, the full ramifications of which we are not yet privileged to grasp. The frustration, alienation and disenchantment of many of the young as expressed in delinquency and the resort to narcotics; the evident breakdown of authority, religion and old ways generally; the questioning of material values that have long dominated man's quest for survival and security; the conquest of nature that now puts man into the position of protecting it against his own depredations, mark these days as ones of great seminal change.

The mushroom cloud that hangs over us all makes it imperative that we pursue ways to avert the Inevitable Decree. We have perhaps seen an end to the series of world wars that have twice plagued the century, just as Viet Nam may spell the end of open wars to control dissidence, marking as it does the emergence of a third world capable of resisting the mightiest armed power the world has ever seen, but without the moral force to impose its will on "backward" peoples.

These are the immeasurables, as they appear to be the concomitants to the totality of antisocial behavior at a level higher than most nations of the world have ever before confronted. No one can know what will ultimately emerge. All that can be hoped for is an appreciation of what is taking place and an intensified search for some understanding of the forces behind the vast and cosmic phenomenon of crime.

Should the time ever come when offenders and prisoners are no longer regarded as captives in a war against society, but rather as persons in need of special dealing by reason of their special needs, we shall then have entered a revolutionary epoch indeed. A few hopeful signs already point in that direction, especially the move in some places to remove the so called sumptuary crimes or "crimes without victims"—alcoholism, prostitution, drug abuse, sex offences, gambling, and vagrancy from the calendar of crimes. Historically, such considerations have been viewed as matters for national concern alone. States have ever been quick to resent interference in such internal matters by outside bodies, however loftily conceived or internationally sponsored.

It is well at this point to recall the wise words of the president of the 1857 Congress of Charities, Correction and Philanthropy, that "universal understanding of penal matters" would be delayed not only because of national differences, but because those differences were cherished. International forums may provide excellent testing grounds for ideas strongly held. But a certain degree of concensus on the part of the public as well as of the experts is necessary before these ideas can begin to be translated into public policy, over and against the "cherished" notions which they aim to replace.

While diversity and conflict are necessary conditions for the growth of any body of knowledge or practice, changes involving a system of justice must first win the approval of lawmakers, bench, bar and penal administrators. In every country such persons tend to be among the most conservative forces in the society, who look rather to commonly held traditional ways and to proposals with a broad base of support than to the innovative and the controversial.

This is not to argue that meetings and conventions which attempt to outlaw inhumane practices in any area should discontinue. The manner in which one country treats its people is today a matter of concern for the entire world, as its manner of dealing with its environment—land, air and water—has implications beyond its own shores or atmosphere. Reciprocally, how one country treats the nationals of another country is today not without repercussions within its own borders.

It is timely to recall that genocide was labelled a crime against humanity in 1948 by the United Nations Convention Against Genocide, to which 69 nations were signatory in 1969. Closely related to the terms of that convention are the provisions of the agreement embodying the Charter of the International Military Tribunal, signed in London in 1945. It was this Charter which resulted, ultimately, in the convening of the subsequent trials at Nuremberg and at Tokyo.

A precedent for calling responsible leaders in the United States to account for war crimes against the peoples of Indo-China may thus be found in the pronouncements which led to the post-World War II trials of war criminals. If the United States, victor of that war, aggressor and hardly the victor in Vietnam, today stands accused in some quarters, it is at least on the same grounds on which it proceeded to try the vanquished leaders of the Axis powers twenty-five years ago.[3] This is but the most recent evidence of the interdependence of all humanity, stemming historically from the men who first conceived the idea of international gatherings to discuss the cause and prevention of crime and the treatment of offenders. Perhaps it is not too much to say that what the world is witnessing today can be seen as an almost unlimited extrapolation of the earlier, humble efforts of jurists, prison administrators and criminologists to deal with traditional crimes within national borders.

Here, aptly, may be cited words printed just 100 years ago, as set down by an observer of several international congresses of crime convened before the London Congress of 1872:

> Far from looking upon those great assemblies as wholly useless, I must acknowledge that the meeting of so many men, so distinguished for their learning and virtuous purposes, and the mutual interchange of ideas, of practical views and projects, cannot fail to give a powerful impulse to the advancement of science, and widen the individual horizon beyond the sphere of each individuality. But this must not be the only object we aim at. The compact, united forces of eminent men, led by such lofty desires, must necessarily and ultimately attain the most advantageous results.[4]

For an examination of those results, it may serve now to consider some of the specific leading questions posed at the 1872 London Congress to see how they fare today. These totalled 26, several relating to the same area (see Exhibit 2). How do we stand now with regard to them?

The first goes to the matter of size of a given prison population. It is fair to say that while today many institutions exist which have inmate populations running into the thousands, the more enlightened view tends toward smaller places. This springs from the realization that the influence of staff on prisoners is the most important single factor in rehabilitation. As in education or religion, the scope of that individual influence is not infinitely expandable.

The answer to the second question is obvious: classification of prisoners has made tremendous strides in the past century. True, 1872 marked a period when penologists, like their opposite numbers in the field of psychiatry, spent more time in classifying convicts—or lunatics—than in treating them. Criminalistics, which now began to call itself "criminology," was taking the first steps taken in the development of any new science: the observation and classification of phenomena within its range of interest. The next steps, the formulation and testing of hypotheses, and the prediction of the occurrence of events, would have to wait the passage of several decades more.

It may be noted at this point, as a measure of the forward strides which prison work has made, that the principle of classification is today universally accepted as basic to the effective functioning of any penal establishment. The same may be said for the concern expressed in 1872 at London for the discharged prisoner, and for means of securing his rehabilitation.

Corporal punishment as an instrument for dealing with prisoners is today no longer debated. This is not to say that it is no longer practiced—on juveniles and adults—in many places in the world. But the fact that the question could no longer be posed for debate in any international gathering is some small gauge of how far we have come. Transportation is in the same category. Not that commitment to islands or to inaccessible penitentiaries is not still practiced. But Devil's Island has been closed, Alcatraz was until recently in the hands of descendants of its original settlers, and no government that calls itself civilized would resort any longer to banishment or exile for condemned felons. International public opinion could be expected to force a reversal of any such action, as the interchange of information about every place in the world makes it increasingly difficult to conceal acts against humanity anywhere.

The question of the desirability of providing professional training for correctional personnel is no longer argued. Such programs are found in every enlightened prison service. Through international effort today, there is greater interchange of correctional personnel in training schemes than could have been imagined when the question of training was first raised at the 1872 London Congress.

The Technical Assistance Program is a prime example of a realistic response by the United Nations to the needs of developing countries. It reflects an awareness that techniques are more easily transmitted or exchanged between countries than are philosophies or even theories, and may provide, in fact, the necessary prerequisites for the later acceptance of related ideas. Technical and scientific cooperation across national boundaries is an important ingredient on the international scene. When it is conducted under the aegis of a world-wide organization, it provides an excellent example of the potential inherent in trans-political cooperation.

The so-called developing countries comprise at least 80 out of today's 127 total membership of the United Nations. The number of persons under 21 years of age is expanding rapidly in many countries, in some of which it may constitute one-half of the total population. In light of the world-wide increases in youthful crime, the significance of the relationship between these two data derives from the potential which they both represent—in terms of criminal careers prevented and human resources conserved—aided by timely and effective programs of technical assistance.

Prison labor today is accepted as a means of training the prisoner, paying him—however minimally—for his work, and using his efforts for productive purposes. This does not mean that the punitive aspects of prison labor have by any means disappeared. But the treadmill, the picking of oakum, the breaking of stone, are no longer found on the schedules of modern penal establishments. Hard labor may still be included as a condition under which a prisoner is sentenced, but like the rule of silence, it is no longer a reality in practice.

While such steps may be viewed as progressive, much remains to be done in the area of the economics of prison labor. For example, some countries, notably the Scandinavian, appear to be moving in the direction of paying to prisoners a wage equivalent to what they would receive in the outside world for comparable work. It is hard to argue against the justice—and even the intelligence—of such a move. For if the burden of the complaint of many prisoners is that they are treated as second-class citizens, what more valid argument could be found to bolster their case than the present pay scales within prisons? One of the characteristics of the convict, as universal as was once the "Gefängnissblick," is his feeling of worthlessness. Token payments for his labor, pittances which are below the dignity even of the outmoded dole, must only contribute to that feeling of self-degradation. In a world where one's status rests in no small degree on what one earns, why should men deprived of liberty be further deprived of economic rewards as well—assuming the quality and quantity of their production to be equal to that of free men? And what better way to raise the level of their output than to pay for its full value? Whether the cost of their keep is to be deducted from their earnings is a subordinate consideration.

At least one government's department of labor has suggested an extension of this advanced economic notion: that men in prison who work be enrolled in the national social security system while they are still under sentence. This would permit them to receive unemployment compensation upon their release, until such time as they had begun to receive wages from their new job on the outside. Whether assistance is paid to a parolee out of unemployment funds or out of a special after-care appropriation is not nearly so important as the fact that placing the released offender in the same category as other unemployed persons helps to remove the stigma of second-class citizenship which follows the released offender like an inescapable shadow of the prison he is supposed to have left behind.

The question asked about the reformation of juvenile offenders was two-thirds down the list at London. Today, with the increase of delinquency among the young in every nation this question is now prime, however little we may have progressed in answering it with any degree of finality.

The provocative question posed about criminal capitalists seems not to have reappeared on any subsequent agenda of an international organization devoted to criminalistics. But in many countries the subject is under more scrutiny than it was when Edwin Hill brought it up in 1872 at London. The subject of white-collar crime is today the concern of those sociologists and criminologists who see in it implications not alone for the field of crime but for the entire societal fabric. Durkheim postulated that a certain amount of crime in any society helped to keep that society moral and on guard against those elements which would destroy it. Today's spread of criminality into all classes of some societies makes it important to develop critiques which will take account of antisocial conduct, not only according to the traditional calendar of crime and the theories derived from studies of the lower socio-economic classes, but also of the wrong-doings against society found in the areas of business, politics, organized crime and the military.

The question of standardizing, gathering and compiling international criminal statistics is little further advanced than it was when first raised. Few subjects have received more regular attention by international crime conference-goers; none has more stoutly resisted any attempt to bring it to fruition.

From the references throughout this work to the Standard Minimum Rules for the Treatment of Prisoners, it might be inferred that it was not until 1926 that they were first formulated. But it would be unfair to the efforts of participants in crime congresses as far back as 1872 to deduce that they did not discuss, and press for dissemination of, a whole host of considerations which were ultimately to find their way into the Standard Minimum Rules as they exist today. In all fairness it should be emphasized that what took place in 1926 was the culmination of a half century or more of discussions of these questions at the international level. At London in 1872 alone, they formed the basis of at least four out of twenty-six questions posed at that initial international crime congress (see Exhibits 2 and 7).

It has been said that "the improvement of the administration of criminal justice in many countries has been often held up by the lack of impartial and constructive criticism."[5] It is equally significant to note that one of the chief obstacles to improved penal treatment has been the very existence of the structure of the penal establishments themselves. Sheldon Glueck once remarked that if poetry is frozen music, prisons are frozen penology. Certain it is that the scores, even hundreds, of ancient penitentiary piles built at the height of the 19th century fervor, stand astride the road to prison progress, blocking it by their weight and the cost of replacing them. Limited in purpose to that for which they were originally designed, they make it impossible to institute the approaches which are being advocated in so many quarters that the present period has been characterized as one of ferment. As pieces of real estate they are desired by no one. Their value can only be enhanced by their removal, for reasons which are cogently put forward in the following:

> The solidity of our prison buildings too often obliges us to apply as well as we can, in nineteenth century surroundings, a regime that is entirely different from that conceived by the builders of these fortresses. In many respects, our old prisons, even though they have been modernized, make one think of a turtleshell into which some other animal has been pushed.[6]

A new fashion is on the way, demanding the design of institutions which shall have built into them a planned obsolescence, or else a possibility of their conversion to a variety of other purposes when they have served their time as penal stations: as hospitals, schools, nursing homes, and technical training institutes.

Our times are marked, as well, by a growing recognition that the mass-congregate institution has largely failed its purpose. We are, perhaps, on the threshold of a new beginning in penology which will see the closing down for good of many of these ancient piles, and their replacement by smaller, more individualized stations. Here intensive programs would be geared to the needs of carefully classified and screened groups of inmates with like needs and a shared potential. No debate between research criminologists as to what constitutes "recidivism," or how precisely to define "failure," can obscure the fact that the overwhelming majority of our penal stations fail to rehabilitate the majority of the persons committed to them.

The argument has been made, and it is hard to counter, that if places could be created which proved to be no more successful with their graduates than are our present jails and prisons, but which in the process somehow managed not to degrade and dehumanize the persons whom they took in hand, that such a step would constitute real penal progress. For what studies of recidivism can measure the effect, during the post-release period, of the indignities practiced upon persons while they had been in confinement? Conversely, it would be hard to gauge the benefits of a long-range nature which might be expected to accrue to a man who, while he was confined, was not made to feel more worthless than when he first went in.

No such discussion can realistically disregard the needs of society to be protected against depredators. The search has gone on down through the century and a half of international interchange and concern in this area, to find, if anything, more effective safeguards for society. But in their zeal to achieve such security, governments have tended to give massive doses of punishment to the many in order to protect itself against the minority. The challenge, therefore, will be to discover, through the development of typologies of offenders and of keener methods of classification and analysis, the truly hardened "dangerous" offender for whom conditions of maximum security may indeed be required. We need to know much more than we now do about the types of personalities which respond to the deterrent effect of punishment, and those whose need to hit out against society is somehow proof against the most drastic of penal sanctions.

This concern is aggravated by the fact that many jurisdictions in the world now report a difference in the kinds of crimes committed which—if only in degree—present a new challenge for both law and corrections. The face of crime is changing: it runs today beyond the usual calendar to include a new dimension—a greater ingredient of anonymity, even of inhumanity than what we have earlier witnessed. As the world's population increases, so the bonds which held communities and even nations together, seem in many quarters to loosen, and the hold of earlier local or tribal ways to relax. We confront, as but one result, not only an increase in the amount of antisocial conduct and an involvement of a larger sector of the population, but what might be called a certain facelessness of crime.

Each war of our century has been followed by an increase in the degree and rate of crime, as if by individual reflection of the increased total power of man to destroy both property and life. Vandalism and crimes against possessions or persons unknown to the depredator, individual and corporate alike, are increasingly manifested. What one author has called "Magnicide"[7]—the killing of persons in high places, what is usually called assassination—is become, in some places, not so much an act of political reprisal or defiance, but one done for individual satisfaction of other, less traditional, if not so lofty purposes. A murder perpetrated by an aggrieved assailant in a fit of passion against his victim is understandable in the sense that it is a personal or "human" response. This is not to condone such acts, but to place them in a setting which appears lacking in many murders committed in some parts of the world, in which the motive is not so understandable, because no personal bond of any kind existed between the dead man and his killer.

The first unthinking response of each of us, when assaulted or otherwise aggrieved, is to react in retaliatory fashion. We yield that claim to vengeance to the state, under an unwritten clause of the traditional social contract. This process of "sublimation" is, after all, the mark of the civilized citizen of a civilized state. But in the act of forfeiting the right to avenge an outrage against our person or property, we do not, by the same token, root out from our primordial heritage the instinctual response: to strike back when struck. Penal sanctions are only the institutionalized form, *in toto*, of the private vengeance that lies in all of us. As long as it does, we must expect—and even look for—the same urge for vengeance to be manifested by the state acting in our behalf: The Crown *vs.* John Doe, the Government of Ruritania *vs.* Mary Roe, the People *vs.* Peter Poe; ten years for robbery—twenty for rape—a life for a life.

As one bit of contemporary evidence of the saying *plus ça change, plus c'est la même chose*, current reports from embattled Northern Ireland may be cited. While the British may have abandoned transportation of convicts a century or more ago, the exigencies of policy today in that troubled zone have brought about a revival of this barbaric practice. Today's news stories describe the arrest—without charge or subsequent trial—of suspected IRA members and their internment aboard ship in Belfast harbor—reminiscent of imprisonment of convicts on hulks in English harbors and river mouths as long ago as 1858, until which time this practice formed an integral part of the English prison system.[8] Punishment rather than persuasion remains the chief reliance when lines are drawn. This is as true today as it has ever been before when we confront one another in wars, whether between nations, classes—or colonies.

Meanwhile, it is to be hoped that the highest common denominator of punitive treatment which exists almost universally today may be considerably lowered. In the end it may be found that less rather than more men need the tight security which is the hallmark of the traditional penal institution, whose value is more keenly questioned these days than it has ever been in the past.

A further hopeful note may be found in the direction of current international efforts to provide technical assistance to workers in the field, The establishment of regional institutes is but one recent and heartening example of this trend. It is devoutly to be hoped that the pioneer United Nations institutes in Italy and Japan will be matched by counterparts in other areas of the world. They represent, in a sense, the application within the field of international action of the precept of reality therapy which is making its way into many institutions for offenders: the idea that in order to effect change it is important to start at the root of that problem which is most pressing. And in the field of corrections this means improved methods of training correctional personnel, not only at the administrative level, but also at the level of guards whose duties hitherto have been all too often limited to custody and security.

Even if in the final analysis all that has been recounted above were to be discounted as totalling to an unimpressive record of results, as a running tally of the agents of change rather than of change itself, there still emerges a residuum which is impossible to calculate. There is an impact which is known to every attendant at an international conference on any subject: the value that accrues to each by reason of the informal interchanges that take place outside the conference halls—in corridor, cocktail lounge or hotel room. It is unjust to assume that most participants in international conferences are moved largely by nonprofessional motives to attend them. There are, after all, many better ways to pass ten days in any summer than in an international conference thousands of miles away. The gregarious instincts of man, heightened in this instance by a commonality of professional interest, is what appears to bring most conferees to conferences. The growth in the totality of professional knowledge which results is equalled only by the number of professional—and personal—associations made, which carry over when participants return home. These are of the essence of international conferences, as the interchange of more effective ways of dealing with the problems commonly confronted is the prize.

Certainly the umbrella of international collaboration in the field of crime has been progressively extended over the years in two measurable ways: both in terms of coverage of subject matter and in the breadth of representation. At the first IPC meeting in London in 1872, 22 countries were represented; the United Nations Crime congress in Kyoto, Japan, was host to delegates and participants from 85 countries, almost four times that number.

It will be recalled that the earliest international crime congresses drew largely from Europe, with some delegates from the United States and an occasional representative from Latin America and from Asia. The League of Nations widened this representation to involve a somewhat larger number of countries from these two last areas. The Soviet Union did not become a League member until September, 1934. It was left to the United Nations, more globally representative than any other world organization before it, to bring in the African countries and the major socialist nations—except China. Now that the People's Republic has finally been admitted to the United Nations, and negotiations are underway (as these words are being written) to begin to build a bridge between China's 800 million people and that part of the world which had for twenty-two years attempted to exclude them, we may hopefully look forward to a fruitful period of truly international, and now universal, collaboration in the field of crime.

Exhibit 5
International Meetings Scheduled for the
Decade of the 1970s

1971 — November — International Society of Social Defence — "Diversion and
Decriminalization" — Paris
— International Center for Comparative Criminology: "Justice in
Megalopolis"
1972 — International Penal and Penitentiary Foundation
— International Center for Comparative Criminology: Symposium on "The
Adaptation of Justice in the Third World"
1973 — September — Joint Meeting of the International Criminal Law
Association, the International Society of Criminology, International
Society of Social Defence and the International Penal and Penitentiary
Foundation — Bellagio
— Seventh International Congress of Criminology — Moscow
1974 — International Association of Penal Law — Montevideo
1975 — Fifth United Nations Crime Congress — Toronto
1976 — International Society of Social Defence
1977 — International Penal and Penitentiary Foundation
1978 — Joint Meeting of the International Criminal Law Association,
International Society of Criminology, International Society of Social
Defence, International Penal and Penitentiary Foundation
1979 — International Association of Penal Law
1980 — Sixth United Nations Crime Congress

Fixed ideas and the habits which derive from national patterns are
not easily moved. It is only by the confrontation of ideas which are different from one's own, even opposed, that one is led to question his basic
precepts. National hatreds are derived from prejudice, which stems largely
from ignorance. If the UNESCO Constitution is correct that wars start in
the minds of men, and that economic and social conditions are at the root
of misunderstanding, then it is indeed fitting and proper for international
action to be encouraged. If the conditions of childhood are ameliorated, we
may somehow succeed in preventing the development in adulthood of the
kind of mentality which leads to enmity, to war and to the destruction of
mankind.

It has been well said before:

All that has been done in the past, in spite of imperfections and in
spite of the fact that it has been carried out on too small a scale, has

undoubtedly had a most beneficial influence on the progress of criminal science and on the shaping of an improved criminal policy throughout the world. It should encourage perseverance in the effort.[9]

In the future perspective:

The proper solution of penal problems in all countries alike will not only make for the welfare of each but will also be a factor in stabilizing international peace. The efficient and enlightened administration of criminal justice is an essential element of social and international security.[10]

Notes

1. John Conrad, *Crime and Its Correction*, p. 301.
2. Hugo Grotius, *Prolegomena*, para. 28; translated in *Classics of International Law* 1 (19):20.
3. See Telford Taylor, *Nuremberg and Vietnam*.
4. Martino Beltrani-Scalia, "Historical Sketch of National and International Congresses in Europe and America," p. 276.
5. Leon Radzinowicz, "International Collaboration in Criminal Science," in Leon Radzinowicz and J.W.C. Turner, eds., *Modern Approach to Criminal Law*, p. 488.
6. International Penal and Penitentiary Commission, *Three Aspects of Penal Treatment*, from the Postface by Paul Cornil, then president of IPPF, p. 87.
7. Alfonso Quiroz Cuarón, and Samuel Máynez Puente, *Psicoanalisis del Magnicidio* (Mexico City: Editorial Juridicia Mexicana, 1965).
8. Henry Meyhew and John Binny, *Criminal Prisons of London* (London: Griffin, Bone, 1858), pp. 199-200.
9. Radzinowicz, "International Collaboration," p. 497.
10. Ibid., p. 495.

Exhibit 6

Declaration of Principles Adopted and Promulgated by the First National Congress on Penitentiary and Reformatory Discipline, Cincinnati — October 1870*

I. Crime is an intentional violation of duties imposed by law, which inflicts an injury upon others. Criminals are persons convicted of crime by competent courts. Punishment is suffering inflicted on the criminal for the wrong done by him, with a special view to secure his reformation.

II. The treatment of criminals by society is for the protection of society. But since such treatment is directed to the criminal rather than to the crime, its great object should be his moral regeneration. Hence the supreme aim of prison discipline is the reformation of criminals, not the infliction of vindictive suffering.

III. The progressive classification of prisoners, based on character and worked on some well-adjusted mark system, should be established in all prisons above the common jail.

IV. Since hope is a more potent agent than fear, it should be made an ever-present force in the minds of prisoners, by a well-devised and skillfully-applied system of rewards for good conduct, industry and attention to learning. Rewards, more than punishments, are essential to every good prison system.

V. The prisoner's destiny should be placed, measurably, in his own hands; he must be put into circumstances where he will be able, through his own exertions, to continually better his own condition. A regulated self-interest must be brought into play and made constantly operative.

VI. The two master forces opposed to the reform of the prison systems of our several states are political appointments, and a consequent instability of administration. Until both are eliminated, the needed reforms are impossible.

VII. Special training, as well as high qualities of head and heart, is required to make a good prison or reformatory officer. Then only will the administration of public punishment become scientific, uniform and successful, when it is raised to the dignity of a profession, and men are specially trained for it, as they are for other pursuits.

VIII. Peremptory sentences ought to be replaced by those of indeterminate length. Sentences limited only by satisfactory proof of reformation should be substituted for those measured by mere lapse of time.

IX. Of all reformatory agencies, religion is first in importance, because most potent in its action upon the human heart and life.

X. Education is a vital force in the reformation of fallen men and women. Its tendency is to quicken the intellect, inspire self-respect, excite to higher aims,

*Reprinted from E.C. Wines, ed. *Transactions of the National Congress on Penitentiary and Reformatory Discipline* (Albany: Weed, Parsons and Co., Printers, 1871), pp. 541-547.

and afford a healthful substitute for low and vicious amusements. Education is, therefore, a matter of primary importance in prisons, and should be carried to the utmost extent consistent with the other purposes of such institutions.

XI. In order to the reformation of imprisoned criminals, there must be not only a sincere desire and intention to that end, but a serious conviction, in the minds of the prison officers, that they are capable of being reformed, since no man can heartily maintain a discipline at war with his inward beliefs; no man can earnestly strive to accomplish what in his heart he despairs of accomplishing.

XII. A system of prison discipline, to be truly reformatory, must gain the will of the convict. He is to be amended; but how is this possible with his mind in a state of hostility? No system can hope to succeed, which does not secure this harmony of wills, so that the prisoner shall choose for himself what his officer chooses for him. But, to this end, the officer must really choose the good of the prisoner, and the prisoner must remain in his choice long enough for virtue to become a habit. This consent of wills is an essential condition of reformation.

XIII. The interest of society and the interest of the convicted criminal are really identical, and they should be made practically so. At present there is a combat between crime and laws. Each sets the other at defiance, and, as a rule, there is little kindly feeling, and few friendly acts, on either side. It would be otherwise if criminals, on conviction, instead of being cast off, were rather made the objects of a generous parental care; that is, if they were trained to virtue, and not merely sentenced to suffering.

XIV. The prisoner's self-respect should be cultivated to the utmost, and every effort made to give back to him his manhood. There is no greater mistake in the whole compass of penal discipline, than its studied imposition of degradation as a part of punishment. Such imposition destroys every better impulse and aspiration. It crushes the weak, irritates the strong, and indisposes all to submission and reform. It is trampling where we ought to raise, and is therefore as unchristian in principle as it is unwise in policy.

XV. In prison administration, moral forces should be relied upon, with as little admixture of physical force as possible, and organized persuasion be made to take the place of coercive restraint, the object being to make upright and industrious freemen, rather than orderly and obedient prisoners. Brute force may make good prisoners; moral training alone will make good citizens. To the latter of these ends, the living soul must be won; to the former, only the inert and obedient body.

XVI. Industrial training should have both a higher development and a greater breadth than has heretofore been, or is now, commonly given to it in our prisons. Work is no less an auxiliary to virtue, than it is a means of support. Steady, active, honorable labor is the basis of all reformatory discipline. It not only aids reformation, but is essential to it. It was a maxim with Howard, "make men diligent, and they will be honest"—a maxim which this congress regards as eminently sound and practical.

XVII. While industrial labor in prisons is of the highest importance and utility to the convict, and by no means injurious to the laborer outside, we regard the contract system of prison labor, as now commonly practised in our country, as prejudicial alike to discipline, finance and the reformation of the prisoner, and sometimes injurious to the interest of the free laborer.

XVIII. The most valuable parts of the Irish prison system—the more strictly penal stage of separate imprisonment, the reformatory stage of progressive classification, and the probationary stage of natural training—are believed to be as applicable to one country as another—to the United States as to Ireland.

XIX. Prisons, as well as prisoners, should be classified or graded so that there shall be prisons for the untried, for the incorrigible and for other degrees of depraved character, as well as separate establishments for women, and for criminals of the younger class.

XX. It is the judgment of this congress, that repeated short sentences for minor criminals are worse than useless; that, in fact, they rather stimulate than repress transgression. Reformation is a work of time; and a benevolent regard to the good of the criminal himself, as well as to the protection of society, requires that his sentence be long enough for reformatory processes to take effect.

XXI. Preventive institutions, such as truant homes, industrial schools, etc., for the reception and treatment of children not yet criminal, but in danger of becoming so, constitute the true field of promise, in which to labor for the repression of crime.

XXII. More systematic and comprehensive methods should be adopted to save discharged prisoners, by providing them with work and encouraging them to redeem their character and regain their lost position in society. The state has not discharged its whole duty to the criminal when it has punished him, nor even when it has reformed him. Having raised him up, it has the further duty to aid in holding him up. And to this end it is desirable that state societies be formed, which shall cooperate with each other in this work.

XXIII. The successful prosecution of crime requires the combined action of capital and labor, just as other crafts do. There are two well defined classes engaged in criminal operations, who may be called the capitalists and the operatives. It is worthy of inquiry, whether a more effective warfare may not be carried on against crime, by striking at the capitalists as a class, than at the operatives one by one. Certainly, this double warfare should be vigorously pushed, since from it the best results, as regards repressive justice, may be reasonably hoped for.

XXIV. Since personal liberty is the rightful inheritance of every human being, it is the sentiment of this congress that the state which has deprived an innocent citizen of this right, and subjected him to penal restraint, should, on unquestionable proof of its mistake, make reasonable indemnification for such wrongful imprisonment.

XXV. Criminal lunacy is a question of vital interest to society; and facts show that our laws regarding insanity, in its relation to crime, need revision, in order to bring them to a more complete conformity to the demands of reason, justice and humanity; so that, when insanity is pleaded in bar of conviction, the investigation may be conducted with greater knowledge, dignity and fairness; criminal responsibility be more satisfactorily determined; the punishment of the sane criminal be made more sure, and the restraint of the insane be rendered at once more certain and more humane.

XXVI. While this congress would not shield the convicted criminal from the just responsibility of his misdeeds, it arraigns society itself as in no slight degree accountable for the invasion of its rights and the warfare upon its interests, practised by the criminal classes. Does society take all the steps which it easily might, to change, or at least improve, the circumstances in our social state that lead to crime; or, when crime has been committed, to cure the proclivity to it, generated by these circumstances? It cannot be pretended. Let society, then, lay the case earnestly to its conscience, and strive to mend in both particulars. Offences, we are told by a high authority, must come; but a special woe is denounced against those through whom they come. Let us take heed that that woe fall not upon our head.

XXVII. The exercise of executive clemency in the pardon of criminals is a practical question of grave importance, and of great delicacy and difficulty. It is believed that the annual average of executive pardons from the prisons of the whole country reaches ten per cent of their population. The effect of the too free use of the pardoning power is to detract from the *certainty* of punishment for crimes, and to divert the mind of prisoners from the means supplied for their improvement. Pardons should issue for one or more of the following reasons, viz.: to release the innocent, to correct mistakes made in imposing the sentence, to relieve such suffering from ill-health as requires release from imprisonment, and to facilitate or reward the real reformation of the prisoner. The exercise of this power should be by the executive, and should be guarded by careful examination as to the character of the prisoner and his conduct in prison. Furthermore, it is the opinion of this congress that governors of states should give to their respective legislatures the reasons, in each case, for their exercise of the pardoning power.

XXVIII. The proper duration of imprisonment for a violation of the laws of society is one of the most perplexing questions in criminal jurisprudence. The present extraordinary inequality of sentences for the same or similar crimes is a source of constant irritation among prisoners, and the discipline of our prisons suffers in consequence. The evil is one for which some remedy should be devised.

XXIX. Prison statistics, gathered from a wide field and skillfully digested, are essential to an exhibition of the true character and working of our prison systems. The collection, collation and reduction to tabulated forms of such statistics can best be effected through a national prison discipline society, with competent working committees in every state, or by the establishment of a national prison bureau, similar to the recently instituted national bureau of education.

XXX. Prison architecture is a matter of grave importance. Prisons of every class should be substantial structures, affording gratification by their design and material to a pure taste, but not costly or highly ornate. We are of the opinion that those of moderate size are best, as regards both industrial and reformatory ends.

XXXI. The construction, organization, and management of all prisons should be by the state, and they should form a graduated series of reformatory establishments, being arranged with a view to the industrial employment, intellectual education and moral training of the inmates.

XXXII. As a general rule, the maintenance of penal institutions, above the county jail, should be from the earnings of their inmates, and without cost to the state; nevertheless, the true standard of merit in their management is the rapidity and thoroughness of reformatory effect accomplished thereby.

XXXIII. A right application of the principles of sanitary science in the construction and arrangements of prisons is a point of vital importance. The apparatus for heating and ventilation should be the best that is known; sunlight, air and water should be afforded according to the abundance with which nature has provided them; the rations and clothing should be plain but wholesome, comfortable, and in sufficient but not extravagant quantity; the bedsteads, bed and bedding, including sheets and pillow cases, not costly but decent, and kept clean, well-aired and free from vermin; the hospital accommodations, medical stores and surgical instruments should be all that humanity requires and science can supply; and all needed means for personal cleanliness should be without stint.

XXXIV. The principle of the responsibility of parents for the full or partial support of their criminal children in reformatory institutions has been extensively applied in Europe, and its practical working has been attended with the best results. It is worthy of inquiry whether this principle may not be advantageously introduced into the management of our American reformatory institutions.

XXXV. It is our conviction that one of the most effective agencies in the repression of crime would be the enactment of laws by which the education of all the children of the state should be made obligatory. Better to force education upon the people than to force them into prison to suffer for crimes, of which the neglect of education and consequent ignorance have been the occasion, if not the cause.

XXXVI. As a principle that crowns all, and is essential to all, it is our conviction that no prison system can be perfect, or even successful to the most desirable degree, without some central authority to sit at the helm, guiding, controlling, unifying and vitalizing the whole. We ardently hope yet to see all the departments of our preventive, reformatory and penal institutions in each state moulded into one harmonious and effective system; its parts mutually answering to and supporting each other; and the whole animated by the same spirit, aiming at the same objects, and subject to the same control; yet without loss of the advantages of voluntary aid and effort, wherever they are attainable.

XXXVII. This congress is of the opinion that, both in the official administration of such a system, and in the voluntary cooperation of citizens therein, the agency of women may be employed with excellent effect.

Exibit 7

STANDARD MINIMUM RULES FOR THE TREATMENT OF PRISONERS AND RELATED RECOMMENDATIONS

U N I T E D   N A T I O N S

Department of Economic and Social Affairs

New York, 1958

NOTE

By resolution 663 C (XXIV) of 31 July 1957, the Economic and Social Council approved the *Standard Minimum Rules for the Treatment of Prisoners* (p. 1) and endorsed *inter alia* the *Recommendations on the Selection and Training of Personnel for Penal and Correctional Institutions* (p. 7) and the *Recommendations on Open Penal and Correctional Institutions* (p. 10), as adopted by the First United Nations Congress on the Prevention of Crime and the Treatment of Offenders, held at Geneva in 1955. According to this resolution, Governments were invited, among other things, to give favourable consideration to the adoption and application of the *Standard Minimum Rules,* and to take the other two groups of recommendations as fully as possible into account in their administration of penal and correctional institutions. The following texts are reproduced from the Report on the First United Nations Congress on the Prevention of Crime and the Treatment of Offenders (United Nations publication, Sales No.: 1956.IV.4).

A. STANDARD MINIMUM RULES FOR THE TREATMENT OF PRISONERS

Resolution adopted on 30 August 1955

The First United Nations Congress on the Prevention of Crime and the Treatment of Offenders,

Having adopted the Standard Minimum Rules for the Treatment of Prisoners annexed to the present Resolution,

1. *Requests* the Secretary-General, in accordance with paragraph *(d)* of the annex to resolution 415(V) of the General Assembly of the United Nations, to submit these rules to the Social Commission of the Economic and Social Council for approval;

2. *Expresses* the hope that these rules be approved by the Economic and Social Council and, if deemed appropriate by the Council, by the General Assembly, and that they be transmitted to governments with the recommendation *(a)* that favourable consideration be given to their adoption and application in the administration of penal institutions, and *(b)* that the Secretary-General be informed every three years of the progress made with regard to their application;

3. *Expresses* the wish that, in order to allow governments to keep themselves informed of the progress made in this respect, the Secretary-General be requested to publish in the International Review of Criminal Policy the information sent by governments in pursuance of paragraph 2, and that he be authorized to ask for supplementary information if necessary;

4. *Expresses* also the wish that the Secretary-General be requested to arrange that the widest possible publicity be given to these rules.

Annex

Standard Minimum Rules for the Treatment of Prisoners

PRELIMINARY OBSERVATIONS

1. The following rules are not intended to describe in detail a model system of penal institutions. They seek only, on the basis of the general consensus of contemporary thought and the essential elements of the most adequate systems of today, to set out what is generally accepted as being good principle and practice in the treatment of prisoners and the management of institutions.

2. In view of the great variety of legal, social, economic and geographical conditions of the world, it is evident that not all of the rules are capable of application in all places and at all times. They should, however, serve to stimulate a constant endeavor to overcome practical difficulties in the way of their application, in the knowledge that they represent, as a whole, the minimum conditions which are accepted as suitable by the United Nations.

3. On the other hand, the rules cover a field in which thought is constantly developing. They are not intended to preclude experiment and practices, provided these are in harmony with the principles and seek to further the purposes which derive from the text of the rules as a whole. It will always be justifiable for the central prison administration to authorize departures from the rules in this spirit.

4. (1) Part I of the rules covers the general management of institutions, and is applicable to all categories of prisoners, criminal or civil, untried or convicted, including prisoners subject to "security measures" or corrective measures ordered by the judge.

(2) Part II contains rules applicable only to the special categories dealt with in each section. Nevertheless, the rules under section A, applicable to prisoners under sentence, shall be equally applicable to categories of prisoners dealt with in sections B, C and D, provided they do not conflict with the rules governing those categories and are for their benefit.

5. (1) The rules do not seek to regulate the management of institutions set aside for young persons such as Borstal institutions or correctional schools, but in general part I would be equally applicable in such institutions.

(2) The category of young prisoners should include at least all young persons who come within the jurisdiction of juvenile courts. As a rule, such young persons should not be sentenced to imprisonment.

PART I. RULES OF GENERAL APPLICATION

Basic principle

6. (1) The following rules shall be applied impartially. There shall be no discrimination on grounds of race, colour, sex, language, religion, political or other opinion, national or social origin, property, birth or other status.

(2) On the other hand, it is necessary to respect the religious beliefs and moral precepts of the group to which a prisoner belongs.

Register

7. (1) In every place where persons are imprisoned there shall be kept a bound registration book with numbered pages in which shall be entered in respect of each prisoner received:

(a) Information concerning his identity;

(b) The reasons for his commitment and the authority therefor;

(c) The day and hour of his admission and release.

(2) No person shall be received in an institution without a valid commitment order of which the details shall have been previously entered in the register.

Separation of categories

8. The different categories of prisoners shall be kept in separate institutions or parts of institutions taking account of their sex, age, criminal record, the legal reason for their detention and the necessities of their treatment. Thus,

(a) Men and women shall so far as possible be detained in separate institutions; in an institution which receives both men and women the whole of the premises allocated to women shall be entirely separate;

(b) Untried prisoners shall be kept separate from convicted prisoners;

(c) Persons imprisoned for debt and other civil prisoners shall be kept separate from persons imprisoned by reason of a criminal offence;

(d) Young prisoners shall be kept separate from adults.

Accommodation

9. (1) Where sleeping accommodation is in individual cells or rooms, each prisoner shall occupy by night a cell or room by himself. If for special reasons, such as temporary overcrowding, it becomes necessary for the central prison administration to make an exception to this rule, it is not desirable to have two prisoners in a cell or room.

(2) Where dormitories are used, they shall be occupied by prisoners carefully selected as being suitable to associate with one another in these conditions. There shall be regular supervision by night, in keeping with the nature of the institution.

10. All accommodation provided for the use of prisoners and in particular all sleeping accommodation shall meet all requirements of health, due regard being paid to climatic conditions and particularly to cubic content of air, minimum floor space, lighting, heating and ventilation.

11. In all places where prisoners are required to live or work,

(a) The windows shall be large enough to enable the prisoners to read or work by natural light, and shall be so constructed that they can allow the entrance of fresh air whether or not there is artificial ventilation;

(b) Artificial light shall be provided sufficient for the prisoners to read or work without injury to eyesight.

12. The sanitary installations shall be adequate to enable every prisoner to comply with the needs of nature when necessary and in a clean and decent manner.

13. Adequate bathing and shower installations shall be provided so that every prisoner may be enabled and required to have a bath or shower, at a temperature suitable to the climate, as frequently as necessary for general hygiene according to season and geographical region, but at least once a week in a temperate climate.

14. All parts of an institution regularly used by prisoners shall be properly maintained and kept scrupulously clean at all times.

Personal hygiene

15. Prisoners shall be required to keep their persons clean, and to this end they shall be provided with water and with such toilet articles as are necessary for health and cleanliness.

16. In order that prisoners may maintain a good appearance compatible with their self-respect, facilities shall be provided for the proper care of the hair and beard, and men shall be enabled to shave regularly.

Clothing and bedding

17. (1) Every prisoner who is not allowed to wear his own clothing shall be provided with an outfit of clothing suitable for the climate and adequate to keep him in good health. Such clothing shall in no manner be degrading or humiliating.

(2) All clothing shall be clean and kept in proper condition. Underclothing shall be changed and washed as often as necessary for the maintenance of hygiene.

(3) In exceptional circumstances, whenever a prisoner is removed outside the institution for an authorized purpose, he shall be allowed to wear his own clothing or other inconspicuous clothing.

18. If prisoners are allowed to wear their own clothing, arrangements shall be made on their admission to the institution to ensure that it shall be clean and fit for use.

19. Every prisoner shall, in accordance with local or national standards, be provided with a separate bed, and with separate and sufficient bedding which shall be clean when issued, kept in good order and changed often enough to ensure its cleanliness.

Food

20. (1) Every prisoner shall be provided by the administration at the usual hours with food of nutritional value adequate for health and strength, of wholesome quality and well prepared and served.

(2) Drinking water shall be available to every prisoner whenever he needs it.

Exercise and sport

21. (1) Every prisoner who is not employed in out-door work shall have at least one hour of suitable exercise in the open air daily if the weather permits.

(2) Young prisoners, and others of suitable age and physique, shall receive physical and recreational training during the period of exercise. To this end space, installations and equipment should be provided.

Medical services

22. (1) At every institution there shall be available the services of at least one qualified medical officer who should have some knowledge of psychiatry. The medical services should be organized in close relationship to the general health administration of the community or nation. They shall include a psychiatric service for the diagnosis and, in proper cases, the treatment of states of mental abnormality.

(2) Sick prisoners who require specialist treatment shall be transferred to specialized institutions or to civil hospitals. Where hospital facilities are provided in an institution, their equipment, furnishings and pharmaceutical supplies shall be proper for the medical care and treatment of sick prisoners, and there shall be a staff of suitably trained officers.

(3) The services of a qualified dental officer shall be available to every prisoner.

23. (1) In women's institutions there shall be special accommodation for all necessary pre-natal and post-natal care and treatment. Arrangements shall be made wherever practicable for children to be born in a hospital outside the institution. If a child is born in prison, this fact shall not be mentioned in the birth certificate.

(2) Where nursing infants are allowed to remain in the institution with their mothers, provision shall be made for a nursery staffed by qualified persons, where the infants shall be placed when they are not in the care of their mothers.

24. The medical officer shall see and examine every prisoner as soon as possible after his admission and thereafter as necessary, with a view particularly to the discovery of physical or mental illness and the taking of all necessary measures; the segregation of prisoners suspected of infectious or contagious conditions; the noting of physical or mental defects which might hamper rehabilitation, and the determination of the physical capacity of every prisoner for work.

25. (1) The medical officer shall have the care of the physical and mental health of the prisoners and should daily see all sick prisoners, all who complain of illness, and any prisoner to whom his attention is specially directed.

(2) The medical officer shall report to the director whenever he considers that a prisoner's physical or mental health has been or will be injuriously affected by continued imprisonment or by any condition of imprisonment.

26. (1) The medical officer shall regularly inspect and advise the director upon:

(a) The quantity, quality, preparation and service of food;

(b) The hygiene and cleanliness of the institution and the prisoners;

(c) The sanitation, heating, lighting and ventilation of the institution;

(d) The suitability and cleanliness of the prisoners' clothing and bedding;

(e) The observance of the rules concerning physical education and sports, in cases where there is no technical personnel in charge of these activities.

(2) The director shall take into consideration the reports and advice that the medical officer submits according to rules 25 (2) and 26 and, in case he concurs with the recommendations made, shall take immediate steps to give effect to those recommendations; if they are not within his competence or if he does not concur with them, he shall immediately submit his own report and the advice of the medical officer to higher authority.

Discipline and punishment

27. Discipline and order shall be maintained with firmness, but with no more restriction than is necessary for safe custody and well-ordered community life.

28. (1) No prisoner shall be employed, in the service of the institution, in any disciplinary capacity.

(2) This rule shall not, however, impede the proper functioning of systems based on self-government, under which specified social, educational or sports activities or responsibilities are entrusted, under supervision, to prisoners who are formed into groups for the purposes of treatment.

29. The following shall always be determined by the law or by the regulation of the competent administrative authority:

(a) Conduct constituting a disciplinary offence;

(b) The types and duration of punishment which may be inflicted;

(c) The authority competent to impose such punishment.

30. (1) No prisoner shall be punished except in accordance with the terms of such law or regulation, and never twice for the same offence.

(2) No prisoner shall be punished unless he has been informed of the offence alleged against him and given a proper opportunity of presenting his defence. The competent authority shall conduct a thorough examination of the case.

(3) Where necessary and practicable the prisoner shall be allowed to make his defence through an interpreter.

31. Corporal punishment, punishment by placing in a dark cell, and all cruel, inhuman or degrading punishments shall be completely prohibited as punishments for disciplinary offenses.

32. (1) Punishment by close confinement or reduction of diet shall never be inflicted unless the medical officer has examined the prisoner and certified in writing that he is fit to sustain it.

(2) The same shall apply to any other punishment that may be prejudicial to the physical or mental health of a prisoner. In no case may such punishment be contrary to or depart from the principle stated in rule 31.

(3) The medical officer shall visit daily prisoners undergoing such punishments and shall advise the director if he considers the termination or alteration of the punishment necessary on grounds of physical or mental health.

Instruments of restraint

33. Instruments of restraint, such as handcuffs, chains, irons and strait-jackets, shall never be applied as a punishment. Furthermore, chains or irons shall not be used as restraints. Other instruments of restraint shall not be used except in the following circumstances:

(a) As a precaution against escape during a transfer, provided that they shall be removed when the prisoner appears before a judicial or administrative authority;

(b) On medical grounds by direction of the medical officer;

(c) By order of the director, if other methods of control fail, in order to prevent a prisoner from injuring himself or others or from damaging property; in such instances the director shall at once consult the medical officer and report to the higher administrative authority.

34. The patterns and manner of use of instruments of restraint shall be decided by the central prison administration. Such instruments must not be applied for any longer time than is strictly necessary.

Information to and complaints by prisoners

35. (1) Every prisoner on admission shall be provided with written information about the regulations governing the treatment of prisoners of his category, the disciplinary requirements of the institution, the authorized methods of seeking information and making complaints, and all such other matters as are necessary to enable him to understand both his rights and his obligations and to adapt himself to the life of the institution.

(2) If a prisoner is illiterate, the aforesaid information shall be conveyed to him orally.

36. (1) Every prisoner shall have the opportunity each week day of making requests or complaints to the director of the institution or the officer authorized to represent him.

(2) It shall be possible to make requests or complaints to the inspector of prisons during his inspection. The prisoner shall have the opportunity to talk to the inspector or to any other inspecting officer without the director or other members of the staff being present.

(3) Every prisoner shall be allowed to make a request or complaint, without censorship as to substance but in proper form, to the central prison administration, the judicial authority or other proper authorities through approved channels.

(4) Unless it is evidently frivolous or groundless, every request or complaint shall be promptly dealt with and replied to without undue delay.

Contact with the outside world

37. Prisoners shall be allowed under necessary supervision to communicate with their family and reputable friends at regular intervals, both by correspondence and by receiving visits.

38. (1) Prisoners who are foreign nationals shall be allowed reasonable facilities to communicate with the diplomatic and consular representatives of the State to which they belong.

(2) Prisoners who are nationals of States without diplomatic or consular representation in the country and refugees or stateless persons shall be allowed similar facilities to communicate with the diplomatic representative of the State which takes charge of their interests or any national or international authority whose task it is to protect such persons.

39. Prisoners shall be kept informed regularly of the more important items of news by the reading of newspapers, periodicals or special institutional publications, by hearing wireless transmissions, by lectures, or by any similar means as authorized or controlled by the administration.

Books

40. Every institution shall have a library for the use of all categories of prisoners, adequately stocked with both recreational and instructional books, and prisoners shall be encouraged to make full use of it.

Religion

41. (1) If the institution contains a sufficient number of prisoners of the same religion, a qualified representative of that religion shall be appointed or approved. If the number of prisoners justifies it and conditions permit, the arrangement should be on a full-time basis.

(2) A qualified representative appointed or approved under paragraph (1) shall be allowed to hold regular services and to pay pastoral visits in private to prisoners of his religion at proper times.

(3) Access to a qualified representative of any religion shall not be refused to any prisoner. On the other hand, if any prisoner should object to a visit of any religious representative, his attitude shall be fully respected.

42. So far as practicable, every prisoner shall be allowed to satisfy the needs of his religious life by attending the services provided in the institution and having in his possession the books of religious observance and instruction of his denomination.

Retention of prisoners' property

43. (1) All money, valuables, clothing and other effects belonging to a prisoner which under the regulations of the institution he is not allowed to retain shall on his admission to the institution be placed in safe custody. An inventory thereof shall be signed by the prisoner. Steps shall be taken to keep them in good condition.

(2) On the release of the prisoner all such articles and money shall be returned to him except in so far as he has been authorized to spend money or send any

such property out of the institution, or it has been found necessary on hygienic grounds to destroy any article of clothing. The prisoner shall sign a receipt for the articles and money returned to him.

(3) Any money or effects received for a prisoner from outside shall be treated in the same way.

(4) If a prisoner brings in any drugs or medicine, the medical officer shall decide what use shall be made of them.

Notification of death, illness, transfer, etc.

44. (1) Upon the death or serious illness of, or serious injury to a prisoner, or his removal to an institution for the treatment of mental affections, the director shall at once inform the spouse, if the prisoner is married, or the nearest relative and shall in any event inform any other person previously designated by the prisoner.

(2) A prisoner shall be informed at once of the death or serious illness of any near relative. In case of the critical illness of a near relative, the prisoner should be authorized, whenever circumstances allow, to go to his bedside either under escort or alone.

(3) Every prisoner shall have the right to inform at once his family of his imprisonment or his transfer to another institution.

Removal of prisoners

45. (1) When prisoners are being removed to or from an institution, they shall be exposed to public view as little as possible, and proper safeguards shall be adopted to protect them from insult, curiosity and publicity in any form.

(2) The transport of prisoners in conveyances with inadequate ventilation or light, or in any way which would subject them to unnecessary physical hardship, shall be prohibited.

(3) The transport of prisoners shall be carried out at the expense of the administration and equal conditions shall obtain for all of them.

Institutional personnel

46. (1) The prison administration, shall provide for the careful selection of every grade of the personnel, since it is on their integrity, humanity, professional capacity and personal suitability for the work that the proper administration of the institutions depends.

(2) The prison administration shall constantly seek to awaken and maintain in the minds both of the personnel and of the public the conviction that this work is a social service of great importance, and to this end all appropriate means of informing the public should be used.

(3) To secure the foregoing ends, personnel shall be appointed on a full-time basis as professional prison officers and have civil service status with security of

tenure subject only to good conduct, efficiency and physical fitness. Salaries shall be adequate to attract and retain suitable men and women; employment benefits and conditions of service shall be favourable in view of the exacting nature of the work.

47. (1) The personnel shall possess an adequate standard of education and intelligence.

(2) Before entering on duty, the personnel shall be given a course of training in their general and specific duties and be required to pass theoretical and practical tests.

(3) After entering on duty and during their career, the personnel shall maintain and improve their knowledge and professional capacity by attending courses of in-service training to be organized at suitable intervals.

48. All members of the personnel shall at all times so conduct themselves and perform their duties as to influence the prisoners for good by their examples and to command their respect.

49. (1) So far as possible, the personnel shall include a sufficient number of specialists such as psychiatrists, psychologists, social workers, teachers and trade instructors.

(2) The services of social workers, teachers and trade instructors shall be secured on a permanent basis, without thereby excluding part-time or voluntary workers.

50. (1) The director of an institution should be adequately qualified for his task by character, administrative ability, suitable training and experience.

(2) He shall devote his entire time to his official duties and shall not be appointed on a part-time basis.

(3) He shall reside on the premises of the institution or in its immediate vicinity.

(4) When two or more institutions are under the authority of one director, he shall visit each of them at frequent intervals. A responsible resident official shall be in charge of each of these institutions.

51. (1) The director, his deputy, and the majority of the other personnel of the institution shall be able to speak the language of the greatest number of prisoners, or a language understood by the greatest number of them.

(2) Whenever necessary, the services of an interpreter shall be used.

52. (1) In institutions which are large enough to require the services of one or more full-time medical officers, at least one of them shall reside on the premises of the institution or in its immediate vicinity.

(2) In other institutions the medical officer shall visit daily and shall reside near enough to be able to attend without delay in cases of urgency.

53. (1) In an institution for both men and women, the part of the institution set aside for women shall be under the authority of a responsible woman officer who shall have the custody of the keys of all that part of the institution.

(2) No male member of the staff shall enter the part of the institution set aside for women unless accompanied by a woman officer.

(3) Women prisoners shall be attended and supervised only by women officers. This does not, however, preclude male members of the staff, particularly doctors and teachers, from carrying out their professional duties in institutions or parts of institutions set aside for women.

54. (1) Officers of the institutions shall not, in their relations with the prisoners, use force except in self-defence or in cases of attempted escape, or active or passive physical resistance to an order based on law or regulations. Officers who have recourse to force must use no more than is strictly necessary and must report the incident immediately to the director of the institution.

(2) Prison officers shall be given special physical training to enable them to restrain aggressive prisoners.

(3) Except in special circumstances, staff performing duties which bring them into direct contact with prisoners should not be armed. Furthermore, staff should in no circumstances be provided with arms unless they have been trained in their use.

Inspection

55. There shall be a regular inspection of penal institutions and services by qualified and experienced inspectors appointed by a competent authority. Their task shall be in particular to ensure that these institutions are administered in accordance with existing laws and regulations and with a view to bringing about the objectives of penal and correctional services.

PART II. RULES APPLICABLE TO SPECIAL CATEGORIES

A. Prisoners Under Sentence

Guiding principles

56. The guiding principles hereafter are intended to show the spirit in which penal institutions should be administered and the purposes at which they should aim, in accordance with the declaration made under Preliminary Observation 1 of the present text.

57. Imprisonment and other measures which result in cutting off an offender from the outside world are afflictive by the very fact of taking from the person the right of self-determination by depriving him of his liberty. Therefore the prison system shall not, except as incidental to justifiable segregation or the maintenance of discipline, aggravate the suffering inherent in such a situation.

58. The purpose and justification of a sentence of imprisonment or a similar measure deprivative of liberty is ultimately to protect society against crime. This end can only be achieved if the period of imprisonment is used to ensure, so far as

possible, that upon his return to society the offender is not only willing but able to lead a law-abiding and self-supporting life.

59. To this end, the institution should utilize all the remedial, educational, moral, spiritual and other forces and forms of assistance which are appropriate and available, and should seek to apply them according to the individual treatment needs of the prisoners.

60. (1) The régime of the institution should seek to minimize any differences between prison life and life at liberty which tend to lessen the responsibility of the prisoners or the respect due to their dignity as human beings.

(2) Before the completion of the sentence, it is desirable that the necessary steps be taken to ensure for the prisoner a gradual return to life in society. This aim may be achieved, depending on the case, by a pre-release régime organized in the same institution or in another appropriate institution, or by release on trial under some kind of supervision which must not be entrusted to the police but should be combined with effective social aid.

61. The treatment of prisoners should emphasize not their exclusion from the community, but their continuing part in it. Community agencies should, therefore, be enlisted wherever possible to assist the staff of the institution in the task of social rehabilitation of the prisoners. There should be in connexion with every institution social workers charged with the duty of maintaining and improving all desirable relations of a prisoner with his family and with valuable social agencies. Steps should be taken to safeguard, to the maximum extent compatible with the law and the sentence, the rights relating to civil interests, social security rights and other social benefits of prisoners.

62. The medical services of the institution shall seek to detect and shall treat any physical or mental illnesses or defects which may hamper a prisoner's rehabilitation. All necessary medical, surgical and psychiatric services shall be provided to that end.

63. (1) The fulfilment of these principles requires individualization of treatment and for this purpose a flexible system of classifying prisoners in groups; it is therefore desirable that such groups should be distributed in separate institutions suitable for the treatment of each group.

(2) These institutions need not provide the same degree of security for every group. It is desirable to provide varying degrees of security according to the needs of different groups. Open institutions, by the very fact that they provide no physical security against escape but rely on the self-discipline of the inmates, provide the conditions most favourable to rehabilitation for carefully selected prisoners.

(3) It is desirable that the number of prisoners in closed institutions should not be so large that the individualization of treatment is hindered. In some countries it is considered that the population of such institutions should not exceed five hundred. In open institutions the population should be as small as possible.

(4) On the other hand, it is undesirable to maintain prisons which are so small that proper facilities cannot be provided.

64. The duty of society does not end with a prisoner's release. There should, therefore, be governmental or private agencies capable of lending the released prisoner efficient after-care directed towards the lessening of prejudice against him and towards his social rehabilitation.

Treatment

65. The treatment of persons sentenced to imprisonment or a similar measure shall have as its purpose, so far as the length of the sentence permits, to establish in them the will to lead law-abiding and self-supporting lives after their release and to fit them to do so. The treatment shall be such as will encourage their self-respect and develop their sense of responsibility.

66. (1) To these ends, all appropriate means shall be used, including religious care in the countries where this is possible, education, vocational guidance and training, social casework, employment counselling, physical development and strengthening of moral character, in accordance with the individual needs of each prisoner, taking account of his social and criminal history, his physical and mental capacities and aptitudes, his personal temperament, the length of his sentence and his prospects after release.

(2) For every prisoner with a sentence of suitable length, the director shall receive, as soon as possible after his admission, full reports on the matters referred to in the foregoing paragraph. Such reports shall always include a report by a medical officer, wherever possible qualified in psychiatry, on the physical and mental condition of the prisoner.

(3) The reports and other relevant documents shall be placed in an individual file. This file shall be kept up to date and classified in such a way that it can be consulted by the responsible personnel whenever the need arises.

Classification and individualization

67. The purposes of classification shall be:

(a) To separate from others those prisoners who, by reason of their criminal records or bad characters, are likely to exercise a bad influence;

(b) To divide the prisoners into classes in order to facilitate their treatment with a view to their social rehabilitation.

68. So far as possible separate institutions or separate sections of an institution shall be used for the treatment of the different classes of prisoners.

69. As soon as possible after admission and after a study of the personality of each prisoner with a sentence of suitable length, a programme of treatment shall be prepared for him in the light of the knowledge obtained about his individual needs, his capacities and dispositions.

Privileges

70. Systems of privileges appropriate for the different classes of prisoners and the different methods of treatment shall be established at every institution, in order to encourage good conduct, develop a sense of responsibility and secure the interest and cooperation of the prisoners in their treatment.

Work

71. (1) Prison labour must not be of an afflictive nature.

(2) All prisoners under sentence shall be required to work, subject to their physical and mental fitness as determined by the medical officer.

(3) Sufficient work of a useful nature shall be provided to keep prisoners actively employed for a normal working day.

(4) So far as possible the work provided shall be such as will maintain or increase the prisoners' ability to earn an honest living after release.

(5) Vocational training in useful trades shall be provided for prisoners able to profit thereby and especially for young prisoners.

(6) Within the limits compatible with proper vocational selection and with the requirements of institutional administration and discipline, the prisoners shall be able to choose the type of work they wish to perform.

72. (1) The organization and methods of work in the institutions shall resemble as closely as possible those of similar work outside institutions, so as to prepare prisoners for the conditions of normal occupational life.

(2) The interests of the prisoners and of their vocational training, however, must not be subordinated to the purpose of making a financial profit from an industry in the institution.

73. (1) Preferably institutional industries and farms should be operated directly by the administration and not by private contractors.

(2) Where prisoners are employed in work not controlled by the administration, they shall always be under the supervision of the institution's personnel. Unless the work is for other departments of the government the full normal wages for such work shall be paid to the administration by the persons to whom the labour is supplied, account being taken of the output of the prisoners.

74. (1) The precautions laid down to protect the safety and health of free workmen shall be equally observed in institutions.

(2) Provision shall be made to indemnify prisoners against industrial injury, including occupational disease, on terms not less favourable than those extended by law to free workmen.

75. (1) The maximum daily and weekly working hours of the prisoners shall be fixed by law or by administration regulation, taking into account local rules or custom in regard to the employment of free workmen.

(2) The hours so fixed shall leave one rest day a week and sufficient time for

education and other activities required as part of the treatment and rehabilitation of the prisoners.

76. (1) There shall be a system of equitable remuneration of the work of prisoners.

(2) Under the system prisoners shall be allowed to spend at least a part of their earnings on approved articles for their own use and to send a part of their earnings to their family.

(3) The system should also provide that a part of the earnings should be set aside by the administration so as to constitute a savings fund to be handed over to the prisoner on his release.

Education and recreation

77. (1) Provision shall be made for the further education of all prisoners capable of profiting thereby, including religious instruction in the countries where this is possible. The education of illiterates and young prisoners shall be compulsory and special attention shall be paid to it by the administration.

(2) So far as practicable, the education of prisoners shall be integrated with the educational system of the country so that after their release they may continue their education without difficulty.

78. Recreational and cultural activities shall be provided in all institutions for the benefit of the mental and physical health of prisoners.

Social relations and after-care

79. Special attention shall be paid to the maintenance and improvement of such relations between a prisoner and his family as are desirable in the best interests of both.

80. From the beginning of a prisoner's sentence consideration shall be given to his future after release and he shall be encouraged and assisted to maintain or establish such relations with persons or agencies outside the institution as may promote the best interests of his family and his own social rehabilitation.

81. (1) Services and agencies, governmental or otherwise, which assist released prisoners to re-establish themselves in society shall ensure, so far as is possible and necessary, that released prisoners be provided with appropriate documents and identification papers, have suitable homes and work to go to, are suitably and adequately clothed having regard to the climate and season, and have sufficient means to reach their destination and maintain themselves in the period immediately following their release.

(2) The approved representatives of such agencies shall have all necessary access to the institution and to prisoners and shall be taken into consultation as to the future of a prisoner from the beginning of his sentence.

(3) It is desirable that the activities of such agencies shall be centralized or co-ordinated as far as possible in order to secure the best use of their efforts.

B. Insane and Mentally Abnormal Prisoners

82. (1) Persons who are found to be insane shall not be detained in prisons and arrangements shall be made to remove them to mental institutions as soon as possible.

(2) Prisoners who suffer from other mental diseases or abnormalities shall be observed and treated in specialized institutions under medical management.

(3) During their stay in a prison, such prisoners shall be placed under the special supervision of a medical officer.

(4) The medical or psychiatric service of the penal institutions shall provide for the psychiatric treatment of all other prisoners who are in need of such treatment.

83. It is desirable that steps should be taken, by arrangement with the appropriate agencies, to ensure if necessary the continuation of psychiatric treatment after release and the provision of social-psychiatric after-care.

C. Prisoners Under Arrest or Awaiting Trial

84. (1) Persons arrested or imprisoned by reason of a criminal charge against them, who are detained either in police custody or in prison custody (jail) but have not yet been tried and sentenced, will be referred to as "untried prisoners" hereinafter in these rules.

(2) Unconvicted prisoners are presumed to be innocent and shall be treated as such.

(3) Without prejudice to legal rules for the protection of individual liberty or prescribing the procedure to be observed in respect of untried prisoners, these prisoners shall benefit by a special régime which is described in the following rules in its essential requirements only.

85. (1) Untried prisoners shall be kept separate from convicted prisoners.

(2) Young untried prisoners shall be kept separate from adults and shall in principle be detained in separate institutions.

86. Untried prisoners shall sleep singly in separate rooms, with the reservation of different local custom in respect of the climate.

87. Within the limits compatible with the good order of the institution, untried prisoners may, if they so desire, have their food procured at their own expense from the outside, either through the administration or through their family or friends. Otherwise, the administration shall provide their food.

88. (1) An untried prisoner shall be allowed to wear his own clothing if it is clean and suitable.

(2) If he wears prison dress, it shall be different from that supplied to convicted prisoners.

89. An untried prisoner shall always be offered opportunity to work, but shall not be required to work. If he chooses to work, he shall be paid for it.

90. An untried prisoner shall be allowed to procure at his own expense or at

the expense of a third party such books, newspapers, writing materials and other means of occupation as are compatible with the interests of the administration of justice and the security and good order of the institution.

91. An untried prisoner shall be allowed to be visited and treated by his own doctor or dentist if there is reasonable ground for his application and he is able to pay any expenses incurred.

92. An untried prisoner shall be allowed to inform immediately his family of his detention and shall be given all reasonable facilities for communicating with his family and friends, and for receiving visits from them, subject only to such restrictions and supervision as are necessary in the interests of the administration of justice and of the security and good order of the institution.

93. For the purposes of his defence, an untried prisoner shall be allowed to apply for free legal aid where such aid is available, and to receive visits from his legal adviser with a view to his defence and to prepare and hand to him confidential instructions. For these purposes, he shall if he so desires be supplied with writing material. Interviews between the prisoner and his legal adviser may be within sight but not within the hearing of a police or institution official.

D. Civil Prisoners

94. In countries where the law permits imprisonment for debt or by order of a court under any other non-criminal process, persons so imprisoned shall not be subjected to any greater restriction or severity than is necessary to ensure safe custody and good order. Their treatment shall be not less favourable than that of untried prisoners, with the reservation, however, that they may possibly be required to work.

B. SELECTION AND TRAINING OF PERSONNEL FOR PENAL AND CORRECTIONAL INSTITUTIONS

Resolution adopted on 1 September 1955

The First United Nations Congress on the Prevention of Crime and the Treatment of Offenders,

Having adopted recommendations, annexed to the present resolution, on the question of the selection and training of personnel for penal and correctional institutions,

1. *Requests* the Secretary-General, in accordance with paragraph *(d)* of the annex to resolution 415(V) of the General Assembly of the United Nations, to submit these recommendations to the Social Commission of the Economic and Social Council for approval;

2. *Expresses* the hope that the Economic and Social Council will endorse these

recommendations and draw them to the attention of governments, recommending that governments take them as fully as possible into account in their practice and when considering legislative and administrative reforms;

3. *Expresses* also the wish that the Economic and Social Council request the Secretary-General to give the widest publicity to these recommendations and authorize him to collect periodically information on the matter from the various countries, and to publish such information.

Annex

Recommendations on the Selection and Training of Personnel For Penal and Correctional Institutions

A. Modern Conception of Prison Service

I. *Prison service in the nature of a social service*

(1) Attention is drawn to the change in the nature of prison staffs which results from the development in the conception of their duty from that of guards to that of members of an important social service demanding ability, appropriate training and good team work on the part of every member.

(2) An effort should be made to arouse and keep alive in the minds both of the public and of the staff an understanding of the nature of modern prison service. For this purpose all appropriate means of informing the public should be used.

II. *Specialization of functions*

(1) This new conception is reflected in the tendency to add to the staff an increasing number of specialists, such as doctors, psychiatrists, psychologists, social workers, teachers, technical instructors.

(2) This is a healthy tendency and it is recommended that it should be favourably considered by governments even though additional expense would be involved.

III. *Co-ordination*

(1) The increasing specialization may, however, hamper an integrated approach to the treatment of prisoners and present problems in the co-ordination of the work of the various types of specialized staff.

(2) Consequently, in the treatment of prisoners, it is necessary to ensure that all the specialists concerned work together as a team.

(3) It is also considered necessary to ensure, by the appointment of a co-

ordinating committee or otherwise, that all the specialized services follow a uniform approach. In this way the members of the staff will also have the advantage of gaining a clearer insight into the various aspects of the problems involved.

B. Status of Staff and Conditions of Service

IV. *Civil service status*

Full-time prison staff should have the status of civil servants, that is, they should:

(a) Be employed by the government of the country or State and hence be governed by civil service rules;

(b) Be recruited according to certain rules of selection such as competitive examination;

(c) Have security of tenure subject only to good conduct, efficiency and physical fitness;

(d) Have permanent status and be entitled to the advantages of a civil service career in such matters as promotion, social security, allowances, and retirement or pension benefits.

V. *Full-time employment*

(1) Prison staff, with the exception of certain professional and technical grades, should devote their entire time to their duties and therefore be appointed on a full-time basis.

(2) In particular, the post of director of an institution must not be a part-time appointment.

(3) The services of social workers, teachers and trade instructors should be secured on a permanent basis, without thereby excluding part-time workers.

VI. *Conditions of service in general*

(1) The conditions of service of institutional staff should be sufficient to attract and retain the best qualified persons.

(2) Salaries and other employment benefits should not be arbitrarily tied to those of other public servants but should be related to the work to be performed in a modern prison system, which is complex and arduous and is in the nature of an important social service.

(3) Sufficient and suitable living quarters should be provided for the prison staff in the vicinity of the institution.

VII. *Non-military organization of the staff*

(1) Prison staff should be organized on civilian lines with a division into ranks or grades as this type of administration requires.

(2) Custodial staff should be organized in accordance with the disciplinary rules of the penal institution in order to maintain the necessary grade distinctions and order.

(3) Staff should be specially recruited and not seconded from the armed forces or police or other public services.

VIII. *Carrying of arms*

(1) Except in special circumstances, staff performing duties which bring them into direct contact with prisoners should not be armed.

(2) Staff should in no circumstances be provided with arms unless they have been trained in their use.

(3) It is desirable that prison staff should be responsible for guarding the enclosure of the institution.

C. Recruitment of Staff

IX. *Competent authority and general administrative methods*

(1) As far as possible recruitment should be centralized, in conformity with the structure of each State, and be under the direction of the superior or central prison administration.

(2) Where other State bodies such as a civil service commission are responsible for recruitment, the prison administration should not be required to accept a candidate whom they do not regard as suitable.

(3) Provision should be made to exclude political influence in appointments to the staff of the prison service.

X. *General conditions of recruitment*

(1) The prison administration should be particularly careful in the recruitment of staff, selecting only persons having the requisite qualities of integrity, humanitarian approach, competence and physical fitness.

(2) Members of the staff should be able to speak the language of the greatest number of prisoners or a language understood by the greatest number of them.

XI. *Custodial staff*

(1) The educational standards and intelligence of this staff should be sufficient to enable them to carry out their duties effectively and to profit by whatever in-service training courses are provided.

(2) Suitable intelligence, vocational and physical tests for the scientific evaluation of the candidates' capacities are recommended in addition to the relevant competitive examinations.

(3) Candidates who have been admitted should serve a probationary period to allow the competent authorities to form an opinion of their personality, character and ability.

XII. *Higher administration*

Special care should be taken in the appointment of persons who are to fill posts in the higher administration of the prison services; only persons who are suitably trained and have sufficient knowledge and experience should be considered.

XIII. *Directors of executive staff*

(1) The directors or assistant directors of institutions should be adequately qualified for their functions by reason of their character, administrative ability, training and experience.

(2) They should have a good educational background and a vocation for the work. The administration should endeavour to attract persons with specialized training which offers adequate preparation for prison service.

XIV. *Specialized and administrative staff*

(1) The staff performing specialized functions, including administrative functions, should possess the professional or technical qualifications required for each of the various functions in question.

(2) The recruitment of specialized staff should therefore be based on the professional training diplomas or university degrees evidencing their special training.

(3) It is recommended that preference should be given to candidates who, in addition to such professional qualifications, have a second degree or qualification, or specialized experience in prison work.

XV. *Staff of women's institutions*

The staff of women's institutions should consist of women. This does not, however, preclude male members of the staff, particularly doctors and teachers, from carrying out their professional duties in institutions or parts of institutions set aside for women. Female staff, whether lay or religious, should, as far as possible, possess the same qualifications as those required for appointment to institutions for men.

D. Professional Training

XVI. *Training prior to final appointment*

Before entering on duty, staff should be given a course of training in their general duties, with a view particularly to social problems, and in their specific duties and be required to pass theoretical and practical examinations.

XVII. *Custodial staff*

(1) A programme of intensive professional training for custodial staff is recommended. The following might serve as an example for the organization of such training in three stages:

(2) The first stage should take place in a penal institution, its aim being to familiarize the candidate with the special problems of the profession and at the same time to ascertain whether he possesses the necessary qualities. During this initial phase, the candidate should not be given any responsibility, and his work should be constantly supervised by a member of the regular staff. The director should arrange an elementary course in practical subjects for the candidates.

(3) During the second stage, the candidate should attend a school or course organized by the superior or central prison administration, which should be responsible for the theoretical and practical training of officers in professional subjects. Special attention should be paid to the technique of relations with the prisoners, based on the elementary principles of psychology and criminology. The training courses should moreover comprise lessons of the elements of penology, prison administration, penal law and related matters.

(4) It is desirable that during the first two stages candidates should be admitted and trained in groups, so as to obviate the possibility of their being prematurely employed in the service and to facilitate the organization of courses of training.

(5) The third stage, intended for candidates who have satisfactorily completed the first two and shown the greatest interest and a vocation for the service, should consist of actual service during which they will be expected to show that they possess all the requisite qualifications. They should also be offered an opportunity to attend more advanced training courses in psychology, criminology, penal law, penology and related subjects.

XVIII. *Directors or executive staff*

(1) As methods vary greatly from country to country at the present time, the necessity for adequate training, which directors and assistant directors should have received prior to their appointment in conformity with paragraph XIII above, should be recognized as a general rule.

(2) Where persons from the outside with no previous experience of the work

but with proved experience in similar fields are recruited as directors or assistant directors, they should, before taking up their duties, receive theoretical training and gain practical experience of prison work for a reasonable period, it being understood that a diploma granted by a specialized vocational school or a university degree in a relevant subject may be considered as sufficient theoretical training.

XIX. *Specialized staff*

The initial training to be required from specialized staff is determined by the conditions of recruitment, as described in paragraph XIV above.

XX. *Regional training institutes for prison personnel*

The establishment of regional institutes for the training of the staff of penal and correctional institutions should be encouraged.

XXI. *Physical training and instruction in the use of arms*

(1) Prison officers shall be given special physical training to enable them to restrain aggressive prisoners by the means prescribed by the authorities in accordance with the relevant rules and regulations.

(2) Officers who are provided with arms shall be trained in their use and instructed in the regulations governing their use.

XXII. *In-service training*

(1) After taking up their duties and during their career, staff should maintain and improve their knowledge and professional capacity by attending advanced courses of in-service training which are to be organized periodically.

(2) The in-service training of custodial staff should be concerned with questions of principle and technique rather than solely with rules and regulations.

(3) Whenever any type of special training is required it should be at the expense of the State and those undergoing training should receive the pay and allowances of their grade. Supplementary training to fit the officer for promotion may be at the expense of the officer and in his own time.

XXIII. *Discussion groups, visits to institutions, seminars for senior personnel*

(1) For senior staff, group discussions are recommended on matters of practical interest rather than on academic subjects, combined with visits to different types of institutions, including those outside the penal system. It would be desirable to invite specialists from other countries to participate in such meetings.

(2) It is also recommended that exchanges be organized between various countries in order to allow senior personnel to obtain practical experience in institutions of other countries.

XXIV. *Joint consultation, visits and meetings for all grades of staff*

(1) Methods of joint consultation should be established to enable all grades of prison personnel to express their opinion on the methods used in the treatment of prisoners. Moreover, lectures, visits to other institutions and, if possible, regular seminars should be organized for all categories of staff.

(2) It is also recommended that meetings should be arranged at which the staff may exchange information and discuss questions of professional interest.

C. OPEN PENAL AND CORRECTIONAL INSTITUTIONS

Resolution adopted on 29 August 1955

The First United Nations Congress on the Prevention of Crime and the Treatment of Offenders,

Having adopted recommendations, annexed to the present resolution on the question of open penal and correctional institutions,

1. *Requests* the Secretary-General, in accordance with paragraph *(d)* of the annex to resolution 415(V) of the General Assembly of the United Nations, to submit these recommendations to the Social Commission of the Economic and Social Council for approval;

2. *Expresses* the hope that the Economic and Social Council will endorse these recommendations and draw them to the attention of governments, recommending that governments take them as fully as possible into account in their practice and when considering legislative and administrative reforms;

3. *Expresses* also the wish that the Economic and Social Council request the Secretary-General to give the widest publicity to these recommendations and authorize him to collect periodically information on the matter from the various countries, and to publish such information.

Annex

Recommendations on Open Penal and Correctional Institutions

I. An open institution is characterized by the absence of material or physical precautions against escape (such as walls, locks, bars, armed or other special security guards), and by a system based on self-discipline and the inmate's sense of responsibility towards the group in which he lives. This system encourages the inmate to use the freedom accorded to him without abusing it. It is these characteristics which distinguish the open institution from other types of institutions, some of which are run on the same principles without, however, realizing them to the full.

II. The open institution ought, in principle, to be an independent establishment; it may, however, where necessary, form a separate annex to an institution of another type.

III. In accordance with each country's prison system, prisoners may be sent to such an institution either at the beginning of their sentence or after they have served part of it in an institution of a different type.

IV. The criterion governing the selection of prisoners for admission to an open institution should be, not the particular penal or correctional category to which the offender belongs, nor the length of his sentence, but his suitability for admission to an open institution and the fact that his social readjustment is more likely to be achieved by such a system than by treatment under other forms of detention. The selection should, as far as possible, be made on the basis of a medico-psychological examination and a social investigation.

V. Any inmate found incapable of adapting himself to treatment in an open institution or whose conduct is seriously detrimental to the proper control of the institution or has an unfortunate effect on the behaviour of other inmates should be transferred to an institution of a different type.

VI. The success of an open institution depends on the fulfilment of the following conditions in particular:

(a) If the institution is situated in the country, it should not be so isolated as to obstruct the purpose of the institution or to cause excessive inconvenience to the staff.

(b) With a view to their social rehabilitation, prisoners should be employed in work which will prepare them for useful and remunerative employment after release. While the provision of agricultural work is an advantage, it is desirable also to provide workshops in which the prisoners can receive vocational and industrial training.

(c) If the process of social readjustment is to take place in an atmosphere of trust, it is essential that the members of the staff should be acquainted with and understand the character and special needs of each prisoner and that they should be capable of exerting a wholesome moral influence. The selection of the staff should be governed by these considerations.

(d) For the same reason, the number of inmates should remain within such bounds as to enable the director and senior officers of the staff to become thoroughly acquainted with each prisoner.

(e) It is necessary to obtain the effective co-operation of the public in general and of the surrounding community in particular for the operation of open institu-

tions. For this purpose it is therefore, among other things, necessary to inform the public of the aims and methods of each open institution, and also of the fact that the system applied in it requires a considerable moral effort on the part of the prisoner. In this connexion, local and national media of information may play a valuable part.

VII. In applying the system of open institutions each country, with due regard for its particular social, economic and cultural conditions, should be guided by the following observations:

(a) Countries which are experimenting with the open system for the first time should refrain from laying down rigid and detailed regulations in advance for the operation of open institutions;

(b) During the experimental stage they should be guided by the methods of organization and the procedure already found to be effective in countries which are more advanced in this respect.

VIII. While in the open institution the risk of escape and the danger that the inmate may make improper use of his contacts with the outside world are admittedly greater than in other types of penal institutions, these disadvantages are amply outweighed by the following advantages, which make the open institution superior to the other types of institution:

(a) The open institution is more favourable to the social readjustment of the prisoners and at the same time more conducive to their physical and mental health.

(b) The flexibility inherent in the open system is expressed in a liberalization of the regulations; the tensions of prison life are relieved and discipline consequently improves. Moreover, the absence of material and physical constraint and the relations of greater confidence between prisoners and staff tend to create in the prisoners a genuine desire for social readjustment.

(c) The conditions of life in open institutions resemble more closely those of normal life. Consequently, desirable contacts can more easily be arranged with the outside world and the inmate can thus be brought to realize that he has not severed all links with society; in this connexion it might perhaps be possible to arrange, for instance, group walks, sporting competitions with outside teams, and even individual leave of absence, particularly for the purpose of preserving family ties.

(d) The same measure is less costly if applied in an open institution than in an institution of another type, in particular because of lower building costs and, in the case of an agricultural institution, the higher income obtained from cultivation, if cultivation is organized in a rational manner.

IX. In conclusion, the United Nations Congress on the Prevention of Crime and the Treatment of Offenders

(a) Considers that the open institution marks an important step in the development of modern prison systems and represents one of the most successful applications of the principle of the individualization of penalties with a view to social readjustment;

(b) Believes that the system of open institutions could contribute to decreasing the disadvantages of short term sentences of imprisonment;

(c) Consequently recommends the extension of the open system to the largest possible number of prisoners, subject to the fulfilment of the conditions set forth in the foregoing recommendations;

(d) Recommends the compilation of statistics supplemented by follow-up studies conducted, in so far as possible, with the help of independent scientific authorities, which will make it possible to assess, from the point of view of recidivism and social rehabilitation, the results of treatment in open institutions.

Bibliography

Bibliography

Abstracts on Criminology and Penology [formerly *Excerpta Criminologica*]. Institute of Criminology, University of Leiden, 1960-.

Ali, Badr-El-Din. *International Survey of Standard Minimum Rules: A Pilot Study*. Prepared under the auspices of the International Prisoner's Aid Association. Milwaukee: IPAA, 1968.

Alper, Benedict S., ed. "Crime Prevention in the Context of National Development." Report prepared for the United Nations Section of Social Defence. New York, 1961. Mimeographed.

American Prison Association. *Proceedings of the 55th Annual Congress of the American Prison Association, Jackson, Mississippi, November 7-14, 1925.* Cheshire, Conn.: Connecticut Reformatory, 1926.

Ancel, Marc. *The Death Penalty in European Countries*. Strasbourg: Council of Europe, 1962.

Augustus, John. *A Report of the Labors of John Augustus for the Last Ten Years in Aid of the Unfortunate*. Boston, 1852.

Barrows, Samuel J. *The International Prison Congress: Its Origins, Aims, and Objects Together with the Program of Questions for the Eighth International Prison Congress to Be Held at Washington, D.C., 1910.* Report prepared for the Secretary of State by the Commissioner for the United States. Washington: Government Printing Office, 1908.

_____. *Report of the Delegates of the United States to the Fifth International Prison Congress*. Report to the President of the United States. Washington: Government Printing Office, 1896.

Basalo, J. Carlos Garcia. *Introducción al Estudio de la* Penologia. Buenos Aires: Dirección Nacional de Institutos Penales, 1967.

Bates, Sanford. "Report on the International Prison Congress." In *Proceedings of the 60th Annual Congress of the American Prison Association,*

Louisville, Kentucky, October 10th to 16th, 1930, pp. 308-20. Cheshire, Conn.: Connecticut Reformatory, 1931.

————. "Report of the American Delegate to the Twelfth International Congress of the International Penal and Penitentiary Commission." In *Proceedings of the Eightieth Annual Congress of Correction of the American Prison Association, St. Louis, Missouri, October 8th to 13th, 1950,* pp. 41-51. New York: Office of the Association, 1951.

Beltrani-Scalia, Martino. "Historical Sketch of National and International Penitentiary Congresses in Europe and America." In *Transactions of the National Congress on Penitentiary and Reformatory Discipline, Cincinnati, Ohio, Oct. 12-18, 1870,* pp. 267-77. Edited by E.C. Wines. Albany, N.Y.: Weed, Parsons and Co., Printers, 1871.

Brill, Jeanette G., and Payne E. George. *The Adolescent Court and Crime Prevention.* New York: Pitman, 1938.

Conrad, John. *Crime and Its Correction* Berkeley: University of California Press, 1965.

Faulkner, Roland P. "The International Criminal Law Association." *Annals of the American Academy of Political and Social Science,* July 1890.

Glueck, Sheldon. "The International Prison Congress of 1930." *Mental Hygiene* 15 (October 1931): 775-90.

Godechot, Jacques. *The Taking of the Bastille.* New York: Charles Scribner's Sons, 1970.

Goring, Charles. *The English Convict.* London: Darling and Son, Ltd., 1913.

Healy, William. *The Individual Delinquent.* Boston: Little, Brown, 1915.

Henderson, Charles R. "The Resolutions of the 1910 International Prison Congress in Their Application to the United States." In *Proceedings of the Annual Congress of the American Prison Association, Omaha, Nebraska, October 14-19, 1911,* pp. 23-30. Indianapolis: Wm. B. Burford, Printer, 1911.

Howard Association. *The Prison Congress of London, July 1872.* London: The Association, 1872.

International Bibliography on Crime and Delinquency. New York: National Council on Crime and Delinquency, 1964-.

International Labour Organisation. *Activities of the I.L.O.: 1947-1970.* Reports submitted to the United Nations. Geneva: International Labour Office, 1971.

————. *Index to Conventions and Recommendations Adopted by the International Labour Conferences, 1919-1966.* Geneva: International Labour Office, 1966.

International Penal and Penitentiary Commission. *Proceedings of the Twelve International Penitentiary Congresses, 1872-1950: Analytical and Name Index.* Prepared under the direction of the Secretary-General of the International Penal and Penitentiary Commission, Thorsten Sellin, by Valy Degoumois. Berne: Staempfli & Cie, N.D. Following are selected documents as listed in this volume.

Prisons and Reformatories at Home and Abroad; being the Trans-actions of the International Penitentiary Congress held in London, July 3-13, 1872, including official documents, discussion, and papers presented to the Congress. Edited, at the request of the International Committee, by Edwin Pears, LL.B., Barrister-at-Law, Secretary of the Congress. London: Longmans, Green, 1873.

Le Congrès pénitentiaire international de Stockholm, 15-26 août, 1878. *Comptes-rendus des séances*, publiés sous la direction de la Commission pénitentiaire internationale par le Dr Guillaume, directeur du pénitencier de Neuchâtel, secrétaire-général du Congrès. Stockholm: Bureau de la Commission pénitentiaire internationale, 1879.

Actes du Congrès pénitentiaire international de Rome, Novembre 1885. Publiés par les soins du Comité exécutif. 3 vols. Rome: Imprimerie des "Mantellate", 1887.

Actes du Congrès pénitentiaire international de St-Pétersbourg, 1890. Publiés sous la direction de la Commission d'organisation par le Dr Guillaume, secrétaire-général du Congrès. *Procès-verbaux des séances.* 5 vols. Saint-Pétersbourg: Bureau de la Commission d'organisation du Congrès, 1892.

République francaise, Ministère de l'Intérieur. *Ve Congrès pénitentiaire international (Paris, 1895). Compte-rendu des séances des quatre sections.* 5 vols. Melun: Imprimerie administrative, 1897.

Actes du Congrès pénitentiaire international de Bruxelles, août 1900. Publiés sous la direction de M.F.-C. De Latour, président du Congrès, par le Dr Guillaume, secrétaire-général du Congrès, et Charles Didion, secrétaire-général adjoint. *Procès-verbaux des séances.* 5 vols. Berne: Imprimerie Stæmpfli & Cie 1901.

Actes du Congrès pénitentiaire international de Budapest, Septembre, 1905. Publiés sous la direction de M. Jules Rickl de Bellye, président du Congrès, par de Dr Guillaume, secrétaire général du Congrès. *Procès-verbaux des séances.* 5 vols. Budapest et Berne: Bureau de la Commission pénitentiaire internationale, 1907.

Actes du Congrès pénitentiaire international de Washington, Octobre 1910. Publiés à la demande de la Commission pénitentiaire internationale par le Dr Louis-C. Guillaume et le Dr Eugène Borel. *Procès-verbaux des séances et voyage d'études, etc.* 5 vols. Groningen: Bureau de la Commission pénitentiaire internationale, 1913.

Actes du Congrès pénitentiaire international de Londres, août 1925. Publiés par le secrétaire-général du Congrès, Dr J. Simon van der Aa, professeur de droit pénal à l'Université de Groningen e. c., secrétaire-général de la Commission pénitentiaire internationale. *Procès-verbaux des séances.* 4 vols. Berne: Bureau de la Commission pénitentiaire internationale, 1927.

Proceedings of the IXth International Penitentiary Congress held in London, August 1925. Edited by the Secretary-General of the Congress, Sir Jan Simon van der Aa, K.B.E., LL.D., Professor of Penal Law at the University of Groningen, o. l., Secretary-General of the International Prison Commission. x, 426 p. Berne: Bureau of the International Prison Commission, 1927.

Actes du Congrès pénal et pénitentiaire international de Prague, août 1930. Publiés par le secrétaire-général du Congrès, Dʳ J. Simon van der Aa, professeur de droit pénal à l'Université de Groningen, e. c., secrétaire-général de la Commission internationale pénale et pénitentiaire. *Procès-verbaux des séances.* 5 vols. Berne: Bureau de la Commission internationale pénale et pénitentiaire, 1931.

Actes du Congrès pénal et pénitentiaire international de Berlin, août 1935. Publiés par le secrétaire-général du Congrès, Dʳ J. Simon van der Aa, professeur de droit pénal à l'Université de Groningue, e. c., secrétaire-général de la Commission internationale pénale et pénitentiaire. *Procès-verbaux des séances.* 5 vols. Berne: Bureau de la Commission internationale pénale et pénitentiaire, 1936.

Douzième Congrès pénal et pénitentiaire international, La Haye, 1950. *Actes* publiés par le secrétaire-général du Congrès. Dʳ Thorsten Sellin, professeur de sociologie à l'Université de Pennsylvanie, secrétaire-général de la Commission internationale pénale et pénitentiaire. Volume I. *Procès-verbaux des séances.* 6 vols. Berne: Commission internationale pénale et pénitentiaire, 1951.

International Penal and Penitentiary Commission. *Les Systemès Pénitentiaires en vigeur dans divers pays.* Berne: IPPC, 1935.

International Penal and Penitentiary Foundation [formerly IPPC]. *Modern Methods of Penal Treatment.* Berne: IPPF, 1954.

———. *New Psychological Methods for the Treatment of Prisoners: Proceedings of the International Colloquium of Brussels, 26-31 March, 1962.* Berne: Staempfli & Cie, 1962.

———. *Three Aspects of Penal Treatment.* 2 vols. Berne: Staempfli & Cie, 1960.

International Society of Criminal Anthropology. Following are the entries, in chronological order, for the *Proceedings* of the seven congresses held by this organization.

Premier Congrès international d'anthropologie criminelle, Rome, 1885. Programme et conclusions des rapporteurs. Rome: Forzani et C., Imprimeurs du Senat, 1885.

Actes du deuxieme Congrès international d'anthropologie criminelle, biologie et sociologie, Paris, août, 1889. Paris: G. Masson, Editeur, 1890.

Actes du troisième Congrès international d'anthropologie criminelle tenu a Bruxelles en août 1892. Biologie et sociologie. Bruxelles: F. Hayez, Imprimeur de L'Académie Royale de Belgique, 1893.

Compte-Rendu des travaux de la quatrième session tenue a Genève du 24 au 29 août, 1896. Geneve: Georg & C., Libraires-Editeurs, 1897.

Compte-Rendu des travaux de la cinquième session tenue à Amsterdam du 9 au 14 septembre 1901. Amsterdam: Imprimerie de J.H. Bussy, 1901.

Comptes-Rendus du VI Congrès international d'anthropologie criminelle, Turin, 28 avril-3 mai 1906. Milan-Turin-Rome: Bocca Frères Editeurs, 1908.

Bericht über den VII Internationalen Kongress für kriminalanthropologie, Köln a Rhein, 9-13 oktober 1911. Heidelberg: Carl Winter's Universitäts-buchhandlung, 1912.

International Society of Criminology. *International Annals of Criminology.* Paris, 1960-.

Klare, Hugh J., ed. *Changing Concepts of Crime and Its Treatment.* Oxford: Pergamon Press, 1966.

League of Nations. *Monthly Summary of the League of Nations: 1921-1938.* 18 vols.

_____. Secretariat. *Auxiliary Services of Juvenile Courts.* Geneva, 1931.

_____. Secretariat. *Child Welfare Councils.* Geneva, 1937.

_____. Secretariat. *Institutions for Erring and Delinquent Minors.* Geneva, 1934.

_____. Secretariat. *Organisation of Juvenile Courts and the Results Attained Hitherto.* Geneva, 1932.

_____. Secretariat. *The Placing of Children in Families.* 2 vols. Geneva, 1938.

_____. Secretariat. *Study on the Legal Position of the Illegitimate Child.* Geneva, 1939.

Leonard, L. Larry. *International Organization.* New York: McGraw-Hill, 1951.

Lopez-Rey, Manuel, and Germain, Charles, eds. *Studies in Penology: Essays in Honor of Sir Lionel Fox.* The Hague: M. Nijhoff, 1964.

Loudet, Dr. Osvaldo. *Actos, Deliberaciónes, Trabajos del Primer Congreso Latino-Americano de Criminología, 25-31 julio, 1938.* Buenos Aires: Sociedad Argentina de Criminología, 1939.

MacLaurin, John [pesud.]. *The United Nations and Power Politics.* London: George Allen & Unwin, 1951.

Mannheim, Hermann. *Comparative Criminology.* Boston: Houghton Mifflin, 1967.

_____. "More International Cooperation and Comparative Study in the Field of Criminal Justice." In *Criminal Justice and Social Reconstruction.* New York: Oxford, 1946.

_____, ed. *Pioneers in Criminology.* London: Stevens, 1960.

National Prison Association. *Transactions of the National Congress on Penitentiary and Reformatory Discipline, Cincinnati, Ohio, Oct. 12-18, 1870.* Edited by E.C. Wines, 1871. Reprinted by the American Correctional Association on the occasion of its centennial anniversary, October 1970.

Pena de Morte, Colóquio Internacional Comerative do Centenário da Abolição da Pena de Morte em Portugal. 2 vols. Coimbra: Faculdade de Direito da Universidade de Coimbra, 1968.

Proceedings of the American Correctional Association. New York and Washington, 1873-1971.

Radzinowicz, Leon. *In Search of Criminology.* London: Heineman, 1961.

———, and Turner, J.W.C., eds. *The Modern Approach to Criminal Law.* London: Macmillan and Co., Ltd., 1945.

Randall, C.D. *The Fourth International Prison Congress, St. Petersburg, Russia, 1891.* Washington: Bureau of Education, Circular of Information No. 2, 1891.

Robertson, A.H. *The Council of Europe.* 2nd ed. London: Stevens & Sons Ltd., 1961.

Rothman, David J. *Discovery of the Asylum: Social Order and Disorder in the New Republic.* Boston: Little, Brown, 1971.

Ruggles-Brise, Sir Hugh Evelyn. *Prison Reform at Home and Abroad: A Short History of the International Movement Since the London Congress, 1872.* London: Macmillan and Co., Ltd., 1924.

Sanders, Wiley B. *Juvenile Offenders for a Thousand Years.* Chapel Hill: University of North Carolina Press, 1970.

Sellin, Thorsten. "Lionel Fox and the International Penal and Penitentiary Commission." In *Studies in Penology: Essays in Honor of Sir Lionel Fox*, pp. 194-207. Edited by Manuel Lopez-Rey and Charles Germain. The Hague: M. Nijhoff, 1964.

Sutherland, Edwin H. *White Collar Crime.* New York: The Dryden Press, 1949.

Tallack, William. "Influence of the Great Prison Congress of 1872." In *Transactions of the Third National Prison Congress held at St. Louis, Missouri, May 13-16, 1874*, pp. 174-84. Edited by E.C. Wines. New York: National Prison Association, 1874.

Taylor, Telford. *Nuremberg and Vietnam: An American Tragedy.* Chicago: Quadrangle Press, 1970.

Teeters, Negley K. *Deliberations of the International Penal and Penitentiary Congresses.* Philadelphia: Temple University Book Store, 1949.

———. "The First International Penitentiary Congresses, 1846-47-57." *Prison Journal* 26 (July 1946): 190-211.

———. *Penology From Panama to Cape Horn.* Philadelphia: University of Pennsylvania Press, 1946.

———. *World Penal Systems: A Survey.* Philadelphia: Pennsylvania Prison Society, 1944.

United Nations. *Report of the First United Nations Congress on the Preven-*
tion of Crime and the Treatment of Offenders, Geneva, 22 August-3
September 1955. New York, 1955. A/CONF.6/1.

————. *Second United Nations Congress on the Prevention of Crime and*
Treatment of Offenders, London. New York, 1960. A/CONF.17/20.

————. "Provisional Draft of the Final Report of the Fourth United Nations
Congress on the Prevention of Crime and the Treatment of Offenders,
Kyoto, 17-26 August 1970." (Mimeographed)

————. *Standard Minimum Rules for the Treatment of Prisoners in the*
Light of Recent Developments in the Correctional Field. Working
paper prepared by the Secretariat for the Fourth U.N. Congress on
the Prevention of Crime and the Treatment of Offenders, Kyoto,
Japan, 17-26 August 1970. A/CONF. 43/3.

————. *Third United Nations Congress on the Prevention of Crime and the*
Treatment of Offenders, Stockholm, 8-18 August 1965. New York,
1965. A/CONF.17/26.

————. *The Young Adult Offender.* New York: (UN/ST/SOA/SD/II), 1965.
See also, on the same topic, *Special Preventive and Treatment Meas-*
ures for Young Adults. New York, 1966. UN/A/CONF.26/6.

United Nations Asia and Far East Institute. *New Horizons in Social De-*
fence Training and Research: A Survey of the First Eight Years at
UNAFEI. Fuchu: UNAFEI, 1970.

————. *UNAFEI: Report for [year].* Fuchu: UNAFEI, 1965-.

United Nations. Department of Economic and Social Affairs. *International*
Review of Criminal Policy. Nos. 1-28. New York, 1952-1970.

United Nations Educational, Scientific and Cultural Organization. "Modern
Methods in Criminology." *International Social Science Journal*
[Paris] 18 (1966).

————. *Report of the Director-General on the Activities of the Organiza-*
tion, 1947-1971. Paris: Joseph Floch, 1972.

————. *The University Teaching of Social Sciences: Criminology.* Paris,
1957.

Veillard-Cybulsky. *Les Jeunes Délinquants dans le Monde.* Neuchatel: Dela-
chaux et Niestlé, 1963.

Wines, Enoch C. *The Actual State of Prison Reform Throughout the Civil-*
ized World. A discourse pronounced at the opening of the International Prison Congress of Stockholm, August 20, 1878. Stockholm:
Central-Tryckeriet, 1878.

————. *International Congress on the Prevention and Repression of Crime,*
Including Penal and Reformatory Treatment. Statement of the objects of the proposed Congress and the result of negotiations with
various Continental governments in relation thereto, with the Proceedings of a meeting held in London, November 3rd, 1871. London,
1871.

————. "International Prison Congresses." In *Transactions of the Fourth*

National Prison Congress held in New York, June 6-9, 1876, pp. 31-52. Edited by E.C. Wines. New York: National Prison Association, 1877.

_____. *The State of Prisons and of Child-Saving Institutions in the Civilized World*. 1880. Reprint. Montclair, N.J.: Patterson Smith, 1968.

Wines, Frederick H. *Punishment and Reformation: An Historical Sketch of the Rise of the Penitentiary System*. London: Swan Sonnenschein, 1895.

World Health Organization. *The First Ten Years of the WHO*. Geneva: WHO, 1958.

_____. *Handbook of Resolutions and Decisions of the World Health Organization and the Executive Board, 1948-1967*. Geneva: WHO, 1967.

Index

About the Authors

Benedict S. Alper, Visiting Professor of Criminology at Boston College, Chestnut Hill, Massachusetts has taught at the Rutgers Law School in Newark and the New School for Social Research in New York City. His initial apprenticeship in the field was as probation officer in the Boston Juvenile Court and as correctional officer in the Massachusetts State Prison. Professional experience includes posts at the state, national, and international levels: as research director of a New York Legislative Committee, Field Secretary of the American Parole Association, chief statistician and special assistant to the Director, Federal Bureau of Prisons, and first Chief of the Section of Social Defense at the United Nations. In the United States Army, at the end of World War II, he administered five prisons in Trieste. He has served as consultant to the American Foundation of Philadelphia and as Research Associate to the Center of Studies in Criminal Justice, University of Chicago Law School. He participated in the Third United Nations Crime Congress in Stockholm in 1965, and was Consultant to the United Nations Consultative Group on Crime in Geneva in 1968 and to the Fourth United Crime Congress in Kyoto in 1970. One of his recent books, *Halfway Houses*, coauthored with Oliver J. Keller, Jr., was published by Lexington Books in 1970.

Jerry F. Boren is on the faculty of the Sociology Department of Merrimack College, North Andover, Massachusetts. He has taught at Colby College and Boston College, where he is currently a doctoral candidate in sociology. He received his BA in sociology from the University of Missouri and holds the MA in religious studies from Andover Newton Theological School. He has contributed chapters on low-income housing programs to a forthcoming book, *Stratagems Against Poverty in America*.